Solo, Yet Never Alone

Swimming the Great Lakes

By

Laura E. Young

ScrivenerPress

Library and Archives Canada Cataloguing in Publication

Young, Laura E., 1963-, author
Solo, yet never alone : swimming the Great Lakes / Laura E. Young.

Includes bibliographical references.
ISBN 978-1-896350-63-9 (pbk.)

1. Long distance swimming--Great Lakes (North America).
2. Swimmers--Canada--Biography. I. Title.

GV837.9.Y68 2014   797.2'10922   C2014-901528-3

Book design: Laurence Steven
Cover design: Chris Evans
Cover photos: Tony Chisholm, Dr. Mark Ghesquiere, Laura E. Young
Author photo: Brent Wohlberg

Published by Scrivener Press
465 Loach's Road,
Sudbury, Ontario, Canada, P3E 2R2
info@yourscrivenerpress.com
www.scrivenerpress.com

We acknowledge the financial support of the Ontario Arts Council and the Canada Council for the Arts for our publishing activities.

Canada Council for the Arts   Conseil des Arts du Canada

ONTARIO ARTS COUNCIL
CONSEIL DES ARTS DE L'ONTARIO
50 YEARS OF ONTARIO GOVERNMENT SUPPORT OF THE ARTS
50 ANS DE SOUTIEN DU GOUVERNEMENT DE L'ONTARIO AUX ARTS

But I told that kid a hundred times "Don't take the Lakes for granted.
They go from calm to a hundred knots so fast they seem enchanted."

...

Now it's a thing that us oldtimers know. In a sultry summer calm
There comes a blow from nowhere, and it goes off like a bomb.

—from "White Squall" by Stan Rogers.

Your Rocky Spine

I was lost in the lakes,
And the shapes that your body makes
That your body makes, that your body makes
That your body makes

And the mountains said I could find you here
They whispered the snow and the leaves in my ear
I traced my finger along your trails
Your body was the map, I was lost in it

Floating over your rocky spine
The glaciers made you and now you're mine
Floating over your rocky spine
The glaciers made you and now you're mine

I was moving across your frozen veneer
The sky was dark, but you were clear
Could you feel my foot-steps
And would you shatter, would you shatter
Would you

And with your soft fingers between my claws
Like purity against resolve
I could tell, then and there
We were formed from the clay
And came from the rocks for the earth to display

They told me to be careful up there
Where the wind blows a venomous rage through your hair
They told me to be careful up there
Where the wind, rages through your hair

Table of Contents

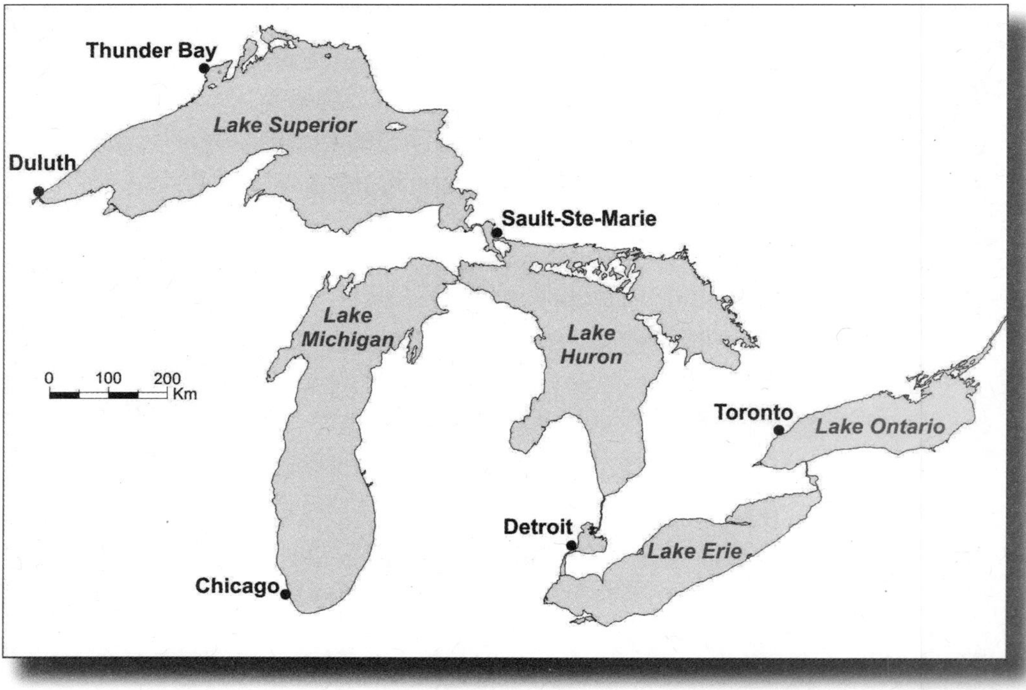

The Great Lakes

Map Credit: L.L. Lariviere—Laurentian University.

Preface

Years ago I discovered *Swimming to Antarctica*, Lynne Cox's incredible account of her journeys on the world's freakingly cold waters. And yes, she did swim to Antarctica. The swims were wild; Lynne's ability to handle increasingly cold water is fascinating reading—the world of open-water swimming blown wide open.

And then I got to thinking. Canadians have done some pretty crazy, wonderful open-water swims: the Northumberland Strait, Lake Winnipeg, Strait of Juan de Fuca. And of course, the Great Lakes. I learned that, beyond a few accounts of Marilyn Bell's historic Lake Ontario crossing in 1954, there was little else to find on Great Lakes swimming. Where was the story of Canadian outdoor swimming, "cross-country swimming" as one athlete called it. And so I set out to capture the essence of what it takes to swim the greatest reservoir of fresh water on an increasingly parched planet.

This book is not a training manual. Nor is it a historical document. It won't rehash old stories or analyze extreme sports and the behaviour of the people who do them. While it'll touch on all these in some way, it's more like a walk along the beach—along the shores of Lakes Huron, Ontario, Michigan, Erie, and Superior—with any of the swimmers who have crossed them.

In "Part One—Sixty Years of Great Lakes Swimming," the story weaves through the decades and through all five Lakes, featuring various well-known swimmers, iconic and odd swims, deliberate first-time achievements, the one-offs, and the recurring faces. Readers are invited to share the mindset that it takes to get to the shore of a Great Lake, let alone across to the other side. The icons and legends of marathon swimming on the Great Lakes—Marilyn Bell, Vicki Keith, Cindy Nicholas, John Scott—they all reflect on what drove them. How did it all begin for Marilyn Bell? Did Vicki Keith ever doubt she would swim five Great Lakes in the summer of 1988? How did Cindy Nicholas and John Scott get across Lake Ontario so fast that few have ever come close to their record-setting times?

In "Part Two—From All Walks of Life ... They Swam," we encounter a host of very special "regular" people, both those whose names are on the exclusive register of swimmers who have completed a crossing of one of the Great Lakes, and those who were pulled out mere kilometres from the other shore. One of the things you'll come to appreciate, though, as you meet these people, is that regardless of whether they completed the crossing or not, their stories are unique and intimate accounts of a journey brimming with love and respect for our magnificent inland seas.

In setting out to write the stories of the swimmers who have tackled the Great Lakes I spoke exclusively with Canadian swimmers and the swims sanctioned through Solo Swims of Ontario Inc., the organization which governs the crossings in Ontario. Canada has a shining history in marathon swimming, one that rocks with gritty, gutsy, sometimes messy performances, the way we Canadians like our sporting events. All the swimmers in this book talk about the currents, waves, unpredictable weather, cold, and glorious nights and mornings on the mighty waters, and in doing so add to the global knowledge of open-water swimming.

Research included interviews with over 40 swimmers, swim masters, navigators, and swim managers. It also included a touch of personal experience: in the summer of 2010 I was "embedded" as an observer on Colleen Shields' attempt to cross Lake Ontario from Niagara-on-the-Lake to Toronto, and I swam with her for about an hour (it felt longer) in the rolling waters off Toronto. As well, every attempt was made to contact as many swimmers as possible for their reflections on the challenge of the Lakes, and success and failure when Mother Nature is in charge of the outcome. For various reasons, not all swimmers opted to be included. Their phenomenal achievements, however, are listed in the appendices at the conclusion of this story. Finally, any errors or omissions are strictly those of the author.

Open water swimming feels like the ultimate. You are going somewhere and you are one with, present in the moment with, wind, water, sky, sun, waves, perhaps even rain and lightning (coupled with a mad scramble to shore or boat) to the point where it feels like you are of the water and merely a set of eyes peering above the surface. Of course any of us can have a version of that experience on a hot summer's day by slipping into the lake or river and just being there. But then there are the people who swim the Great Lakes. This is their story.

But this is also a story for one nameless, even faceless swimmer from a small northern Ontario community north of the watershed, where the rivers flow north to James Bay. In fact, though, he could be any swimmer in small-town Canada. One morning, before the start of another age-group meet, a mom related to me how the swimmer they were billeting was being harassed for swimming. He was so upset with the chirping that he wanted to quit the sport.

And so, I write for him, and for all the other swimmers who know that while it's hard (and even sometimes like watching paint dry), there's nothing like swimming.

Acknowledgments

Like a Great Lakes swim, the writing of this book has been a team effort.

First and foremost I thank all of the swimmers and their families who entrusted their stories and photos to me; in particular Bryan Finlay, Colleen Shields, Vicki Keith, Marilyn Bell Di Lascio, Marilyn Korzekwa, and the team at Solo Swims of Ontario Inc., who keep swimmers safe and crossing. So many of you gave remarkably of your time and attention. You know this book couldn't have happened without you.

Sincere thanks to Alex Baumann, Lynne Cox, and Vicki Keith for agreeing to read the book prior to publication and offer comments.

Laura E. Young

I express my sincere appreciation to the Ontario Arts Council for all its support, especially the Writers' Works in Progress and Writers' Reserve grant programs.

Thank you to Ariel Rogers of Fogarty's Cove Music and Tony Dekker of the Great Lake Swimmers, for their immediate support and kind permission in using lyrics to the brilliant songs quoted in this book.

As well, to Laurence Steven, publisher and editor of Scrivener Press, and to cartographer L. L. Lariviere of Laurentian University: thank you for making this a beautiful book.

In the Aquatic World: thanks to my fabulous, "hard-core" teammates at Laurentian Masters Swimming and the Lake Nepahwin Swimmers, other amphibious friends at the Jeno Tihanyi Olympic Gold Pool, and in the great wide world of swimming. And, to the guard team at R.G. Dow Pool.

Thanks to my dear readers across Northeastern Ontario and to *The Sudbury Star* for "the pulpit" in my Personal Best sports column.

Thanks to Greg Zorbas. And to DBS Computers.

With so many other supporters on this project, I am likely missing someone. Please consider yourself covered with this big hug of gratitude: especially Lise (and Erik), Paulette, France, Karen, Jen, Diane, and Laurene, and The Pomegranate & Rum Book Club: Brenda, Janice, Josette, Judy, Micheline, Sheila, and Sue.

Thanks to dearest Evelyn (with Kerry), on our beloved Nova Scotia coast.

I want to express my appreciation to my extended, beautiful family: my parents, Carolyn and Michael Young, my mother-in-law, Vanda, and my siblings Catherine (Howard) and Douglas (Cindy), Jamie, Erik, and Meghan; Iva, and Chelsie, Jon, Kingsley, Kini, Pam, Riley, Robbie, Tallianna, and Tysen.

And most of all, heartfelt gratitude goes to my team in the canoe with the towels and the house keys: Glen, Neal and Roberto.

Prologue

The Heart of a Marathoner
Marilyn Bell Takes Atlantic City

Early on the morning of July 1, 1954, Marilyn Bell filled the 10 glass bottles she had bought at her local pharmacy with a sticky blend of corn syrup and water. Then she caught the streetcar down to the Credit River in Toronto. She was about to break the number one rule of swimming: never swim alone. There was no choice.

This swim was no ordinary dip for the 16-year-old Toronto high school student and lifeguard. Down on the dock where the open water swimmers of the Lakeshore Swim Club trained, her teammates were talking about the inaugural Atlantic City Championship that July. The 26-mile (41.8 km) second annual marathon swim in the Atlantic Ocean around Absecon Island on the U.S. east coast was part of the 100th anniversary celebrations of Atlantic City (Wennerberg 137). Marilyn's teammate, her beloved 'big brother' Cliff Lumsdon, was already a superstar in marathon swimming, and he had been talking up going to the race. There was prize money and the chance to see a hero: Gertrude Ederle, the first woman to swim across the English Channel—who returned home after her swim to a ticker tape parade normally reserved for baseball heroes—would be the official race starter in Atlantic City. The women's race at the Canadian National Exhibition (CNE) at the end of that summer had been cancelled, so Marilyn asked her coach, Gus Ryder, if she could go to Atlantic City instead.

Marilyn had never swum more than three miles (4.8 km) in competition;

in training, perhaps 10 miles (16 km). Nor was she the brightest star in the Lakeshore Swimming Club constellation. Her parents had already seriously considered removing her from swimming altogether. The cost was high, even in the 50s, for the Bell family. Lakeshore's coach Ryder asked her parents, Grace and Syd, for more time for Marilyn, explaining that she was developing at her own speed.

In fact, Gus was already considering Marilyn for the Atlantic City marathon. Gus told her father he would only enter her if she could swim for 10 hours straight. And there wasn't much time to get that trial in. She had to swim the Friday of the Dominion Day weekend. If she could go to Atlantic City she'd realize her lifelong dream of representing Canada in swimming. A good showing might also earn a spot on a relay race across Lake Ontario in September.

All this came before Marilyn Bell's swimming career changed and reached heights few Canadians ever see, long before any collection of stories on Canadian sports heroes included her story, or a Toronto Island ferry was named after her. Canadians may not know all their history but most do know that Marilyn Bell became Marilyn Bell on September 8-9, 1954 as the first person to swim across Lake Ontario. A legend grew out of the crossing: she bested the great American swimmer Florence Chadwick, defeated lamprey eels at the peak of their population in the Lake, and worked through severe fatigue to complete the crossing. There is speculation that she actually swam further than the 51 kilometres, having battled currents that pushed her too far west.

And though 60 years have passed since her iconic swim, the sunrise on Lake Ontario remains as vivid as it was the morning it lit her path to Toronto. She likens the play of light on Lake Ontario to an Easter morning for the glory and sense of rebirth she discovered in the sunrise, September 9, 1954 (Solo Swims).

But long before her Lake Ontario crossing, before she dared challenge Chadwick, she had a swim to do in the Credit River.

The Great Lake headwaters begin in tiny park ponds, in rock crevasses and depressions, in forest rivulets, and neighbourhood creeks before flowing ultimately into the big waters themselves. The sheer magnitude of the Lakes tends to deflect our attention from their sources. Similarly, it's one thing to interview Marilyn Bell, historical figure and Canadian icon; it's another to find the headwaters of her swimming career. She has said that much that was written about her at the height of her career wasn't accurate, nor was the swim in the river stressed. Yet that swim had a drama of its own. In fact, without Marilyn's singular determination it wouldn't have happened at all. And perhaps that would have been the end of the Marilyn Bell story. Adding to the drama, to the pressure of a 10 hour swim in the Credit River, was the fact she would be alone. Just the night before the scheduled swim, when everything was in place, her father told her he had to work—he couldn't get away in time to supervise the entire swim. He wouldn't be able to row the support boat alongside her. Marilyn watched her last opportunity before the Atlantic City registration deadline evaporating. Marilyn recalls how upset her father was with her "bullheadedness," but he promised to get there as soon as he could. Coach Ryder didn't know she would be alone; he thought her father would be watching.

The next morning she headed to the Credit River anyway. The river was familiar to Marilyn since the Lakeshore club held all its open water training sessions here, swimming up and down, even to Lake Ontario, even in late May, when the waters were frigid. "We would be swimming out there like crazy people. Never complaining. Never complaining," Marilyn says. Coach Ryder would tell them to swim and Marilyn would get into the icy waters. Cliff Lumsdon would tell Gus he was nuts and swim back to the dock.

At the dock that July 1st, Marilyn shed her clothes to her swimsuit, explaining her plan to the man who rented boats, that she would swim between the highway bridge, about 100 yards to the south of the dock, then up to the railroad bridge. "Are you going to be here?" Because he was always there, she says. She told him her father was coming.

"I'm not going anywhere," he said.

"Okay. I have 10 bottles of corn syrup so I have to drink one of these every hour and I have to swim for 10 hours. If I swim from the dock to the hydro wires, then I turn around and swim down to the bridge, you'll be able to see me if you're here."

He promised to stay and watch out.

Scared to death, she recalls, Marilyn left her towel and clothes on the dock, slipped in with the eels and fish, and started swimming: to the wires, down to the bridge. To the wires, to the bridge. The boatman whistled every hour. She came in, swallowed the diluted corn syrup and resumed swimming. This first long swim seemed endless. She wondered if she would make it, when her father would show. She tried to keep track of how many times she went up and down the course, but since she didn't wear a watch she couldn't gauge how much, or how little, time was passing. "I think that was probably more depressing than anything. If my Dad had been in the boat he would have been telling me the end of an hour."

Her father arrived around the seventh hour, stunned that Marilyn was still in the water, still swimming away. Marilyn figures he expected to find her on the dock crying. She was on her way up the river, breathing on the opposite side so she didn't see him until he came alongside in the boat. Eventually Gus arrived, and learned that she had been swimming alone in the river for about seven hours.

But for Marilyn, there was no choice. She needed to do the swim. The Olympics would never happen for her. But, Atlantic City was an international race. She could still represent Canada. And, after so many years of swimming for the social aspect, of winning ribbons and a rare medal, she was actually hungry, actually wanting to achieve as a competitive athlete.

She would never have asked Gus if he thought she would make it. "But I think he did. Otherwise, I don't think he would have set the limits so high. He was really, really testing me. But he also knew so much about the way I processed stuff."

When she finished her trial swim, she had only three weeks to train for Atlantic City and learn to swim with goggles for the first time. Then one of her long-time rivals, Shirley Campbell, also entered the Atlantic City race, and joined Lakeshore to train. The renowned Canadian swimmer had always beaten Bell in the past CNE races. She was a glamorous, talented athlete who had spent the winter teaching swimming in Florida and often drove Marilyn home in a brand-new car purchased with her earnings. They were friends, sure, but also rivals—and now here she was down at the Credit River on the dock with Marilyn.

"So I had this inner turmoil going on because I liked her," Marilyn says. "We were friends but I also was really threatened by her because she was successful. And, she was older than me. So," Marilyn laughs, "here was this usurper in my river, with my coach, and with my Cliff."

In the end Shirley helped Marilyn toughen up, making her swim stronger. And, Marilyn was determined to get to Atlantic City regardless of who was training in her river. "That energy, that motivation that was coming inside me, which up until then hadn't been all that evident... I hadn't had any reason before."

Marilyn worked hard to convince Gus to say they were going to Atlantic City. "I wanted to prove that he was right. He always told me I had the potential to be a winner but I never really bought into that. I had to discover that. It was only after I did that 10-hour swim on my own that I believed that I really could do this." These were heady days for long-distance swimming. Cliff Lumsdon dominated the marathon swimming scene, winning the 1949 Lou Marsh trophy as Canada's athlete of the year, and gaining friends with his warm, generous personality (Wennerberg 103). In 1951, Winnie Roach Leuszler became the first Canadian—female or male—to swim across the English Channel. She was a mother who clearly was ahead of her time: in 1949 she won an eight kilometre race while four months pregnant (Solo Swims). In 1951, she triumphed in the Channel and returned home to a ticker tape parade. She was a Canadian heroine as far as Marilyn was concerned.

By 1952, Marilyn had turned professional, hoping to win the money necessary for her to keep swimming. She could swim forever. Coach Ryder had noticed this, and how she never complained. In pool training, he would tell her the workout was done, to cool down with another 100 metres, then go home. She would swim another 100 metres and get out of the water, thanking her coach. "Thank you, Gus. Thank you for helping me," she would say. She would do whatever he asked, happy that the Gus Ryder was paying attention to her, this kid who just liked to hang around the pool.

Now at 16 she was off to Atlantic City with Cliff, Cliff's girlfriend and future wife, Joan Cooke and Cliff's mother Violet Lumsdon, who was also a chaperone. (These were the 50s, Marilyn says.) In the week leading up to the

Atlantic City marathon, Marilyn managed little training in the ocean, swimming only to get used to goggles. At the time, the only ones available were a rigid rubber that limited the swimmer's visibility and had to be so tightly fastened to avoid leaking that Marilyn's head would bleed. She had been practising at home with them; in Atlantic City, she would swim a 50 metre course parallel to the beach to test her goggles in the ocean.

Throughout the week she formed a friendship with the beach lifeguard captain, Floyd Hunt, a friendship that would last a lifetime. It was a surprising and happy event considering Marilyn believes she must have looked like she didn't have much going on, especially after word got out about her first real dip in the ocean. The beach captain directed two lifeguards to take her out to train in an area known as the inlet. It was one of the rougher patches the swimmers would encounter on race day. She waded out as far as she possibly could then started swimming. Treading water, she asked the lifeguards if there were any fish around. "And, of course, these two guys were college men and here I am this little high school kid that's really dumb from the country. And I'm asking, 'Are there fish in the ocean?'"

They laughed. Then one of the guards, Joe "Chipper" Di Lascio told the petite Canadian swimmer: "Well, you won't have to worry about the fish. But don't put your feet down too far because there are crabs and they will bite you." With that Bell sprinted to shore faster than she had ever swum in her life. That was it. She wasn't going back in the ocean if she could help it. As these things go, Joe would later become her husband.

When coach Gus Ryder arrived shortly before the race he could tell Marilyn was upset. Finally he cornered her: "What's bothering you? Have you been training?"

"I've been working with the goggles but I haven't been doing much training," she replied.

"Why? Why haven't you been swimming?"

She stammered: "You know, there's fish in there and I'm really afraid of the fish." She was spooked. She was the smallest swimmer among these adults. She recognized faces, Winnie Roach among them, but they were all mature, grown women who, Bell figured, weren't afraid of much. The rest were men, big burly men and there was a lot of joking around about why Bell was even at the race. Was she the mascot, or what? By this point, Bell was utterly psyched out.

Gus gave his teen swimmer a pep talk. "You're in a good place. No one is expecting anything from you." He told her to prove them wrong. "You just have to put your mind to it. You'll be on top of the water. You don't have to worry about what's underneath. Don't tread water. Just keep swimming."

In Atlantic City, Bell says Gus's race strategy used her also-ran status to her advantage. She had always been one of the pack, a swimmer who liked the social aspect of the sport but who rarely won a medal. Medals came on the relays if they came, she says. But now it wasn't so bad being in the background. Shirley Campbell was no longer a factor. She didn't even compete. Liese Putt was there. She had twice defeated Bell in Lake Ontario at CNE swims. Gus wanted Marilyn to stay out front and away from Putt.

"With Liese," Ryder said, "I'm not going to let you get into a competition with her. When you swim I'm going to take you away from her. You don't have to be concerned about what she's doing." Ryder didn't want Marilyn to partner with Liese because Marilyn might have stayed with her. She liked Liese. She would have been comfortable swimming with Liese. Gus worried that Bell would swim Putt's race, and that, eventually, the older swimmer would wear Bell down. Ryder wanted Bell to drop the Montreal swimmer. "Of course I didn't process that until after the swim when we actually talked about what had happened," Marilyn recalls.

Race conditions were ideal, the ocean gently swaying, supporting the swimmers. Water temperature was a perfect 21C for the 25 entrants. And the race was on. Cliff Lumsdon pulled away with fellow Canadian, Hamilton, Ontario's Tom Park. After two hours, they had covered five miles. If they could keep up that blistering pace, they'd circle the island in about 10 hours. The two waged a series of attacks, like a breakaway of two cyclists in the Tour de France, before Park wore down Lumsdon and Cliff could not respond to Park's final attack. Park finished in 9 hours, 21 minutes, 42 seconds (Wennerberg 141). Cliff Lumsdon stroked in nearly four minutes later.

Because of the swim's layout, the swimmers could be seen from shore for the entire race. The local radio station broadcast updates. People were partying at the homes along the bay as the swimmers went by. As she moved along, Bell could hear people hollering her name, yelling: "Go Canada. You Canadians are great."

Behind her male teammates, Marilyn felt the first inkling of success tickle under her swim cap. She was passing Ventor Pier. The first woman to pass this pier would win $100. From his perch in the rowboat, Gus wrote on the chalkboard that she had just won the money. It was a huge amount to a 16-year-old in 1954. "That $100 kept me going for a long time."

As she headed into the treacherous Absecon Inlet, the tide was running. Gus yelled to just keep swimming, follow the boat. Each swimmer had been assigned two lifeguards who were familiar with the tides. Marilyn's lifeguards were in the rhythm of the swim, adopting the young Canadian and making her their own.

Swimming the narrow channel along the back of the island, she began picking off many of the male swimmers. American Jerry Kerschner, who had qualified for the 1944 Olympic team (there were no Olympics during World War II), had beaten Cliff Lumsdon and George Bevan, of Manitoba at CNE's 1951 sixteen kilometre race. Marilyn recalls how prior to Atlantic City, Jerry had openly wondered why Marilyn was even in the company of the race professionals. As she moved along, Gus scribbled on his chalkboard: "You're catching Jerry."

When she passed Jerry, he stopped in the water. Shortly afterwards, Marilyn paused for a feeding. Gus told her Jerry had just quit. Before the race, Jerry had said he'd get out if a woman was beating him. When Marilyn swam by, his crew yelled that a woman had passed him. "It was very funny to me, but the fact is that I actually beat this guy who won the Ex [CNE] swims, and that, for me, was just, 'Oh. Wow, this is really great.' That was real motivation for me".

Gus continued to motivate her that way, making a commotion on the chalkboard each time she passed yet another male swimmer. "Another one down. Another one down." She passed through a nasty patch of raw sewage spewing out of a pipe, the odour terrible, the water temperature spiking to 26.6C, a dip in a hot tub for an open-water swimmer. Then back into the colder ocean with the changing tide. For the last quarter of the 26-mile (41.8 km) race, she swam through a slimy mucky mess of jellyfish, the goo slipping under her bathing suit. Her lifeguards told her, "Keep going, they won't sting. Keep going!"

"So I did! I swam through it. Then I knew I was the first woman to finish." Her time was 10 hours, 7 minutes, 20 seconds, less than a minute out of sixth place. Her paycheque of $1,150 was significantly less than Tom Park's winnings. And he had a trophy. Eventually somebody realized the poor optics of the women's winner not getting a trophy and Marilyn received her trophy. But being the first woman was an incredible realization. All the negative aspects of the swim, all the unpleasantness strengthened Bell. She was finally first at something. She had competed and won for Canada. She was named an alternate on the relay team for the Lake Ontario crossing at the CNE. Eventually Gus Ryder came up with the idea of putting Marilyn's name forward for the solo challenge of Lake Ontario that would ultimately blossom into a battle royal between Chadwick, Bell and Winnie Roach Leuszler, with only Marilyn completing the first-ever solo swim across Lake Ontario. Marilyn bought into the idea because Gus believed she could do it. "I never bought into the idea that I could be the one." Even she wasn't sure if anyone could do it. Her own motivation was to try and swim further than Florence Chadwick. Marilyn believes the swims in the Credit River and then in Atlantic City, were critical to her success in Lake Ontario (McAllister 97). The joy, the sense of herself as a competitive athlete, that she took from her fresh and saltwater swims brought her to the point where she could challenge for the solo crossing, for that shot at being the first ever.

At first, she recalls, swimming solo across Lake Ontario hadn't even occurred to her. Who did that, anyway? Even nearly 60 years on, people still ask. During interviews Marilyn Bell Di Lascio remembered how, as a 12-year-old, she had been strolling with her father along the Toronto waterfront. As they watched the CNE's professional swim races on set courses parallel and point to point, she asked her father if anyone had ever swum across the Lake. "Oh, no. I don't think anyone would do that," he replied. "It's much too far."

Part One

Sixty Years of Great Lakes Swimming

Lake Ontario 1

Too Far, Indeed...

Too far, too cold, too wide, too deep, too much water and weather. Only the glaciers that carved them could be considered more massive than the Great Lakes, the beating heart of North America, interlocking, connected pools with their own climates. But the glaciers retreated in the melt some 10,000 years ago; the Lakes remained—25 percent of the planet's fresh water. Much has been said, written, and photographed about the largest collection of freshwater lakes in the world. From any vantage point, they are gargantuan—inland seas. Over 40 million people in Canada and the United States rely on them, one in three Canadians and one in seven Americans, for their fresh water (Science North). They are under threat, polluted, ambushed by flying carp among other invasive species. And yet, they can take down a freighter and keep it down. Lake Superior—the name says it all—has sucked down its share of heaving, cargo-laden tankers and never coughed them back up. Champion swimmers consider themselves fortunate after Superior has picked them up and tossed them back unceremoniously onto its rocky beaches.

Swimming the Great Lakes is certainly an obscure thing to do in life. Many have stared at the big waters and wondered. But few have tried it. In 2012, 500 people reached the summit of Mt. Everest (Jenkins), more than five times the number of crossings of all five Great Lakes combined, ever. While each Lake has its characteristic features, the marathon swimmers, swim masters, and their crews who do set out have their very own Mount Everest. Lake

Ontario—despite being the smallest of the Great Lakes in area—is the pinnacle, the pride of the tradition, a rolling body of currents that push swimmers towards their destination, then toss and roll them back, water at first enticingly warm, then cold enough to chill a swimmer to the marrow, mere kilometres from the finish. And then there's the lightning, or the cold, or the wind. Even with GPS—online dot navigation allowing anyone in the world to follow a swimmer's track hour by hour on social media—and advances in training, fitness, nutrition, and boats, the chances of success remain 50-50, at best.

In 2012, twelve people inquired with Solo Swims of Ontario Inc., the governing body of marathon swimming on the Great Lakes, about making a crossing; ten officially put their names forward, and seven swims actually happened on Lake Ontario (Solo Swims), with the hope that in 2012 the records for the oldest and the youngest swimmers would be reset. Of those seven attempts, only three were completed, and only one of those was along the longer, traditional route from Niagara-on-the-Lake to Toronto. In that swim, 14-year-old Annaleise Carr became the youngest to cross the Lake. Lake Ontario retained its reputation as one of the world's toughest open-water swims. By comparison, the English Channel, also an exclusive club of swimmers, saw 180 swimmers cross successfully in 2012 (Channel Swimming). Unlike so much else on the Great Lakes, when it comes to swimming, the Lakes remain in charge.

They are as powerful as they are unpredictable. All the guesswork can drive a swimmer mad: When will they change? Or will they, perhaps this once, stay steady? What about fog? In the lower Great Lakes especially, heat, humidity and the sheer size of the water bodies trigger lightning. Any extra humidity can set up weird weather patterns, sending up white squalls, says Bryan Finlay, a swim master with Solo Swims, Inc., whose own attempt on Lake Ontario ended six hours into the crossing due to weather. He says Lake Erie is generally more predictable, and swimmers can get in towards the end of June, perhaps. As long as the wind isn't blowing…

On Lake Ontario, the window is narrow, roughly mid-July to late August, perhaps early September. But then the nights are getting shorter as Canadians brace themselves for the arrival of winter. And virtually nobody will complete the 51-kilometre traditional Lake Ontario crossing in under 14 hours,

Bryan says. That means some swimming in the dark. Bryan has plotted winds at Dover, England, departure and arrival site for the crossing of the English Channel, where the winds are predominately southwest, he says. That doesn't diminish the effort it takes to swim across the Channel as Bryan knows so well, having been plucked unconscious out of it. "As far as Lake Ontario is concerned, I plotted the thing out and there's no established wind direction." The wind can rotate clockwise, move from the north to south, then by its tail end be going south to north. And somewhere else in between. In other words, random winds. "The chances of having a steady southerly breeze behind you for 12 to 20 hours is pretty remote on Lake Ontario. The weather patterns don't seem to last that long," Bryan says.

There are patches of cold, especially if a Laker steams by and churns up ancient waters from the depths of the Lake. And, did Bryan mention the currents? He wonders if people who swim the Lake truly appreciate the difficulty of crossing Lake Ontario, and how lucky they were to get a good day. Without marathon training and expertise, jumping into Lake Ontario is a big challenge, he reflects. "It's one of the toughest marathon swims in the world."

The temperature inversion on Lake Ontario makes it unpredictable, Bryan adds. Along the shoreline of the Toronto side, strong northerly winds and cyclical Lake currents mix and mingle. One summer he measured a temperature range from 23.3C at Niagara-on-the-Lake down to 7.2C at Toronto. It can take a week for the temperature to return to something more swimmable. Swimmers know this inversion will happen during the summer, Bryan says. The question is when.

Marilyn Korzekwa is Solo Swims' medical person and a swim master who has crossed Lake Ontario dozens of times perched on the side of a Zodiac support boat or driving a larger powerboat. Ironically, she is a psychiatrist; athletically, she is also the first person to swim Lake Ontario in both directions, first south to north in 1983, then north to south in 1984. She is the most senior Canadian woman to complete the Catalina Channel, in 2013, and the English Channel, in 2011.

With Lake Ontario, Marilyn says, cold remains the big problem, making it one of the toughest swims in the world. "If the wind picks up it can turn over the surface layers. The layer of warm water rarely gets more than six feet deep." The water temperature tends to plummet the closer the swimmer draws to Toronto: "Coming into Toronto the prevailing wind is northwest. The wind blowing offshore from Toronto takes the warm layer out to the middle of the Lake and the cold water wells up. The last 4.5 kilometres is where the swim really begins, where the test begins, not just for fatigue reasons, but for the cold."

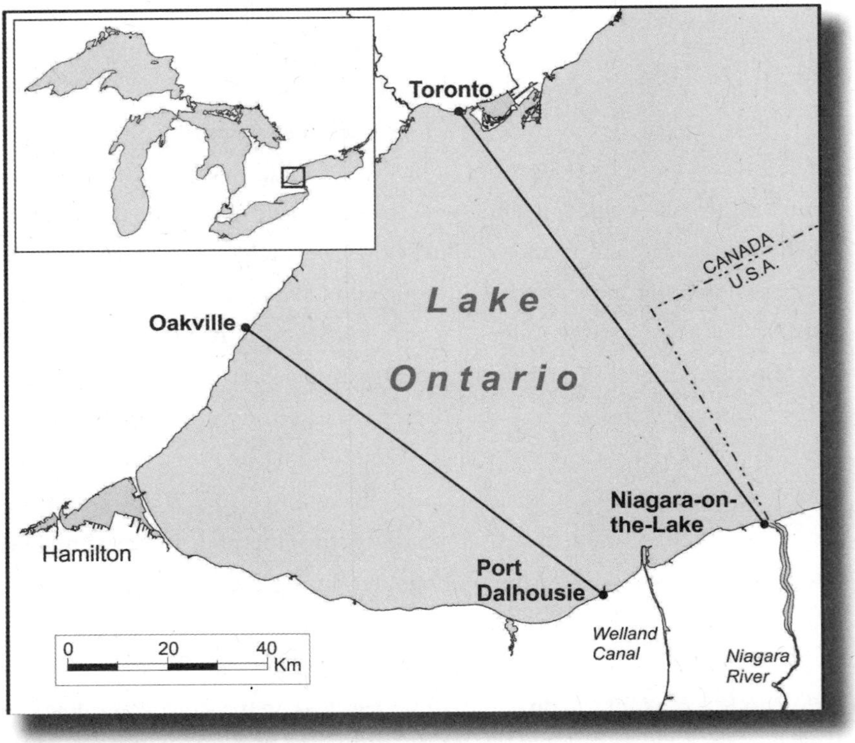

Lake Ontario west end crossing routes. The traditional route leaves from Niagara-on-the-Lake, (directly across the Niagara River from Youngstown, NY, where Marilyn Bell started) and finishes in what is now Marilyn Bell Park near Ontario Place in Toronto. The route from Port Dalhousie to Oakville was developed by the Lake Ontario Swim Team (L.O.S.T.). Map Credit: L.L. Lariviere—Laurentian University

Marilyn Bell—First Lady of the Lake, 1954

On September 8, 1954, it was nearly 11:00 p.m. and Marilyn Bell was wondering what she had gotten herself into. She stood under a tree, taking shelter from the rain in Youngstown, NY, on the shores of Lake Ontario. Winnie Roach Leuszler, the first Canadian ever to swim across the English Channel and Marilyn's friend and heroine stood with her. They exchanged a few words.

With them was a benefactor unknown to them who had driven Marilyn to the coast guard station and who was excited to have played her part in what was already feeling like an epic battle. The woman asked Marilyn for something to remember her by but they had neither pen nor paper for an autograph. Finally Marilyn pulled a tassel from her slipper and handed it to her. They exchanged hugs and the woman told her she thought Marilyn would swim the Lake. Years later they met again; the woman told Marilyn she still had that tassel. Marilyn was full of trepidation: "I had issued the challenge so I had to follow through with it."

In 1954 the Canadian National Exhibition, the late summer festival in downtown Toronto, was shaking up its regular CNE swims in Lake Ontario. The swims began in 1927, buoyed by the success of the Wrigley gum company's sponsorship of the Catalina Channel swims in California (Wennerberg 96). Over the years, a series of distances were raced along the Toronto waterfront with the 15 miler (24 km) being the most popular. In 1954, the CNE organized and sponsored a 32-mile (51.4 km) across the Lake swim relay, and a solo swim (Toronto in Time). That solo swim, the ensuing celebrity status at becoming the first-ever to complete the Great Lake crossing, and a $10,000 pay day were offered famously only to Florence Chadwick, the world-class American marathon swimmer (Wennerberg 106).

Here myth and legend mingle with reality. To some extent, Florence has been vilified; in the movie on Marilyn Bell's life that invented much of the drama of the CNE sponsorship and the ensuing newspaper wars, the legendary swimmer was one-dimensional at best. In real life, her invitation to the CNE was legitimate and deserving. Florence, a 32-year-old "swimming coach" ("Florence Chadwick") from San Diego, California, was the first woman to swim the Catalina Channel and the first to swim the English Channel in both directions. In her day, the English Channel was considered the greatest challenge for open-water swimmers. She swam three complete crossings of the Channel and each time set a speed record, including shattering the record of Gertrude Ederle, the first woman to ever swim the Channel, by over one hour. Such was Florence's natural ability in open water and marathon swimming that she did not make the 1936 Olympic team because the distances were too short ("Florence Chadwick").

What irked the Canadians was that only Florence was offered the prize money (Toronto in Time). The winning relay team would also receive $10,000. Marilyn checked the line-up of the relay. She was alternate behind the four guys, and figured it was unlikely she would be needed. Only after choosing to try the solo crossing, did she learn that her teammates had decided to split any prize money they won on the relay five ways, whether she was an alternate or not. "That was a very kind thing to do. I was their mascot, too. They really watched out for me and were really good to me."

Marilyn convinced Gus and her parents to let her make the solo attempt. Winnie Roach Leuszler, a mother of three and eventual hall of famer, also stepped up to the challenge. There was to be no money for them, even if they completed the crossing, so when the news broke about the Canadians not getting the money offered to the American, it struck a chord. The story went, as we say now, viral in an ensuing newspaper war between the Toronto papers.

Toronto businesses began to pitch in money for the Canadian teenager if she could complete the swim (McAllister 108;Wennerberg 106).

Florence dictated the start time as per her contract with the CNE. This being Lake Ontario, the weather delayed the start from Monday, September 6th to Wednesday, September 8th. The relay crossing of the Lake was switched to a race in front of the CNE grounds. Florence decided she would leave at 11:00 p.m.

Prior to the swim, CNE officials had told Gus they would give Marilyn's team a certain amount of time to prepare once Florence had decided when she was going to swim. "I'm assuming the reason they did that was to avoid any more adverse publicity about the treatment of the Canadians," Marilyn recalls. Somehow Marilyn's team learned of Florence's departure time. Her father and Gus had gone for a walk that rainy evening, figuring nothing would happen that night. Over on the escort boat the *Mona Four* the team was in a frenzy preparing the food; Marilyn was anxiously getting ready to swim—and no one knew where her coach Gus and her father Syd could be.

When they returned there wasn't enough time to get the support boats over to Youngstown for the start, so Gus decided to stay on the *Mona Four* and head across the lake, while Howie Anderson, a photographer, agreed to take Marilyn to the Youngstown Coast Guard Station where Florence was leaving—if he could find a car to take them…

Thus far the plan seemed simple… except that there still wasn't time to get her support boat close enough so Marilyn would see the boat from the start. She was going to have to swim for it and have her team find her. "Yeah, really," she laughs, so many years on. Still, she agreed and believed Gus. "When I think about it, oh my God."

With Marilyn waiting in swimsuit, sweats, and a raincoat, Howie tried to get wheels to take them to Youngstown. He stopped one car and explained he needed a lift. The driver told him no way, he had to get to Toronto for a big story that was breaking. The driver didn't know that this swimmer needing a ride was part of the story, Marilyn says. "Later on I met him and he said he'd never forgive himself."

In truth, though, nobody would recognize her, in what were ironically her final hours of anonymity. It's unlikely that the reporter was expecting "this person who was being so obnoxious in terms of coming to the party uninvited," Marilyn recalls. Howie stopped another car. This time Howie explained the who and what. The woman said she'd be delighted to help.

And so they arrived at Youngstown, in time to see Florence slipping into Lake Ontario. Marilyn made her way to the water's edge, and purposefully dove in. "I decided I was diving. That was probably the first time I ever tried to be a hot dog," Marilyn laughs.

She surfaced, opening her eyes to the almost pitch dark. She could just make out Florence's flotilla ahead in the distance. Gus had told her to keep swimming and he'd find her. Marilyn had implicit trust in Gus and swam, petrified at being in the water for the first time at night in her swimming career. Gus would later say that he knew how afraid she was to swim at night. He purposefully decided he wouldn't go there with her anytime beforehand, that he knew she could handle it at the time on the day.

Winnie Roach Leuzsler left 17 minutes later but swam around for an hour looking for her support boat. She returned to shore and restarted her swim at 6:00 a.m. (Wennerberg 107). Marilyn faded into the rhythm of swimming, the breath, the reach, roll and pull back of each arm stroke. She may not remember actually finishing the historical swim—but, she says, "I don't think I've forgotten a stroke of night swimming, even now." Gus shone a flashlight forward from the side of his boat and Marilyn swam towards it which helped, but it also attracted eels, which they didn't know would happen until the eels appeared. She speaks in a detached manner about the eels. And that's literally how she dealt with them, detaching the critters and swimming on towards Toronto. "You know, they were part of it," she recalls. In the first hour she removed her goggles. Ninety minutes into the swim, she would pass Florence (Wennerberg 107).

It would be a long night of misery on Lake Ontario for Florence Chadwick, in a summer of incomplete crossings for the legendary swimmer. Seasickness affects some swimmers out on Lake Ontario and some not, but they never know until they're out there. As the rolling waves tossed Florence in the lake, she was increasingly ill and vainly trying to hang on. Before 6:00 a.m., her team hauled her into the boat. Over the radio waves it was announced that

Florence had been pulled out. Listeners wanted know what had happened to Marilyn. Winnie Roach re-entered the Lake at 6:00 a.m., but restarting took its toll and she ended the swim about 12 kilometres short of Toronto (McAllister 115). The only man in the field, the same Jerry Kerschner who had been overtaken by Marilyn in Atlantic City, also didn't finish. He lasted 14 miles (22.5 km) and 8 hours ("One may be…"). Now there was only Marilyn.

The memory of the coming dawn has stayed with Marilyn. She breathed to her right side only, to the east. "I was seeing these yellow streaks, streaks of light way, way far away in the distance." There was no moon that night. Clouds made it impossible to distinguish between sky and water. There was only black. As she took her breath she couldn't figure out what the light was. At first, it seemed like a search light only that didn't make sense because the light wasn't moving up into the sky; it was parallel to her movement in the water. Marilyn had never seen a sunrise. On Lake Ontario, she was low to the horizon looking up to flashes of light that grew brighter and brighter; then the sun rose. "It was magnificent. I've never forgotten it. All I could think was, 'Oh my goodness. It's Easter morning.' For me, the highlight of my Lake Ontario swim was the sunrise. And it was so hopeful." And with the dawn came the realization that she had swum through the night, through the eels, rain, and the waves. She was happy. As the sun burnt off the morning mist from Lake Ontario, they could see ahead into the distance at last, encouraging. "But, the sunrise for me, that was the greatest gift on that swim."

The rest was slogging it in to shore and she was tired. She'd spent two nights on the boat without a good night's sleep waiting for Florence to announce her departure. She'd been up early the morning of the swim and awake all day. There was the stress of waiting. They had thought of going to the movies, anything, but couldn't really leave because they had to be ready when Florence was ready. "There's always tension before a long swim or any kind of an event like that. But when you're not in control of the timing I guess that added extra pressure; I realize that now," Marilyn says. "At the time I think I was oblivious."

Getting into the water at 11:00 p.m. the night before and actually turning the circus into an athletic event had brought a measure of relief. Yet as September 9th wore on sleep deprivation joined the swim. She would doze off only to hear Gus yelling at her to bring her back to reality. During the final hours of the swim she lost any sense of time and struggled with the powerful currents just off Toronto (Toronto in Time). Above and beside her, Gus and her father Syd argued about taking her out. With Canadians across the country glued to radios, Marilyn remained in the Lake, fuelled on pablum and corn syrup (McAllister 115).

She came ashore in a blaze of faces, 20 hours and 55 minutes after starting, the swirling currents having pushed her west of Toronto. "The end of the swim was really anticlimactic for me." When she was taken into the boat, there were medical concerns. Then she was transferred to the accompanying yacht where a doctor examined her. Having swum 20 hours without goggles her eyes were in rough shape. Her mother Grace was trying to administer eye drops in an attempt to clear her eyes. There was a lot of commotion and talk but nobody told her she had completed the crossing, she says. Eventually, as she was in an ambulance being transferred to the Royal York Hotel, she began to realize she had made it. "Did I finish?" she asked. The swim had stopped at the breakwall, so in the confusion she wondered whether she had touched land. Joan Lumsdon, who had

Marilyn Bell completed the first crossing of Lake Ontario, September 8-9, 1954. Photo courtesy of *The Toronto Star*/QMIAgency.

leaped in to pace her on Gus's command, wearing only bra and underwear, said "Of course, you made it. You were the only one."

Everything went crazy after that. "Oh, my gosh. My life was never the same."

It continues to astound Marilyn that her swim has remained such an integral part of Canadian folklore. Over the years she and her husband Chipper Di Lascio would reflect on the enduring legacy of her swim, especially when she would receive a phone call about an award, or when she was inducted into the Canadian Sports Hall of Fame—"To me, that was just unbelievable. Unbelievable." Chipper would tell her that she didn't understand the impact of her story. That it wasn't just a sports story, that this was a story in Canadian history and it was always going to be that way. Marilyn would look at him and say, "I think it's because you're an American that you think like that. Canadians aren't like that."

She would meet people and hear their accounts of what they did while she swam, people who ate beans on toast because their mother wouldn't leave the radio to cook dinner that night. "All these wonderful, wonderful stories that I've heard over the years and still I couldn't get my head around it, that this swim had made that much difference in peoples' lives."

In 2009 a ferry that runs passengers to Toronto Island was named after her. Before she went to Toronto to see the ferry, she had tried to downplay it and tell her family and friends it wasn't a big deal. It's not a huge ferry crossing after all. When she saw the ferry coming around to the dock, then she got it. Chipper was right. "The swim itself did capture the imagination," she says.

She remains unsure why everything happened the way it did: the combination of the hours of her swim, the suspense of a little girl (all five feet one inch of her) out in the middle of a Great Lake and what might happen to her. "It was almost like I became everyone's daughter."

She reflects that perhaps the swim came at a time when Canadians didn't have a complete sense of who they were and what a great country they were. The feeling was that to be successful, if you had talent, you went to the U.S. "Then I think it was just in the 50s, there was something about the times, and this 16-year-old kid that came from nowhere, who had a dream and worked to bring that dream to fruition," she says.

Marilyn Bell proved it was possible. She was an experienced open-water swimmer when she swam the frigid, temperamental, beautiful, uniquely blue waters of Lake Ontario. It seemed the Lake was, as they say, "conquerable." Yet successful crossings remained sporadic: in 1956 John Jeremey of Canada and England's Brenda Fisher swam across. Bill Sadlo of the U.S. in 1957. Jim Woods, also of the U.S., swam three days after Sadlo and took seven hours off Sadlo's crossing time. Woods would go again in 1961, becoming the first King of the Lake. Then nothing until 1974 when Cindy Nicholas stepped up to the shores of Lake Ontario at Youngstown and lucked out with time, water temperature, and weather, a swim that remains the bar for women—and most men—to clear.

Cindy Nicholas and the Women's Speed Record

Remarkably, Cindy Nicholas, now a semi-retired estate lawyer in Toronto, only tested her luck with Lake Ontario once. Conditions that day in 1974 were perfect, seemingly pristine, rare. Years later she still feels gratitude for the weather, while knowing the Lake doesn't give gifts. She may well have been phenomenally lucky though her friend Marilyn Bell says luck had nothing to do with it; Cindy was that talented and that fast. Still, some unnameable force was at play August 17th, for Cindy's one crossing of Lake Ontario, all 15 hours and 10 minutes of swimming, literally launched her life.

On the statistical side, she became the first woman in 18 years to cross Lake Ontario, stripping three hours from England's Brenda Fisher's 1956 record of 18 hours, 50 minutes (Solo Swims). Cindy flung away clinging lamprey eels and dodged boats to set a formidable bar in marathon swimming on the Great Lakes.

But that didn't seem to matter when Cindy Nicholas exited Lake Ontario in 1974 with the women's amateur record. Instead, reporters wanted to know whether she going to swim the English Channel. Come on, was the attitude, anyone who is anyone in swimming has to swim the English Channel. Despite Cindy having just reached the summit of swimming's Mount Everest in record time, everyone wanted to know what was next for Cindy, then a few days shy of her 17th birthday. "I was barely standing up straight because I'd been up all night," she recalls, laughing. In hindsight she thinks that moment on the beach with the reporters swarming around helped her decide not to try out for the Olympic swim team but instead to challenge open-water and marathon swimming. "But it wasn't my initial thought. I didn't even think about the English Channel again for several months until I got a call out of the blue from CFRB." The radio station was thinking about her Channel swim and how they wanted to have a reporter along to document her journey. "I was caught off guard and sort of spluttered, 'Oh, oh, yeah. Well, yeah, someone did say I should do that.' And that's how I fell into it."

Nicholas was a club swimmer in Toronto who wanted to represent Canada at the Olympics. She went to the 1972 Olympic trials but did not qualify for Munich. Though she planned to try for the 1976 Montreal Olympics instead, sometime in the late spring of 1974, her focus began to shift. Another type of swimming was increasingly mentioned in her home. The family could see Lake Ontario from their dining room. Over many a meal her father James reminded her how Marilyn Bell had swum across that very lake. "You know, Cindy, you could do that," he would say. "When are you going to do it? Marilyn Bell did it. I think you should give it a go."

When she came to swim Lake Ontario in the summer of 1974, she needed only to adjust her training for open water. She headed north of Toronto to Lake Rosseau to swim four miles per session, morning, noon and night. Practising for ten miles straight didn't suit her. She loved to go fast, but the longer she swam, the more her speed was adversely affected. Instead, she'd swim out to an island in Lake Rosseau, flip around and swim back. Repeat. Repeat. "Each one was just over a mile and a half (2.4 km). It would be a 45-minute swim." She might rest for a few seconds, which would break the routine and make her swim faster.

In the meantime, her teammates were returning from summer nationals where the world-class swimmers completed a mile (1.6 km) in about 17 minutes and kept their eye to the calendar—two years left to the 1976 Montreal Olympics. They would hear about Cindy's training and her goal to swim Lake Ontario. They thought she was crazy. "They were totally intimidated by swimming three miles (4.8 km) together. But if you gave them three, one-mile repeats on 17 minutes, they'd be fine with that."

Her team was talking about Cindy attempting to break Marilyn Bell's time record, because she did not think she could swim for 22 hours. She was either going to break the record or not make it. Such was the pattern for her career. "I had trouble once I went over 20-some hours. I did a 22 hour miserable, awful, swim across the English Channel and back. For the most part, I like to keep my swims under 20 hours." By hour 20 of any swim Cindy needed to see the end, otherwise that swim wasn't likely to succeed. "A lot of people, they can swim 30 to 40 hours. But I aimed to do the same swim in a lot less time. That's what I tried for, anyway."

In August 1974 she went to Youngstown, NY to wait for just the right moment, the day, the pocket of time when summer seems endless. She was a well-trained swimmer, with other skills so necessary for challenging Lake Ontario: she wasn't afraid of open water, except for weeds; she preferred not to see the bottom, which wouldn't happen anyway, what with Lake Ontario being hundreds of feet deep. Finally, she could handle cold water, so that wouldn't be an issue if the Lake waters inverted. At this time Lake Ontario crossings started at Youngstown, NY, just across the mouth of the Niagara River from Niagara-on-the-Lake on the Canadian side. That had been the start point for Marilyn Bell's crossing in 1954, and the tradition continued. But in Youngstown no one knew who Cindy was, let alone that she was coming.

Over the course of the weeks leading up to Cindy's swim, coach Al Waites had searched for a sponsor to provide an escort boat for the swim. Despite talking up how she would be the first swimmer to conquer the lake in nearly 20 years, he had no luck. Regardless, by Thursday August 15th the swim was on. As the team gathered in Youngstown, they hoped the U.S. Coast Guard might offer an escort. *The Globe and Mail* reported, however, that Richard Price, chief of the U.S. coast guard at Youngstown, said Cindy would not be leaving from the Coast Guard station dock if he had anything to say about it. At first it seemed that the coast guard was refusing to cooperate with the swim, though the *Globe*'s Christie Blatchford, who accompanied the swim, noted that arrangements are supposed to be made well in advance for escort boats on these types of swims. Later the coast guard said it had been taken by surprise when Cindy and her crew showed up at 2:00 a.m. They wanted to help, maybe even offer an escort, but had feared bureaucratic reprisals (Blatchford). After middle of the night discussions on the dock in Youngstown in which the U.S. Coast Guard declined to escort the swim into Canadian waters, the Canadian crew decided to go ahead without an escort boat, but simply with Cindy's dad James, coach Waites, his son Bruce who acted as Cindy's pacer, and Christie Blatchford in the support motorboat.

The escort boat problem was solved at the last minute, thanks to the kindness of strangers. Nearby was a sailboat with four young men on it. Shortly after 2:00 a.m. Cindy and her father asked if they could take her out in Lake Ontario a little ways. "I'm a young, blonde 16-year-old," Cindy laughs. She didn't know Jeff Carver, Chris Doyle and Andy Joyce of Williamsville, NY, or Mark Jaireitano of Youngstown (Blatchford). They were sailors preparing for a regatta the next day at the CNE. Agreeing to help out, they also fed a starving Cindy bread and spaghetti sauce. Then she began stripping down to her swim suit. Understandably stunned, the guys asked what she was doing. Oh, she replied, she was just going for a swim alongside the sailboat while the guys took her out into the Lake.

Under a clear night sky, and with a 14-foot motor boat for her crew and a coincidental sailboat as the escort, Cindy slipped into Lake Ontario at 2:20 a.m. The sailors promised to lead them for two hours; they stayed until 6:45 a.m., Cindy following their sail through the night at a steady 70 strokes per minute, a stroke rate that stayed the same throughout the entire crossing (Blatchford, "Race...").

Of course, years later Cindy would never recommend crossing Lake Ontario this way, with two boats, so last-minute. Her crossing came just prior to the launch of the sanctioning body Solo Swims. "When I look back on this it was the stupidest thing we ever did. My father was there condoning the actions all the way. We had an outboard motorboat, an old wooden one." On Lake Ontario, their boat was like a matchstick, said Coach Waites (Waites). When the sailors departed in the early morning, Cindy was in Lake Ontario and her entire support crew sat in a 14-foot boat. Hours later, a CFRB radio boat arrived and began broadcasting her progress; gift pledges started coming in: $3,000 cash, an Arabian horse, 50 gallons of ice cream, her favourite food. The

CFRB boat guided the team the rest of the way (Martin). Cindy reflects that she could have swum a straighter course with better equipment, but "my father is a pilot of small planes so he's very familiar with a compass. But we couldn't see the other side."

In 1974, the Toronto skyline was barely visible, hardly the giant cluster of buildings it is today, visible from 51 kilometres away in Niagara-on-the-Lake. The CN Tower was still being built. Eventually Cindy could see pipes down by Commissioner's Street. At one point, her escort boat was headed in one direction and Nicholas was yelling at him to go the other way. They were zigzagging back and forth, a horrible situation for the swimmer. Finally, Cindy had had enough, yelling that she wanted to go as straight as she could.

The only real crisis on the lake crossing came 16 kilometres off Toronto when they thought they only had half that distance to cover. "A mere jaunt," Waites shouted at Cindy, "to my tiger in the water; let's go sweetheart, eight to go." But within a stroke of freestyle, perhaps two, word came that, no, they were really 16 kilometres off shore. In a classic case of if you don't have anything nice to say, Waites and James Nicholas waffled, trying to decide whether to tell Cindy or just say nothing. When Cindy stopped for a feeding, she did a porpoise dive, a swimmer in joy and rapture, and asked how much further. Waites paused. "Tiger," he told her, "I'm wrong. It was 16" (Waites).

Cindy simply continued. She asked to be taken the shortest way to Toronto. When it seemed she was really suffering, Coach Waites hopped in the water with her but she refused his support, picked up her stroke rate and swam ashore. Crowds were now appearing, cheering her on. The boats that had eluded the team at the beginning of the crossing were interfering with the finish, blocking her view of shore, which she hated. Then a lamprey latched onto the back of her leg. People started yelling from the flotilla. Mortified, again, she grabbed hold of the eel's head and squeezed it off.

Despite the eels and the interference, Cindy still laughs hard over a story from this point in the swim. People described how she seemed to struggle at the end of the 51-kilometre crossing, how exhausted she must have been. After all, she kept stopping. But not quite for the reason people suspected. Like the astronauts on their lunar voyages, she drank Tang on her crossing... lots of it.

She literally was brimming with Tang and sloshing in the waters off Toronto. She kept stopping in order to go. Everyone was encouraging her to keep swimming. Finally her father James called out from their motorboat. "Let her alone. She has to go."

"I was very lucky. I was charmed, because, I mean, everything could have gone wrong. It was crazy." Cindy tries not to think about that too often. "I have tried to mask that from my memory bank because I wouldn't want anyone to think this is the way to do it." Coach Waites later wrote that her character carried her through, and her real advantage lay in "an extraordinarily placid Lake Ontario." Her conditions, simply, were ideal.

At 5:40 p.m. Cindy came ashore at Ontario Place on the Toronto waterfront, 15 hours and 10 minutes after starting. She told everyone she felt great, maybe she could even swim a few more kilometres. Then she collapsed. Rushed to a nearby St John's Ambulance station, she was soon declared fit. "The little tiger beat the lake last night," Blatchford wrote of the swimmer (Blatchford, "Tears..."). Though Nicholas was the first person to cross since Jim Woods in 1961, she was not the only person to cross Lake Ontario in 1974. On August 30th-31st, American Diana Nyad, then 24, attempted the first double crossing. She swam south from Toronto to Youngstown but was pulled unconscious early in the return swim (Nyad 14). She was credited with the first north to south crossing, a 49-kilometre swim, in 18 hours, 15 minutes.

For Cindy Nicholas, there was little time to rest on the laurels of her crossing of Ontario. From the day of her victory the media was asking, "What's next? You gonna swim the English Channel?" She didn't just swim the Channel; she owned it! By 1976, she was the world women's international swimming champion. She would swim the English Channel 19 times, including five double crossings, and in 1975 would set the record for crossing the Channel in 9 hours and 46 minutes. In 1977 she was the first woman to swim the English Channel both ways nonstop. She set a new world record of 19 hours, 55 minutes, beating her then boyfriend, the great American marathon swimmer Jon Erickson, by over 10 hours.

After her fifth crossing of the English Channel, she was named Queen of the Channel. Odd as it sounds, as a young girl, Cindy had always wanted to be a princess when she grew up. "Then I found out you had to marry a prince." Princes being limited, she figured the Channel might be the right place at the right time to meet Prince Charles of England. She's reminded that she was also blonde and 19. "Don't joke," she says, laughing. "I was waiting for him to meet me at the beach. So anyways I eventually concluded that I wasn't going to be a princess the natural way so I wouldn't mind being Queen of the English Channel, so I went after the five crossings."

Cindy credits her parents for her swimming career and swimming for her good life. "My parents gave up so much of their own life and money for my swimming. What they gave up allowed me to be the champion I became."

Swimming Lake Ontario, then owning the world of marathon swimming, opened doors, as clichéd as that sounds. She achieved a level of celebrity as she worked with Alan Eagleson, the former agent for hockey superstar Bobby Orr. Eagleson took Cindy under his wing, finding her sponsors, offering his law firm as the site for her articling as a lawyer. Notwithstanding the downward spiral that became Eagleson's career and subsequent criminal record, he still helped. Swimming brought fame and fortune in a Canadian way. Thanks to Eagleson and the speaking engagements he arranged, she made money as a world champion marathon swimmer. As she was growing up, the family income had been invested in her swimming until she was 20. After that Eagleson had a knack for getting Cindy funding and her swims paid for themselves. He would find her $5,000 here, another $5,000 there. Not exactly professional hockey money but she was able to retire from swimming and graduate from law school debt free. "He thought I was a great Canadian and a true example. He wanted to help me. He was proud of me as a Canadian. He was proud to be Canadian. I was very fortunate".

She loved hanging out with former Canadian Prime Minister, the late Pierre Trudeau. He became her hero but it was a mutual thing. "He encouraged me and he loved swimming. Anytime I was around him, he would say: 'Cindy, did you bring your suit?' I'd give him the look, 'Did I bring my suit? Of course I brought my suit!'" Trudeau would then invite her for a swim in the pool at the prime minister's residence. In 1979, Trudeau was no longer prime minister but he was there when Nicholas received the Order of Canada, the nation's highest civilian award. "He came over and said, 'I just thought I'd walk over and say congratulations.' He'd come and touch my shoulders, and say 'I always liked to touch your shoulders,'" Cindy recalls, laughing. "He thought they were so strong, strong like bull."

In 1982, those same shoulders were finished with swimming, and she retired when she was still in love with the water. By 2010, she was slipping back into public swimming pools. "It's a big achievement for me now just to swim because, when I go in the pool, people will know it's me, and they want to race me, right? I'll want to race them back. Because that's me. You can't let anybody beat you," she laughs.

Decades after her one crack at Lake Ontario, Cindy finds it remarkable that her time for the crossing still stands as the women's record. "I was lucky. I proved that I had the speed. But we got lucky with the Lake." Marilyn Bell Di Lascio says the crossing was part of Cindy's destiny. "She has the true heart of a marathoner. I have such admiration for Cindy. She's a cool, cool woman, so well-rounded, a good example of a modern woman."

There were some big swims in Cindy's future: the 19 crossings of the English Channel, and Lac St. Jean, and the Baie des Chaleurs in Quebec, and awards from the Order of Canada and the International Swimming Hall of Fame. For Cindy, Lake Ontario was not her toughest swim; certainly not her coldest. She swam through pollution, garbage, and other hazards in the English Channel. Lake Ontario was relatively clean by comparison. But in Lake Ontario, everything came together in the lucky bounce that is, rather simply, the mystery of sport. "And maybe it was better that I never did it again because I did it so well the first time. Until I did another swim I was second-guessing myself, wondering whether it was just a one-time thing. My whole life changed that summer."

Solo Swims of Ontario

Cindy Nicholas's record-setting swim in 1974 signalled change on the shimmering blue horizon of Lake Ontario. As the sun set on the summer of 1974, Lake Ontario was busy. Angela Kondrak came within 2.4 kilometres of finishing her swim before being pulled. About one week later, Diana Nyad, then 24, attempted to become the first swimmer to complete the historic first double crossing of the Lake, coached by Cliff Lumsdon. Loreen Passfield, then 16, was trying to become the youngest swimmer to cross the Lake. Al Waites, her coach, struggled to find the support boats; then the weather postponed everything anyway. Finally, on September 1st, she came within 16 kilometres of Ontario place before her attempt was pulled. It was a double-edged sword. Media coverage of these swims and the ensuing popularity of Cindy Nicholas after her crossing had perhaps created a sense that Lake Ontario could be had. Considering that media then meant newspaper and radio, the crossing attempts were covered extensively, including the delays. The Lake was in the news, but whether that was a good thing was another matter.

Neil MacNeil had been talking about swimming Lake Ontario for years. In 1974 the 17-year-old competitive swimmer in the Scarborough neighbourhood of Toronto decided to make the attempt to cross the Lake and optimistically said he was out to break Cindy's record. He ran to build his fitness, according to reports. On the afternoon of September 7th, he set out from Youngstown, NY with one 12-foot long boat for support. Early in the attempt the boat's motor broke down. His coach waved him back to the boat but MacNeil chose to forge on. That was the last time he was seen alive.

By then Al Waites, coach of Cindy Nicholas, Loreen Passfield, and Angela Kondrak, and Cliff Lumsdon, who had retired from his legendary marathon swimming career and was now coaching, lobbied hard for a governing body similar to the Channel Swimming Association in England. The proposed name was the Lake Ontario Swim Association. Neil MacNeil's father Rod also wanted a similar organization.

In such a body, requirements would need to be met before swims would be sanctioned and recognized. Crucially, an appropriate escort team would need to be in place. The overarching intention was safety for everyone involved. The media would need to stop releasing names until the attempt had been officially sanctioned. Perhaps, Waites was reported as saying, that would stop "wild catters" from making crossing attempts. He and Lumsdon hoped that Neil MacNeil would be the last swimmer to drown on a Lake crossing.

A coroner's inquest was held, with the ensuing list of recommendations, many of which were based on the Gus Ryder Plan (presented during the inquest) for distance swimming which stated unequivocally that the safety of the swim is "an absolute must. Fatalities should not happen." In 1975, under the sponsorship of the Ontario Government, the not-for-profit Solo Swims of Ontario, Inc. (sso) was founded. For 20 years, the Ministry of Citizenship, Culture and Recreation gave sso an operating grant. Over years of government cutbacks, the grant began to fade until it was discontinued in 1996. Since 2004, sso has been a charitable, volunteer organization.

Solo Swims governs open-water, solo swimming of the marathon variety in Ontario, specifically the Great Lakes. sso is charged with keeping everyone—both athlete and support team—safe on the Lake. It also ensures, coordinates, and files the necessary paperwork. In theory, and usually in practice, no one can touch the Toronto side without the authority of Toronto Harbour. sso gets the paperwork in for that, notifying the Coast Guard and shipping. sso says the Coast Guard can stop a swim if the swim doesn't have sso's approval.

Back in the day, swimmers set out with a motorboat, a weather report and, it seems, not much more than a wing and a prayer. When the swimmers talk about their crossings in the early days, they still can't believe it, reflecting from their vantage point as adults with life-experience and as parents. But that was then and this is now. Today, as with most things in sport, the arts, even something as simple as cleaning up trash in a park, there are waivers and pages of requirements. At its website, Solo Swims has posted a 66-page document covering all the details from whom to contact (marine unit of the Metro Toronto Police for one) to the wind speeds that might delay a crossing, to the fees. Every swimmer is assigned a swim master who oversees the preparation and crossing. A trial swim of one third the distance applied for is required and it can all end at that point if the swim master isn't confident the crossing of a Great Lake can be completed. All the while that's going on, somebody needs to be organizing a flotilla to follow the swimmer across. It's a cumbersome set up and it's here that the logistics seem more daunting than the actual swimming.

Nowadays a crossing sets out looking like a compass, with the swimmer

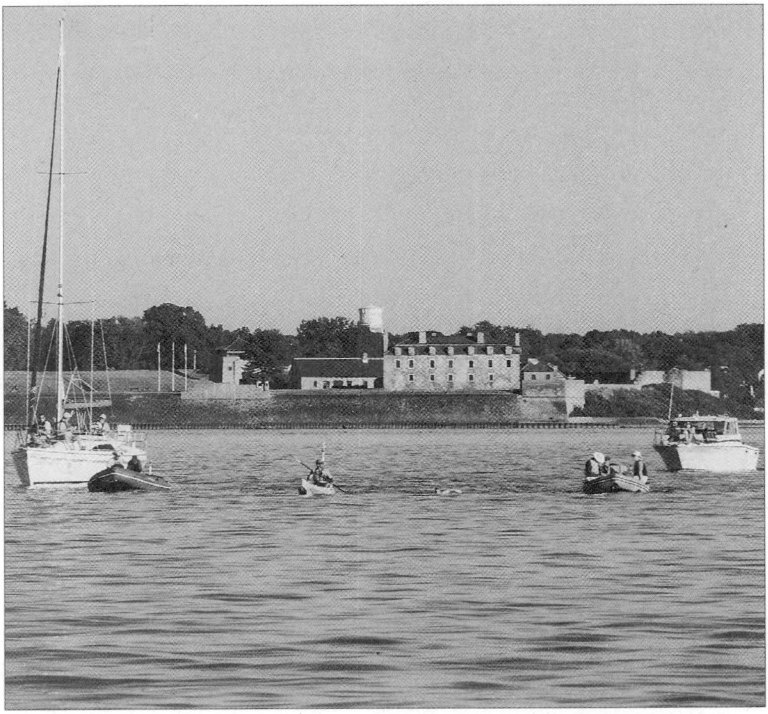

Annaleise Carr sets out with her Solo Swims-approved flotilla from Niagara-on-the-Lake, with Youngstown, NY in the background. August 18, 2012. Photo courtesy Dr. Mark Ghesquiere.

From left: Shelagh Freedman, Cindy Nicholas, Marilyn Korzekwa, Kim Middleton, Vicki Keith (hand on stone), Christine Arsenault, and Greg Taylor, of Solo Swims, Inc., celebrate SSO's 2011 plaque rededication at Niagara-on-the-Lake. Photo courtesy of Laura E. Young.

as the needle pointing in one direction, with the occasional waver. Four boats must accompany the swim and fill in the compass points to the north-south-east-west. At the north point is a sailboat at least 30 feet long, serving as a mothership and doing a mix of everything from setting the course to providing a place for crew to sleep. At the south point or tail is another large powerboat. A Zodiac with the swim master is always beside the swimmer at the east point on the right with the second Zodiac on the other side at the west end. This boat serves for drop off and delivery of crew, food, pacers. There can also be a sea kayak in the mix but no canoes. At least one boat should be capable of speeds of at least 15 knots and be ready for evacuation. Every boat must have the requisite safety equipment. The bottom line is always safety, according to Solo Swims. And knock on wood, so far so good… Heading into 2014, there have been 66 successful crossings of Lake Ontario, 19 of Erie, 5 of Huron and Georgian Bay, 2 of Michigan, 2 of Superior, and over 40 unsuccessful attempts. All were safe.

Five Lakes, One Swimmer—Part I

Vicki Keith and the Penguins that Fly, 1988

When I grow up maybe I'll be a swimmer in the lake
And I'll swim however long as it takes
To get to the other side
And I'll race against the waves and tides
While the boat goes 'chug, chug chug'
And the people go 'clap, clap, clap'
And thank you, Vicki!

—from "See you on the Moon!"
Reproduced with the kind permission of the Great Lake Swimmers

Certain names thread their way through the annals of Great Lakes and open-water marathon swimming the way the waters of the Lakes flow through one another. Vicki Keith is one of those names. In 2010, Queen's University in Kingston, Ontario, where Vicki lives, awarded the world-renowned marathon swimmer an honorary doctorate. Overdue perhaps. While Marilyn Bell was the first to cross Lake Ontario, in August 1987 Vicki was the first to complete a double crossing: 95 kilometres. And then there was the summer of 1988:

Lake Erie, July 1-2, 26 kilometres, 10 hours, 24 minutes;
Lake Huron, July 17-19, 75 kilometres, 46 hours, 55 minutes;
Lake Michigan, July 26-28, 72 kilometres, 52 hours, 45 minutes;
Lake Superior, August 15, 32 kilometres, 17 hours; and finally

Lake Ontario, August 29-30, 45 kilometres, 23 hours, 33 minutes. And over $548,000 raised for Variety Village to help build a swimming pool.

The Great Lakes Summer, as she so aptly named it, began on Lake Erie and the beginning was sobering. In the summer of 1988 Vicki Keith was 27, already an accomplished marathon swimmer, and one who over 61 days would swim across all five Great Lakes. But here she was on July 2nd ending her Lake Erie crossing sitting on a boat, not swimming, not coming ashore doing her trademark butterfly. Vicki sat in the boat, wrapped in a sleeping bag, and tried to come to terms with what had just happened. She had indeed just swum across Lake Erie from Port Colborne, Ontario to Sturgeon Point, New York, an official 26 kilometre swim. The first Great Lake on her list was done, checked off, but ah… come on. Erie was supposed to be easy. In fact, for the person who had done a 95 kilometre double crossing of Lake Ontario the previous year, Erie's 26 k just seemed too easy. What kind of challenge was that? So, a few weeks before her Erie crossing she'd decided to go for the double!

She was most of the way back when Lake Erie, perhaps slighted at being taken so lightly, literally stopped her double crossing cold, and chased her into a boat. She completed the first crossing at night, touching the shore according to the rules. She asked her father Brian Keith which direction she had to go. He pointed and Vicki left. Just like that. Brian Keith, and Ken McGowen, who was sponsoring the swim and who had first introduced Vicki to Variety Village, had to drag the boat off the beach and back onto Lake Erie. Then it took them several minutes to locate her, by the faint light from the glow stick attached to her bathing suit. Vicki continued through the night and was perhaps only two miles from shore—and a successful double crossing of a second Great Lake—when the wind switched dramatically and forced the current—and Vicki—out into the Lake. She swam in the same spot for another four hours. By now there was a small craft warning on Erie. The swim was pulled.

On the boat she was left wondering: "Holy Crap. I couldn't finish Lake Erie. How am I supposed to finish Huron when I can't do Erie? How can I do five when I can't do one?" For about 30 long minutes it went on like this, wallow, moan, process. Then she told herself, "Stop this stupidity. You can't think this way. You need to look forward and focus on Lake Huron."

Over that summer of 1988 as she pegged off five of the greatest bodies of freshwater in the world, the newspapers who followed her all reported that Vicki Keith didn't allow negative thoughts to enter the equation. She would be successful. Every photo showed a beaming Vicki; on one occasion, she carried a reporter on her shoulders in Superior. Another time she was sipping champagne in Chicago in her robe. And she never doubted. Failure, they all implied, didn't enter her brain.

Years later she would say she let everyone believe that. She wouldn't tell anyone she had that mental, all-too-human struggle after Lake Erie. "I had to organize it in my brain and deal with it because I hadn't been successful. I had always believed that I would succeed at whatever I undertook." Finally she resolved the Erie issue by telling herself that while it wasn't everything she had set out to achieve, she had crossed the Lake. It was what she had to do. Onward.

"1988. I remember it well," Vicki says. A summer of 61 days. An estimated 30 pounds gained and lost that summer. Perhaps more than once. Having discovered Dairy Queen Blizzards, she consumed them daily, something she still sounds happy about. She shrunk from a size 15-16 to a size 11-12. She says she could see the weight difference from the start to the end of a long swim. Her shoulders even cooperated, in part she figures because she designed her own workouts. She adjusted accordingly as each day went. "I remember one day I showed up at the pool; I stood and talked to the lifeguards for three hours, then left. I never got in the water. Yeah, procrastinating, I'm good at that." But she figures her body probably needed something else, like rest.

While training for the Great Lakes she also worked out on the universal gym in her home, without warming up. "I knew if I didn't just start right in I would procrastinate." Then she swam, ate lunch, and swam some more. No question: she was overtraining. "It's what I needed to do mentally as opposed to physically." She was swimming 3.2 km an hour, heart rate between 65 and 75 that whole time, focused on having a strong stroke, 16 strokes per length of the 25-metre pool, each stroke as long and slow as possible, keeping her heart rate down.

This five-lake swim had begun as a joke, she laughs, still delighted after all these years. Her central focus had always been to challenge herself. Though raising funds for charities like Variety Village became increasingly important, the core goal remained to prove that nothing was impossible. Her own story exemplified that goal: the non-athlete who becomes an athletic legend with 16 world marathon swimming records (Openwaterpedia).

She wasn't a natural sportswoman but took to swimming happily, falling in love with the water. Still, she didn't race until age 15 when her older brother Donald's coach asked her to join his swim team, which needed an eighth swimmer so it could have two senior girls' relay teams.

A few years into her career she began thinking about marathon swimming. She had seen the *Guinness Book of World Records* and the records for crazy swims like ten miles (16 km) of butterfly. "I said, I could do that." She procrastinated for several years, but then got into the water and swam 12 miles (19.3 km) of butterfly. Her interest was piqued. She started reading the *Guinness Book* and seeing what other records she could go after.

She loved all the strokes but ended up doing butterfly much of the time because—and this is key—she had been told repeatedly that butterfly was not a marathon stroke and that it was impossible to complete certain swims using the butterfly. "I just have this problem with the word impossible. So I find it really important to change how people think about that word."

When Vicki came to swim the five Great Lakes, she had already crossed Lake Ontario three times on two swims, first in 1986, swimming north to south in 26 hours, 59 minutes, and then in 1987, for the supposedly impossible double. Over 56 hours, 10 minutes, from August 5th to 7th, she completed the 95 kilometre, north-south-north, double crossing of Ontario. The closest anyone else had come was in 1974 when the famed American marathon swimmer Diana Nyad, then 24, was stopped by the Lake on the return leg of her attempt.

Of the 1987 double crossing, certain images remain clear in her mind: looking up from the bottom of a three-metre swell at the bottom of her sailboat escort, then looking down from the top of the swell onto the deck of the sailboat; re-greasing at the halfway point by chomping down on a Big Mac; treading water, finishing her burger, and rolling back into the swim north to Toronto; the muscles in her back trying to pull her body into a pretzel shape while she coaxed it to relax; the sight of the Leslie Street Spit on the Toronto waterfront, after 95 kilometres. The impossible achieved.

Vicki Keith and the Toronto skyline. Photo courtesy Lisa Lowry.

She also remembers that in the celebrations afterwards some friends approached her, laughing their heads off. So what if she had just achieved the impossible on the Great Lake? In current parlance, that was so yesterday. "This was a joke to them. They decided I should swim across all five Great Lakes in one summer. They thought of what was the most ridiculously impossible thing and just tossed it at me," she recalls.

Apparently, these friends didn't know Vicki all that well. The next day she bought a map of the Great Lakes, pinned it to her wall, and drew a line across each one where it seemed like a reasonable crossing could be made. She knew she was going to do it. Why? Because it was ludicrous to believe it was possible to do five marathon swims in one summer, and on the Great Lakes no less. And she would swim for Variety Village, with the goal of raising $300,000 for the aquatic wing of the charity's Sport Training and Fitness Centre.

Some days she would stare at the map, visualizing. Other times, she'd just peek at it. She got to the point where she could believe it was possible, that she would swim all five Great Lakes in one summer, 1988. "Once you believe it's possible, then you just have to keep reminding yourself why you're doing this, the important reasons." That's why the charity was the key cog in the mental game. "Though at times, when the swimming didn't seem important enough to me, the kids were always important enough."

So in July 1988 there she was, with Erie done. Though not the double she'd hoped for, it was still the first of five summits of swimming that she had created for herself that summer. Time now to move on, to Huron.

Lake Huron is the second largest Great Lake by surface area (Ontario MNR) and the third largest by volume (Great Lakes Information Network). Sitting strategically at the centre of the five, it has the longest coastline (Ontario MNR). Currents can wreak havoc with a swimmer, as can the shipping. But what Vicki remembers are the hallucinations, and the mental struggle simply to finish in the warm embrace of the people who live along Lake Huron, specifically in Goderich, the town that waited all night on the shores of Huron for her to swim ashore after 75 kilometres from Harbor Beach, Michigan.

Vicki was a stickler for time: she liked to wake up at a certain time and be in the water about 15 or 20 minutes later. At the start of the July 17th swim she was at the beach on time, sitting on a tub of lanolin, and waiting for everyone to show up. "I wanted to get going because sleep deprivation is not a friendly place. But everything was laid back. No one was stressed about anything," she recalls, laughing wryly. Huron was beautiful, calm. So, despite starting an hour late, the team was probably close to their estimated finishing time; "but you never know what you're going to face in the lake," Vicki stresses. They estimated three kilometres an hour, but "whatever current you get will adjust your speed. Thankfully, the weather was great that summer."

The first day was fine, relatively uneventful. On the second afternoon the hallucinations began, first creeping into her peripheral vision at the corner of the eye, then between her ears. She knew they were nothing... maybe. Vicki seemed to be swimming through mountains, following a path, when she saw a castle off to one side. "I thought it was funny." She offered it to her parents who, she says, knew not to buy it. "It's kind of like swamp land in Florida," she laughs.

The hallucinations were funny, but then things turned serious. From about midnight until sunrise she waged a mental battle with her arms. At one point she lay in Huron with her arms frozen above her head, refusing to move. Lying in the big, dark Lake, for what felt like forever, she eventually looked at her arms, and began talking to them, reminding, urging them into action: "right arm, you've got to go around once. Left arm, you have to go around once." This became her focus, one stroke, one arm at a time. As the time passed and her arms listened, her brain took a break. "I discovered that the pain wasn't really in my arms. It wasn't that I was that physically tired, I was mentally tired." It was her second lake in a month with three more to go; she couldn't allow her head to go there. Just finish Huron. "I was really mentally struggling until I got through that."

As the sun rose she took a feeding and performed her morning routine, brushing her teeth: "That pattern of waking up in the morning, that's what you do anywhere." Someone put on a tape of bagpipes, figuring to appeal to Vicki's Scottish heritage. "Those are the kinds of things that make you want to keep going. And when you can't find that strength in yourself, you need to be able to look to your crew and say to yourself, 'they believe in me; I know I can do it.'"

Then, about five miles off shore, she could hear and see them, the people of Goderich. A fire truck was flashing its lights to her from shore. The town had heard about her swim and had waited all night for her to come in. "I don't know about the personality of the Lake, but the people there were spectacular." She was later than anticipated for the landing in Goderich. She laughs heartily at how every swim seemed to take longer than planned. As she finished, she picked up her pace. With just under a kilometre left on this massive 75-kilometre swim, she finished the final 800 metres swimming butterfly.

On shore, a reporter commented on how the burst of butterfly was like showing off. Vicki was taken aback. He didn't understand. Doing fly meant she had something left. "The Lake had nothing left. I beat the Lake, right. It wasn't a tie. I had something left."

On July 19th, 46 hours, 55 minutes after starting in Harbor Beach, she came ashore for the best welcome she ever received. She hung about on the beach with the crowd, then headed into the town to rest in a century-old hotel. After receiving congratulations she mounted the stairs to her third floor room. "And it took me half an hour to get up three flights of stairs." She curled up in a ball and went to sleep. About an hour later she awoke moaning. "Everything hurt so bad."

She was the first officially to swim Huron, according to Solo Swims. She refused to think about the three Lakes remaining, with one named Superior. It was one Lake at a time: finish the swim, get a good sleep, prepare for the next one, loosen the muscles, get going: "Ignore what was in the past and focus on the future." Even preparation for a swim involved controlling what her brain focused on. The famous map on the wall of her apartment showed all five Lakes, but she would focus on each one as an individual, as an entity unto itself. "There was nothing in my brain related to what I'd done the week before or what I was going to do in two weeks. Just the task at hand."

Actually it was 6 days and 23 hours after crossing Huron that she was walking into Lake Michigan to start the swim. Her father Brian headed out in an escort boat to get into position. He was in the galley making soup with Carol, Vicki's mom, when the waves hit and he caught the soup mid-air without spilling a drop, Brian Keith recalls proudly. The swim was postponed.

Eventually, Michigan settled just enough for the swim to start on July 26th. Michigan is the second largest of the Great Lakes by volume (Great Lakes Information Network), with its northern tier colder than the south where Vicki would be swimming. Vicki stepped into the hypnotic blue waters at Union Pier, on the eastern side of Michigan and began to swim west to Chicago, 72 kilometres away. The team battled waves, and then the cold northern waters of the Lake blew down into her swim. The winds shifted from the north and the surface water was now moving Vicki south to Gary, Indiana, instead of west to Chicago. Brian Keith, plotting the course every 15 minutes, decided not to worry. The wind would stop. And miraculously it did, the water began moving back north and Vicki was en route to Chicago again.

Then there was the fatigue. This was the third lake and everybody was hallucinating. The entire crew saw land way out in the middle of Michigan. The trees and land were so vivid that they sent a boat out to investigate. "There was no island there of course," Brian Keith laughs. "We were the tired-est ever."

Coming into Chicago the crew was exhausted, with several members flaked out on the bow of the Zodiac. Vicki came into the city swimming her trademark butterfly. The approaching Chicago skyline was something else to see. At the time, her final mile (1.6 kilometres) into Chicago was more of a sprint, the second-fastest mile she had ever swum. "They clocked it. Because I was so mentally gone I chose a beat in my head, forgot about the exhaustion and the only thing I heard was that beat."

Sporting a white robe and ball cap and eating a Big Mac as her first solid food in 53 hours (Canadian Press), she wanted to party and sleep. She had become the first woman to cross Michigan; American Ted Erikson was 33 in 1961 when he swam Michigan (Openwaterpedia), a 59 kilometre race he finished in 36 hours, 37 minutes. Vicki's team came ashore and left the boats on the beach before heading over to the Ritz Carleton Hotel which had offered to put them up. Drenched and carrying garbage bags into the Ritz, the crew checked in.

Then it was on to Superior, on August 15th. The headlines after this crossing would read that it was easy, a piece of cake, the mighty lake had gone down to the Kingston swimmer. Really?

There was a long wait in Orienta, Wisconsin, for Superior to settle down. The name says it all: the largest of all the Great Lakes, the largest in the world, and holding so much water it could burst, fill all the other lakes, and three more Eries for good measure (Great Lakes Information Network). The day before she crossed Vicki went down to look at the Lake and Superior was in fits, angry, grey and in charge. "My perception of Lake Superior and somebody else's would be very different because of the days we were there." As she stood watching the Lake, a huge storm was pounding through and waves were crashing to her right, right up a cliff. She gazed at Superior and thought about the swim: "I can't believe I'm going to swim across this."

On the day, August 15th, Superior was smooth, relatively warm at 16C, and clear way down into its unfathomable depths. The crossing—a mere 32-kilometre, 17-hour jaunt from Orienta to Two Harbors, Minnesota—was designed to be done mostly in the daylight. The relatively shorter crossing meant it was likely that sleep deprivation would not be a factor. Perhaps that made it seem easier, Vicki says.

And yet, she was about three-quarters of the way across when she hit a

Vicki Keith playing in Lake Superior, August 15, 1988. Photo courtesy Vicki Keith.

wall of cold water. "There was a line and at that point the water temperature dropped to 12.5C right then and there." Her father could see the colour and texture of Superior change with the cold. Vicki had been joking with her crew and turned her smiling face back into the water. Her face froze. For the rest of the swim she was smiling. She couldn't move her face she was that cold. So it looked like she was enjoying it. Her face? Not so much. It was perception versus reality indeed. Still, she finished seven hours ahead of schedule (Kennedy). She figures the media following her was trying to share the same message she was; her intention with Superior was to conquer her personal challenge as opposed to conquering the Lake, she reflects. "The Lake on any given day can give you anything it wants to give you. The choice of words was more about the challenge and the goal as opposed to the Lake itself." As she says, Superior is superior. "The history of Lake Superior stands alone."

And then it was home to Lake Ontario. She set out to complete the longest butterfly swim but three days of weather, including the August thunderstorms that roll over Lake Ontario, delayed the start of her attempt.

Leaving Niagara-on-the-Lake on August 29th, she began swimming the

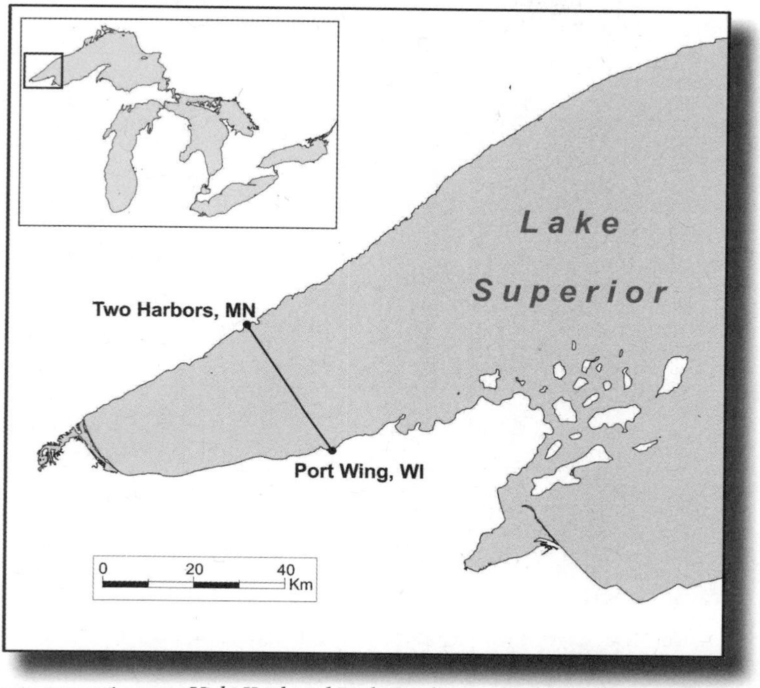

One route, two swimmers: Vicki Keith and Paula Stephanson both left from roughly the same place: Port Wing, WI for Paula, and Orienta, WI (immediately adjacent) for Vicki. Both finished at Two Harbors, MN. Map Credit: L.L. Lariviere—Laurentian University.

double-arm over the water recovery that makes butterfly so beautiful, yet oh so draining. She swam for 38.6 kilometres of the 51 that comprise the traditional route on Lake Ontario (Solo Swims). Then she switched to freestyle, battling fatigue and Lake Ontario's strong currents on the Toronto side to land at the rocky outcrop of the Leslie Street Spit on the Toronto waterfront. Later the spot that would also come to be known as Vicki Keith Point in honour of her achievements (Solo Swims), including raising over $548,000 for a new pool at Variety Village (Kennedy).

Brian Keith believes the swims were successful because they had the time to wait for the right weather. When the weather delayed the crossing, and their escort boats had to leave, they were always able to scrounge and persuade other escorts to join them, he says. Out on the water, he relied on his experience navigating with the Royal Canadian Air Force Reserve and plotted their course regularly. They stayed tuned to marine forecasts and kept an eye on the swim's drift. Vicki could handle waves; in fact, as her father says, she could handle them better than some people in the boats.

The Great Lakes Summer rolled into 1989 and the Butterfly Summer—a mix of fresh and salt water swims around the world. She would circumnavigate Sydney Harbour in Australia, and cross the English Channel, Juan de Fuca Strait, Lake Winnipeg, Lake Ontario, and the Catalina Challenge—all swum with butterfly. She set another record for butterfly on Lake Ontario, this time swimming the entire 51 kilometres butterfly. In her career she would swim Lake Ontario a record five times. In 2003 Vicki was inducted into the International Swimming Hall of Fame for her legendary swims and for her passion for coaching athletes with disabilities. She has raised over one million dollars through her swims (Penguins Can Fly).

In 2001, she founded the Y Abilities Programs at the YMCA of Kingston. She coaches swimmers with disabilities from the grassroots to the world stage. If the cause was right she could be coaxed out of retirement for another mammoth swim. In 2005 she was back in the water, training for a butterfly swim to raise funds for a new pool at the Kingston YMCA where she still works.

Vicki believes that she would not be coaching if she hadn't swum the Lakes. She would have worked with people with disabilities, regardless. She loves coaching these athletes in part because she finds that the parents place their children with disabilities in sport for reasons other than the path to elitism: for fun, to find friends, to participate. Her success swimming open water—fresh and saline—gave others the reason to believe she actually knew what she was talking about, she reflects. "I think it gave me a confidence to be able to stand up for myself and say I believe this."

Despite conquering the five Great Lakes and seemingly owning Lake Ontario, she has never lost her awe of Lake Ontario. Every year she can't wait to hop in for a swim, for her own pleasure. She has lived—appropriately—on an island near Kingston and is a daily witness to the Lake's moods, the way the colour of the water changes with temperature and time. Despite her intimate knowledge of Lake Ontario, she has yet to take it for granted. "Every day it's beautiful and awe-inspiring; I think you gain more respect from swimming it."

Lake Ontario 2

Colleen Shields Catches a Break, 1990

In 1989 Rick Wood answered the call of a swim across Lake Ontario. Along as a pacer was Colleen Shields, then 37, and a good friend of Rick. She would stay in the water with him for over 15 hours straight, inspiring his crew and drawing promises from them that they'd be with her the next summer when she did it.

Right, Colleen thought. Certainly she would not be doing a crossing of her own. "But then I thought if my 'icky Ricky' can do it—so can I."

In May 1990, she started training—twice a week—for a swim set to go in August.

The swim would hurt—like hell, in fact. Her injured left shoulder was in agony, but more painful was the fact she had "totally" underestimated the challenge of the crossing. She came into Lake crossings as the 1989 world masters champion in 50-metre backstroke and took for granted that she could get across Lake Ontario. "I was cocky and felt I was good enough," she reflects. After all, really, how hard could it be?

She didn't have the respect she now deems necessary for the Lake and for a crossing. "Yes, the Lake let me cross her even though I had no business doing so—but I had asked permission. She threw some obstacles at me—there was no way I deserved anything less."

She set out from Niagara-on-the-Lake at 9:00 p.m., facing the clashing waves over the sandbar at the mouth of the Niagara River where it spills into

Lake Ontario. Waves came from all directions. She was vomiting early in the swim as she rode three-foot swells. She felt like ending it all, giving up.

When she finished, a respectable 17 hours, 56 minutes later, she was then the oldest woman to complete the crossing at a mere 38 years. She came ashore at the Leslie Street Spit, also known as Vicki Keith Point, and pledged she was done with Lake Ontario crossings. She had done it, after all.

Colleen Shields learned to swim at the Gus Ryder Pool in Toronto, then trained with the Hamilton Aquatic Club before joining the national team and racing at the 1968 Olympic Trials. She was a backstroker who preferred short distances, 50, maybe 100 metres. "I didn't like to swim anything more than eight lengths. I would argue. That's a pure sprinter." When she didn't make the national team that summer she retired and was sent to Switzerland to finish Grade 13, her last year of high school. She stopped swimming for about 16 years. She joined masters swimming on the suggestion of Sandy Goss, a Canadian Olympic medallist swimmer. "He told me it's for the really old people," Colleen laughs.

Then came 1990 and a Lake Ontario swim she feels she had no business completing. It turned out to be the start of a remarkable distance swimming career. Since then she has moved on to swim Lake Huron, to become a swim master and a medal-winning masters swimmer, and in 1997, to receive the Cliff Lumsdon award from Solo Swims for her accomplishments and support of other swimmers. As a master, as one of those "old people," Colleen is both a mentor for and example to other distance swimmers.

Still it's Lake Ontario that continues to grip Colleen's heart, soul, and mind. She has arguably spent more time in the Lake than most swimmers. For open-water swimmers, Lake Ontario holds a particular interest in the echelon of Canadian Lake swims. For Shields, her 1990 swim didn't seem official in her mind because she had not made the same crossing as Marilyn Bell. "Every Lake crosser starts at Niagara-on-the-Lake with the plan to go to Marilyn Bell Park. That's the traditional swim," Colleen explains. She would be back.

John Scott and the Amateur Men's Speed Record, 1992 and 1994

There is a perfect image in John Scott's mind, a flat, open-water expanse of Lake Ontario, blue as only the Great Lakes can be. When he dreams of that, then maybe he might just take a third crack at Lake Ontario.

But for now, he's done. There's the fact of his family, and his career as a financial planner to consider, not to mention the time he'd have to dedicate to training. Then there's the matter of his times: back in 1992 and 1994 John set the two top amateur times on his crossings. Still, when he thinks of what could be, he would never say never.

Heading into the 2014 open-water swimming season John Scott held fast to the top two amateur times (and third fastest overall) for swimming across Lake Ontario. Fifty-one kilometres: 14 hours, 50 minutes in 1992, and 14 hours, 42 minutes in 1994 on a swim where he made a deliberate attempt at the overall record of 13 hours, 49 minutes set by professional marathon swimmer John Kinsella in 1978. Scott's record swims raised nearly $100,000 for Special Olympics, and his 1991 aborted Lake Ontario crossing raised another $10,000 for the Children's Wish Foundation.

Growing up in Southampton on the shores of Lake Huron, John followed a well-worn path, from swimming lessons with the Red Cross, into age-group swimming on a club team, and then on to varsity swimming at University of Calgary during 1992 Olympic Champion Mark Tewksbury's day. After that he drifted away from the sport for a few years before returning as a masters swimmer.

In 1990 John was asked to help out on Rick Wood's double-crossing of Lake Erie and frequently paced Rick on that swim (35 kilometres in 16 hours, 46 minutes). "I was just blown away by his spirit and heart and perseverance," John says. At the end of that swim, John thought if Rick could do it, then he could do it. And, considering his respectable swimming background, he expected to do it fast. That sense of his ability propelled him into training, with an eye to beating the record for swimming across Lake Ontario.

On August 24, 1991, John Scott failed at his first attempt, and hated that he had failed. He had swum 19.3 kilometres in seven hours. He had thought incorrectly at the time that this type of swim was a personal journey. If he was fit, healthy, and could swim, he could make it. And here he was, fit, healthy, and an excellent swimmer, and he failed. The swim was stopped due to weather; he was told to get out of the water. He had not been concerned for his own safety, bouncing around in the waves. But he accepted that it was impractical to go forward. The conditions were extremely difficult; the majority of the support crew was sick, and boats were at risk in waves often reaching 3.5 metres. He says it really came home to him that the picture was much bigger than just the swimmer. Emotionally he wanted to go forward. Intellectually and responsibly it did not make sense to continue.

And lake swimmers get that. Most have to be informed, then urged, then ordered, to come out. They need to have a swim master touch their hand, or they need to be shown the flashes of lightning striking the CN Tower. "Stopping and getting out is counter to the whole reason you're there," says Scott. Swimmers block the conditions: they're here to swim Lake Ontario, after all. "The moment came when I said 'I'll get out.' Then I sat on the boat and cried for awhile."

Failure. But what's in a word, really? Failing made Scott rethink his approach to the crossing. He realized that "failing" was a better way to understand what had happened than "giving up" would have been, especially if he never tried again. He is fond of two famous quotations from Winston Churchill: "Never, never, never, never, give up," and "Failure is not fatal: it is the courage to continue that counts." He thought he would do the next swim differently. "I changed a few things and I made some conscious decisions to plan for a better swim."

The opportunity came the next weekend, but what occurred then really tested his patience and perseverance. Conditions on Lake Ontario were ideal, even sparkling. But John couldn't find his powerboat captain. The window of opportunity was lost as the day disappeared. Mired in despair over the waste of ideal open-water swimming conditions, John confronted the captain: "How could you do this? How could you do this to me?" Then he walked away. "I'm driving home, just looking at the lake; it was such a beautiful day to swim. But it wasn't to be, so I got it together the next year."

He rallied for the following summer and set big goals: he would aim for a world record, make it a team effort, and raise at least $25,000 for the Special Olympics. At 11:00 p.m. on August 7th John and his team of 46, positioned on two large sailboats, three big cruisers, and two 12-foot Zodiacs set out on a Lake not inclined to hand him the record. Ontario threw what it could at him: five-foot waves, a steady chop-chop-chop of swells, and wind. In response, he threw up often for the first half of the swim. And he couldn't concentrate. "For the first seven hours my mind was very active with all kinds of thoughts. 'Did I forget something at work? What on earth am I doing in this lake?'" Negative thoughts swarmed, always bad for a swimmer. The swim wasn't just hurting, it was killing him. When would it end? How long would it take to end?

He was cold and descending into trouble. It was all distracted, unfocused. Early in the morning, when the sunrise on Lake Ontario is often the part of the swim crossers are most fond of, John was cold, frustrated and sick. He stopped treading water on his feeding and began sinking. He desperately wanted a break. As the water level rose, he told himself he was done. "I'm just going to sink," John recalls thinking. But as the water reached his nose, he awoke from the weirdness. "What was I doing? That was crazy."

From the boat, a crew member called to him. Take a stroke, just one stroke.

In response, he told them how hard it was.

Just take another stroke, take another stroke.

His brother David was in the Zodiac support boat watching him intently from the period of failure to the point he started getting back into his swim. As John took a stroke, he met his brother's eyes. They continued this intimate connection, as John calls it, for awhile, as he progressed, as his strength built up again, as he realized love for his brother, and felt pride in himself for getting his head together again. As he came around, his arm high in recovery, he made a thumbs-up, holding his hand at the top of his stroke to show his brother. They were both crying. Then John put his head down and went for it. He decided to stop eating: no food would mean no vomiting, though it was counter to keeping himself fuelled. He recalls stopping a few times to take a small drink but he has no recollection of stopping to actually eat even though his crew often told him to stop and eat and he would decline.

"It all doesn't seem plausible. But that's what I believe to be the truth. I'm somewhat humbled and understated about that particular crossing in part because I'm not sure how I did it given the significant challenges. But the fact is I did it. And I must say, it was one hell of a swim."

As John got his swim back together that day in 1992, and began surging over the waters of Lake Ontario, the negative noise in his head faded. Only one thought remained, a simple *you can do it*. He searched his mind for any remaining negative thoughts and found nothing. "I remember thinking, 'This is so weird. I can't even think up a negative thought.' I was kind of weirded out by that." He decided to go with it and from that moment there was only one voice and one focus, to finish well.

His stroke rate stayed at 62 per minute. He felt clear, in touch with an energy source: God, or something. Fourteen hours, 50 minutes after he started the 51-kilometre crossing, he touched at Marilyn Bell Park, the traditional landing for these swims, swimming butterfly from the breakwall to shore to honour his craziness, he laughs. He wasn't sure if he had set the record. He saw the crowd, felt hands wanting to help him out of the water. He put up a hand to let everyone know he needed a moment. He turned to the Lake, raised his fist in triumph and amazement. "I saw the lake and I saw the waves crashing over the breakwall and I just thought, 'Yeah, I did it.'"

He told people he'd felt like getting out a few dozen times. He said it was a "good" swim. "For me, that was much more than it sounded. It was a big effort." He was grateful to Mother Nature, the Lake, his crew. A few days after the swim he stood in his hot shower and revisited how great it all felt at the end, how wonderful his time was, and wondered how in the hell he had swum across

Lake Ontario without eating for the final seven hours. "I was burning some kind of fuel. I guess I was burning fat. So, I would say it was a very positive feeling. It was clarity of vision and sort of a connection with some source, plugging myself into an outlet of vibrant energy or something."

He had the fastest amateur time. Then he started chewing on it. Hmmm. Conditions weren't ideal. There was still the fact that American John Kinsella held the fastest record: 13 hours, 49 minutes. Had John Scott been at that event on August 16, 1978, he would have been second: his time, as an amateur, was still faster than the other professionals in that race. Never mind that the professionals were all under the age of 28, while he'd been 31 when he first crossed.

And so, like athletes of all abilities and experience, he wondered "what if?" If he was in better shape, if he ate better, if conditions were better, if the gods were smiling, he could swim it faster. "I told myself, 'I've learned more. I'm smarter. I could do it faster.'" And so he was back on Ontario on August 12, 1994, on a beautiful, calm day.

When it's obvious the swimmer is casting an eye at a record on the Lake, often something odd occurs. For John, as the swim progressed, drawing nearer to the traditional landing point at Marilyn Bell Park, a freighter crossed in the distance. The ship churned up the lake, replacing the thin, precious surface layer of warmth with bitterly cold, ancient water from the bottom. In an instant Lake Ontario transformed from a warm, pleasant, endless summer swim, to biting and bitter cold, leaving John gasping, with shrinking muscles. It was only like this for about 1.5 km, out of a total of 51, and he hung in, hoping he wasn't complaining too much to anyone in the crew. Then he crossed another line and was back into warm lake water. "Oh God. Thank you."

After six hours he was halfway across the lake, 26 kilometres done; he was swimming over four kilometres an hour. The speed comes in part because of a push from the Niagara River current, but there was also his training and natural ability as a swimmer. He was eating well, feeling fantastic, strong, loving it, this was great and he was going to get the record. Up in the boats his crew had a pool and were taking bets. By how much he would beat Kinsella's record?

In the final hours of his swim, though, a storm brewed over Lake Ontario, blowing in wind and rain. Lightning shot across the sky. Technically that meant—as John well knew—that the swim would be stopped. John sensed his crew's agitation but kept his head down in the water. During his 1992 swim his brother David's support brought him through his darkest moment; this time he avoided eye contact. He didn't want to give anyone even the faintest notion that he was worried, that he needed to come out and abort the swim. Later he would learn that even his crew was ignoring the weather, saying, "That's not lightning; it's just really bright right now."

What the crew couldn't ignore was the dropping away of the time record. Waves were coming off the breakwall near Marilyn Bell Park. The Humber River flows into Lake Ontario, spinning a crazy current into the water just off Toronto. That current was even stronger with the rain. The Lake temperature was dropping, along with the hopes for a record swim.

He could ignore the lightning, but not the chill, the numbness and tingling, and the looming, sobering thought of hypothermia. At one point he stopped, he was so cold. The water temperature was likely below 15C, he says. A friend he'd known for 25 years slipped in to swim with him and told him to get going. John looked at him and said, "I don't know who you are." He continues, "And I think he said his name and I thought, 'Shit. I should know him and I don't.' Something in my brain said that's a problem and you better get going."

John opted to not care at that point that he didn't know the name of his pacer. He turned to Toronto and put the hammer down. His crew, realizing the Kinsella record was now out of reach, told him he would break his own record if he could keep up this pace. He finished again with butterfly—"which I intended to do to add a sense of being crazy." His time of 14 hours, 42 minutes was eight minutes faster than in 1992.

It wasn't the world record he had sought, but when he was done he had raised nearly $100,000 for Special Olympics, and his 1991 aborted Lake Ontario crossing raised another $10,000 for the Children's Wish Foundation. And besides, there is little the swimmer and the team can do about the weather. It happens. It was a good swim, a really good effort. "I made some jokes: I'm two years older and eight minutes faster. Any way you look at it, 14:42 is the second-best time, ever. I was proud of that."

Carlos Costa: first with a disability, 1993

Carlos Costa was born without tibia, the largest bone in the lower legs. He learned to crawl but it rapidly became clear that without the tibia, the bones he was born with would not support a growing, active child. When he was two, his left limb was amputated through the knee, and the right leg was cut off one inch above the knee. He was fitted with artificial limbs and was walking within a week. His mom recalled how he always wanted to remove the limbs.

The pool, the water, gave him freedom to move without any support. He loved swimming. Growing up he wished all walkways were paved with water so he could swim them rather than walk. He took swimming lessons, eventually tried competitive swimming, and joined Variety Village when he was 16. He competed at the national level for para-swimmers. He liked to challenge himself and began to swim longer distances.

Then he happened to meet Vicki Keith at a banquet in her honour. Those were the glory days of her marathon career when she was swimming the Great Lakes or the harbour in Sydney, Australia, or the English Channel. "She was everywhere," Carlos says, and he leapt at the opportunity to meet her. "I was just a punk. I was really surprised she took some interest in me." The first thing out of his mouth was, hey Vicki, I want to swim across Lake Ontario. "And for some reason she thought I was serious." She said she'd contact him.

Carlos went home that night and wondered what he had done. Initially he thought it was a novelty, but that quickly turned into something more serious.

"I realized I needed to prove something to myself, and to society as well, to say, hey, I'm an individual. Yeah, we have our limitations but that doesn't mean we can't do anything."

The more they talked, the more sense marathon swimming made to Carlos. He started telling his friends he was going to take a shot at swimming across Lake Ontario. Naturally everybody thought he was nuts and told him so. But for Carlos—and this is a trait he shares with Vicki Keith—when people put limitations on him he feels like he is being handcuffed. He doesn't just want to escape them; he wants to break them off. So despite the naysayers, he wasn't deterred. "It gave me more ammunition because I knew I could do it."

Carlos swims without his prosthetics and doesn't kick his legs. In swimming, the kick is deceptive. A strong kick makes some difference but not compared to the sinking feeling a weak kick gives swimmers, literally dragging them down so it feels like they're swimming on a diagonal through the water. Since he didn't kick them, Carlos' legs would dip and create drag, slowing him down. He corrected that by taking longer, more efficient strokes, reaching further forward with his hands and arms. "I had to have really good technique to compensate." So as he swam he held both of his legs together, his stumps, as he says. His legs floated directly behind him at the surface of the water. Doing so was also psychological. He felt like a bullet penetrating the water.

His journey to swim across Lake Ontario began in 1992. He made two attempts to cross the Lake that summer, first in July, then in September. In July the swim started too perfectly, the Lake was too flat and the weather too bright and sunny. It was absolutely gorgeous. "Everybody was in a great mood. I was making really good time." Then the clouds formed, the lightning cracked in the sky ahead of them, and Vicki ended the swim because of safety. He had swum 38 kilometres of the 51. On September 6th he completed 26 kilometres, halfway, before cold water ended the swim.

He told the media he was going again. That was more than just 19-year-old youthful bravado. He saw completing the Lake swim as a way to develop both his own character and society's awareness of people with disabilities. "Today we generally have more openness and acceptance of people, including people with a disability." Back in the late 80s and 90s people were starting to open up to the abilities people with a disability have but pioneers were needed to break the ice. Carlos thought he could be such a pioneer. "At the time there were a lot of people who would say 'What's he doing in the pool? He's disabled. He's got no legs.' Meanwhile, just by being in there swimming, I was in effect saying, 'As a matter of fact, I can probably do better than you.'"

With two incomplete attempts at Lake Ontario stewing in his mind, the winter of 1992-93 could not pass fast enough for Carlos. He looked forward to May 1993 when he could ramp his training up more to bigger distances in preparation for Lake Ontario.

He did not doubt his ability to swim, nor was he nervous about being in the water, but he did have concerns about the support required for the swim and whether, with his track record of two incomplete crossings, the support and infrastructure needed to get across—the boats, the people—would be there. The weather wasn't helping his cause. As the team gathered in Niagara-on-the-Lake, they were forced to wait a night. The waves on Ontario were too high for them to depart.

Even when they set out at 6:00 a.m. on July 22nd conditions were barely acceptable for swimming and then the waves picked up seemingly the moment he left shore; the wind was strong. Uh, oh, he thought, here we go again. As he swam, hour after anxious hour, he persistently wondered if the conditions were ever going to improve.

Before the swim he and Vicki had come to an agreement. Out on the Lake, he could ask her anything and Vicki had to tell him the truth. The only caveat in this odd game was he could not ask if he was halfway or even further, unless he felt sure that he really and truly had swum that far. As he rode the eight-foot swells, he knew he didn't want this swim to be a repeat of all the other so-called failures. He held off asking Vicki and kept swimming. The weather worsened. Near supper time he finally asked her point blank if they were halfway. She said yes.

He needed a positive answer at that point. He knew that Lake conditions had obliterated their forecast of a 24-hour swim. He would have to swim through the night. "I knew I was going to be in there for a long time." He figured that if he ended it there, halfway through the Lake and facing the night ahead, everyone around, and all the voices in his head too, would be silently saying I told you so. "I didn't want to give them that opportunity. And besides, deep down I knew I could do it. So I just kept chugging along, hour after hour."

Carlos had not practised a lot of night swimming, but he would come to enjoy his overnight crossing of Lake Ontario. As July 22nd rolled into the 23rd, the weather began to settle. "It was almost like we were part of a mission out there." Vicki and her husband John Munro were especially encouraging. Carlos had purposefully surrounded himself with positive people because it is too easy to focus on the negative in Lake Ontario if the swim is not going to plan. Since he wasn't going for a speed record, his time didn't matter. It meant a lot to him just to know he would have the two records: the youngest male and the first disabled swimmer. "Completing that swim would break a stereotype. That was a big deal because there weren't many positive role models out there" for people with disabilities at the time, and he was trying to achieve something not even most able-bodied athletes have done. "I thought if I could hang on and swim across, it would mean something."

It was an intimate evening, even though they were in the middle of Lake Ontario. "I never felt alone. Every stroke of the way I had encouragement." Vicki would tell him regularly to keep going, that he could do it. He hardly looked to the night sky above, but around him the scene was pretty, with the sailboat's night-time running lights twinkling beyond him to the front of their flotilla and his support crew regularly shining flashlights on him in the water. Equally he kept his eye on them. "I wanted to make sure they were okay. Even though I was the one swimming, doing it, I didn't view it that way. For me, we were part of a team. They were helping me reach my goal but we were reaching it together." When the day dawned the weather was settled, the sky brighter.

Around 4:00 p.m., as he was nearing the northern shore of Lake Ontario near Toronto, it seemed odd to him that he could now see land. It was as if the water was being encroached upon by the land, its broad expanse thinning as the shore quickly approached after 50 kilometres and 32 hours. "Wow, this is actually going to end," he thought. When he touched land he could only think that this was the greatest thing ever. John and Vicki picked him up. He told them: "'This is the best day of my life.' And it was."

As he transitioned back into life as a land mammal, Carlos felt like he needed a crowbar to pry the goggles off his face. He looked like a blue racoon, eyes sunk into his head from the pressure of his goggles; his lips and skin were the colour of the sky. Warming up in the shower on the sailboat, was like pouring hot water on a block of ice. Other than being exhausted and sore, he had no major medical issues. But still, the return to being upright was a struggle. It was difficult to put on his prosthetic legs. He needed assistance to walk afterwards. He had spent so much energy focused on preparing to complete the swim that he never thought about what he would do afterwards. "It was all about finishing it."

On November 7th, Carlos became the fourth Canadian to complete the 32-kilometre Catalina Channel swim off California. He wanted to capitalize on the media attention and take the opportunity to do something else right after Lake Ontario. He completed the crossing in 15 hours and 3 minutes and learned almost as soon as he hit the water that he loved swimming in the salty ocean. Swimming itself gave him a measure of freedom but salt water seemed to negate his disability. The extra buoyancy of the ocean leveled him off into perfect streamline with no extra effort on his behalf. He was trained and experienced now and swam as if he had a motor on his back. Not that it was an easy 15-hour swim, but Lake Ontario had prepared him well; he simply knew how to do it. And the buoyancy from salt water proved to be an added benefit. The Catalina swim became his consolation prize for what he had endured on Lake Ontario.

In 1994 he did a double crossing of the straits of Messina in Sicily, a 60-kilometre crossing, and raised more awareness about the abilities of swimmers with a disability. There would be no more marathons after that. He moved on to life outside marathon swimming and now works for an agency of the Ontario government.

He threw himself into masters swimming for awhile and competed regularly, including trips to national championships. He remembers flying over Lake Ontario one year, seeing its beauty, and thinking, "I can swim across it." He finds a thunderstorm on Ontario is a gorgeous thing to behold, though he doesn't want to be in the water when lightning strikes. On a break from work, he may walk down by Lake Ontario and look out over its ever-changing waters. "My heart jumps a beat or two because part of my life was trying to conquer it. It's beautiful. It's just a really nice thing to see."

From his incomplete attempts at Lake Ontario, Carlos learned that success can come after one fails. "When you fail, it's not pretty and it hurts. It's a setback. It's negative. At the same time, it gives you the tools to succeed if you're able to put that aside and go at it again."

Lake Huron

Lake Huron stands at the centre of the Great Lakes system. Fed by Superior and Michigan, it's the fifth largest lake in the world (depending on how you measure), and perhaps the prettiest. It boasts 30,000 islands, and the longest shoreline of the Great Lakes—at 6,157 kilometres it's equivalent to a jaunt across Canada and partway back. Huron was the first Great Lake encountered by the European explorers, in 1615, and it became a major transportation route to western Canada prior to rail. Huron is home to its fair share of shipwrecks, especially in the crystal, ice blue waters near Tobermory, at the mouth of Georgian Bay. With prevailing winds from the west, Huron rocks and rolls through this channel into Georgian Bay. But wind is not the worst of problems for a swimmer. The water temperature can be something else. If cold had a colour, it would be Lake Huron blue.

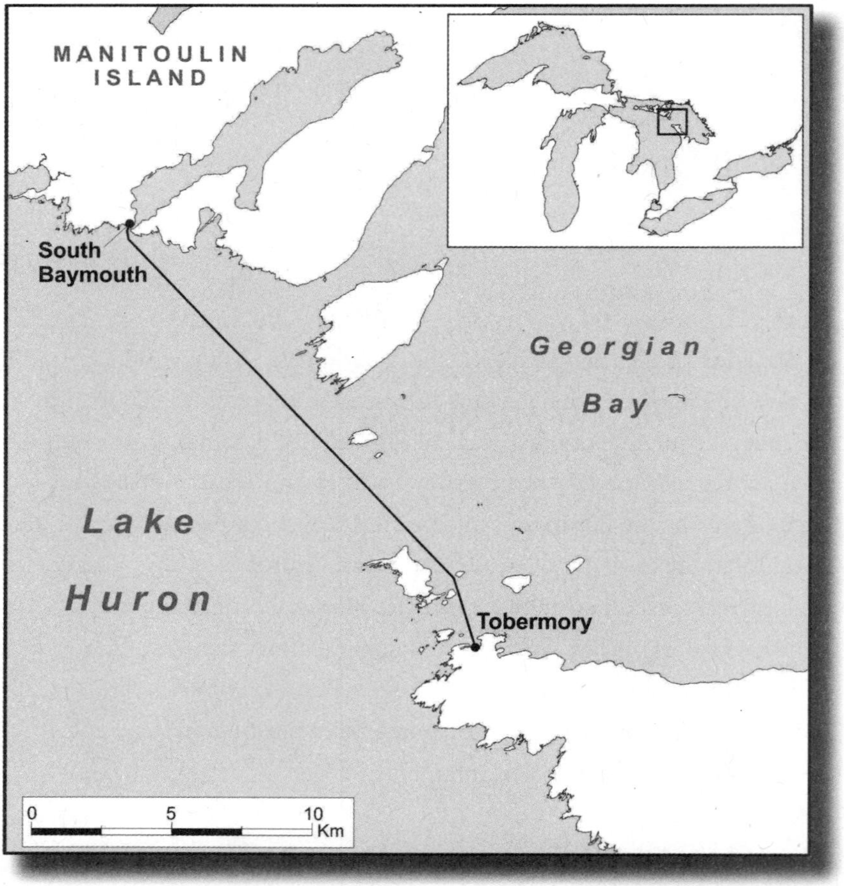

Route followed by Colleen Shields from Tobermory, Ontario to South Baymouth, Ontario, on Maniotulin Island. Map Credit: L.L. Lariviere—Laurentian University.

Colleen Shields: Tobermory to South Baymouth, 1992 and 1993

From his boat, John Scott called to Colleen Shields: "Can you see the landing point?"

Up the waves of Lake Huron she rose: "Yes, I can see it."

Then down she shot into the cold-blue waters where Georgian Bay and Lake Huron mix and mingle. No, she couldn't see it anymore, no more rocky white shore of Manitoulin Island. Then back up the waves she went, and there the Island was again.

It was "third time is the charm" for Colleen Shields on her personal crossing of Lake Huron. In fact it was her second attempt in 1993 alone to complete the crossing from Tobermory—a mecca for divers, home of Fathom Five National Marine Park and shipwrecks —to South Baymouth on Manitoulin Island, the same route along which the *Chi-Cheemaun* ferries cars and passengers every summer.

In terms of Great Lakes swimming, Lake Ontario remains the most popular, perhaps because of its accessibility, but definitely because it is the "tradition," as the place of Marilyn Bell's triumph. Despite its own special challenges, Erie is approachable too, the half-marathon sibling to the longer ones, and a worthy place for one's first attempt at swimming a Great Lake. Then there are the big three: Superior, Michigan, and Huron. With these three, everything is about size: the longest, the deepest, the widest, the most rugged, the coldest (generally, though Ontario is a chiller), and so on.

In his iconic "The Wreck of the Edmund Fitzgerald," Canadian folk singer Gordon Lightfoot sings that Lake Huron rolls, and indeed it does: cold, dark piles and walls of water, usually prevailing from the west. Lake Huron speeds and spills into Georgian Bay, also known as the sixth Great Lake (Ketcheson) and large enough to be numbered among the world's 20 largest lakes. The opening between the two, from a Great Lakes perspective, is but a sliver. It takes the *Chi-Cheemaun* ferry less than two hours to cross the 48-kilometre gap in Highway 6, a route running from Port Dover on Lake Erie to Espanola north of Manitoulin Island and hailed as the most scenic and popular highway in all of Ontario. And it was in that 48 kilometre gap that Colleen Shields found herself in 1992 and 1993, for very personal reasons.

By that time, Colleen had recorded a complete crossing of Ontario, and held the title of the oldest woman to do so. Her ability to stay warm in cold water was legendary. By that time she had also been a swim master on even more crossings of Ontario and Erie. And yet, it's this classic swim on Huron that stands out.

Colleen's reasons for swimming the lake had nothing to do with any of Huron's unique challenges. The Tobermory-South Baymouth swim was in honour of her mother, Audrey, who died in Tobermory at age 56, in 1973, when Colleen was 21. Audrey, a member of the Neilson chocolate family, had been a swimmer with the Canadian Dolphinettes in Toronto and had never smoked a day in her life. "We weren't allowed to eat chocolate growing up," Colleen smiles. Audrey was very active and, Colleen says proudly, had one of the healthiest hearts. According to the coroner's report, however, one vessel gave way and she died of a heart attack. Colleen hasn't taken her mother's engagement and wedding rings off her finger since she died. It's another way she brings her mother along on all her swims.

Colleen's 1990 swim in Lake Ontario would seem like a walk in the park compared to the Tobermory swim, though, she says. She needed three attempts to come to terms with the water temperature. The first time in 1992, the waters were a stark 11C. "The first time I didn't even get in the water. It flipped over to 8.8C." In 1993, the signs were encouraging: Huron was flat and calm, temperature a balmy 17.7C. She took one stroke in 17.7 degree water

Aquatic bloodlines: Colleen Shields (right) and her mother Audrey, back when Colleen was still a sprinter. Photo courtesy Colleen Shields.

and the next stroke the water was 11C. "I didn't even know what hit me." She lasted about three and a half hours, then couldn't do it anymore. She got out. Two weeks later she returned. Over the time she spent preparing for this crossing she had made friends with the crew of the *Chi-Cheemaun* who sent water temperature readings from four metres below the surface. The readings were encouraging: 16.6 to 17C. "I was telling myself, over and over, 'I can do this; I can do this.'" The ferry took a detour around Cove Island near Tobermory in order not to add to the challenge of her swim by stirring up more cold water. She set out on Saturday, August 21st at 6:30 p.m., swimming through Huron's blue waters into the dark, the theory being that water is flatter, calmer, at night.

As it went, though, Huron served up enough that night with 1.8-metre high waves and strong winds blowing in from the south (Nolan). Towards the end of the crossing, the waves were coming broadside, hitting her left side, her bad shoulder. She touched at Huntington Point at 10:45 a.m. on the Sunday morning, 40.5 kilometres and 16 hours, 15 minutes later. She burst into tears and pledged never to take another marathon swim, which, she adds, laughing, she says after every marathon. "It was so personal," she reflects. "It wasn't for any records, it was for my mom." For 20 year's she had thought of Tobermory as a negative place, seeing the picturesque town as the site of a horrible personal tragedy. Now, while it was still the site of her mom's death, happier memories were attached. She laughs. "That's where I did a really crazy swim which nobody else has done."

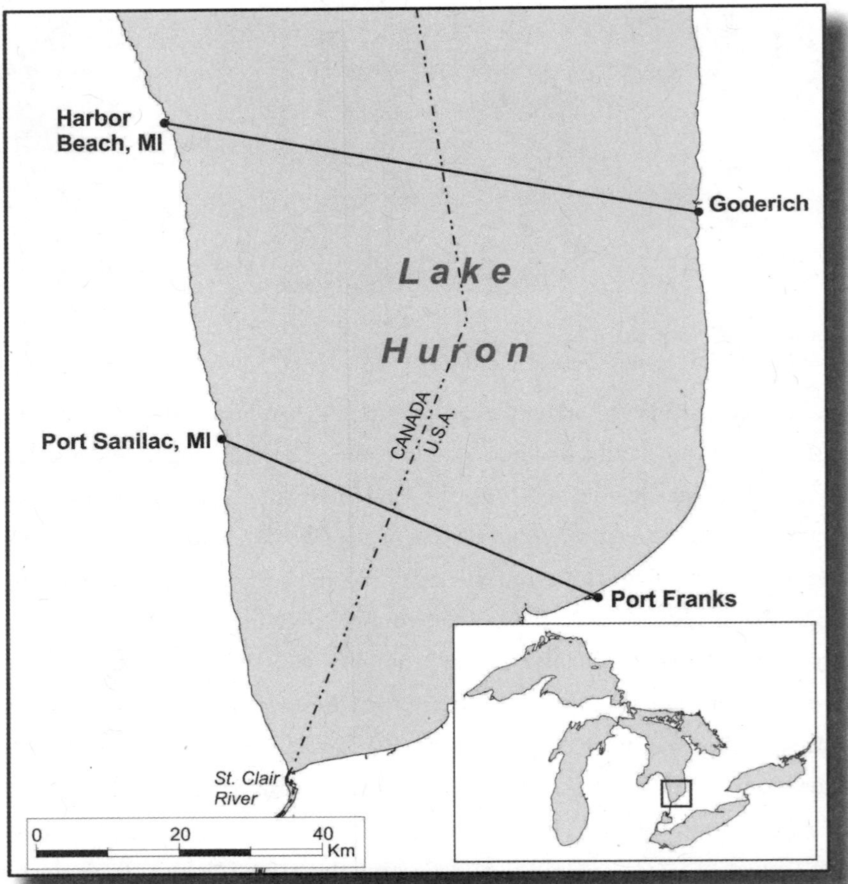

Two routes followed by three swimmers: John Bulsza and Paula Stephanson took the southern route from Port Sanilac, MI to Port Franks, ON, while Vicki Keith swam from Harbor Beach, MI to Goderich, ON. Map Credit: L.L. Lariviere—Laurentian University.

John Bulsza: The first man to swim Huron, 1996

John Bulsza, a high school teacher from London, Ontario, swallowed his final slices of pizza and headed down to the shore of Lake Huron where he took a moment to select a stone from the water's edge. He gave it to his crew for safe-keeping, then stood while crew members layered lanolin onto him to keep in the heat and prevent chafing, and zinc oxide to minimize sunburn on his back. As he stared out over the early morning expanse of Huron, he was at once a turtle about to swim home to his beach, a deeply devoted Catholic raising money for his pro-life causes, and a whimsical 45 year old determined to show a dubious former girlfriend that he was not only good-looking but in great shape. In shape enough to believe he could swim from Port Sanilac, Michigan to Port Franks, Ontario, 55 kilometres across Lake Huron, the second largest of the Great Lakes.

Though it may seem counter intuitive to non-lake crossers, the start of the swim was a palpable relief. For Great Lake swimmers organizing a crew and assembling everyone on the shores of the Lake at the precise moment the weather gives the opportunity is often more draining than training and even crossing. John's start on August 31st was his third attempt that summer to get the crew to the beach. Over the summer people had bailed at the idea of spending over a day bobbing at a swimmer's pace in a boat on a Great Lake. People who had committed to John's crossing were losing pay and John covered their lost wages. He stayed patient, got frustrated and disappointed, then recovered his patience. What was a few more weeks, a few more phone calls? Still, it was sheer relief to take the first strokes in Huron and know that the swim was finally, for real, underway. As he set off, Lake Huron was a balmy 21-23C, liquid blue and big.

John grew up on the shores of Lake Huron and remembers the exact spot where he first fell in love with the Lake. He likens his situation to the hatchling that swims away only to return a full grown turtle, returning again and again to the same spot. "I have it on my coordinates, 43 degrees, 00 minutes, 12 seconds north; 082 degrees, 24 minutes, 13 seconds west. It's my favourite part of the universe." The seed to actually swim Lake Huron, however, was planted as he served as a lifeguard at Sarnia's beach at Canatara Park. As part of his routine, he would swim what was then the grand distance of 500 metres down the shore to the guard stations. As he sat in the guard chair, he looked across, thinking how he'd like to swim to Port Huron. Could he tackle the challenge? Then there was Gail, a girlfriend at the time. She smirked at the suggestion, telling him that when he was 45 he'd be out of shape and ugly. That stuck with him, providing an impetus to stay in shape and a simmering reminder that perhaps he would one day collect on the $5.00 bet they made. He swam masters, everything leading him towards staying in shape, to one day swimming a Great Lake.

In 1991 he decided to go for it, to begin preparing for a Lake Huron crossing. He'd be 45 in a few years, and knew that the Lake would demand more than being in shape and great-looking, though they were nice side effects to proving a point to Gail. He was friends with Bryan Finlay, a record-holder on Lake Erie and fellow masters swimmer in London. As he picked Bryan's brain for tidbits on marathon swimming, John told Bryan he had the credentials to swim Huron because he had raced in rivers, downstream. Bryan laughed.

John would spend five years preparing mentally and physically for Lake Huron. The first two years passed with John knowing Huron was his goal and swimming three times a week in the pool. Three years prior to the swim he got serious, kept a log, built up to swimming 62 kilometres, what he estimated his crossing distance on Huron to be. He would swim 62 kilometres over training and then started again, gradually narrowing the window of time in which he swam the distance. In 1996, he tried to swim 62 kilometres over the school March Break. With mere months to go before summer, he threw out the muscles underneath his left shoulder. Still, there would be no postponing the swim until 1997. For two months John trained with his left hand tucked into his bathing suit and swam one-arm. He spent a lot of time just kicking his legs.

By June, his patience and physiotherapy had paid off and he was swimming with both arms again, careful with the left, especially as he rolled to the left side to breathe. He completed his trial swim without incident and then he began to pray deeply over the matter, to ensure that yes indeed this crossing was really going to happen. For John it was important to know that this dream was attainable, that the swim was not something that could ruin him for life. "Too often swimmers have real major shoulder issues. I didn't want to be crippled. I did not want to have an injury that would cause me to be a disability for my family." Assured through prayer that the swim was meant to be, he carried on, his ear buzzing from phone calls as he tried to secure and assemble a crew for the crossing; the swim was postponed twice before it finally launched on August 31, 1996.

It takes a village to swim a Great Lake: Here's John Bulsza's Lake Huron team in 1996. Photo courtesy John Bulsza.

As the swim curved across the blue swirl of Huron's waters, John knew there were challenges with being in the Great Lake for more than a day. He left in the morning at 8:30 a.m. with water temperatures at a warm 21C. The water even became warmer to him as they headed out into the deep blue of Huron. Setting out in the morning isn't the usual way to start. The wind is supposed to be lighter at night so swimmers usually launch then. Still, John worships the sun and wanted to soak up as much of it as possible. By night, without the sun's warmth, the swim went downhill psychologically. For an hour he swam stuck in a current, going nowhere. Wind from the southeast caused issues, slapping his face as the waves topped half a metre. He reflected on the zinc oxide still coating his body and pondered how bad things would have been without the sunscreen.

To maintain John's focus, his team carried a progression of signs on board the boat. One sign read: front crawl. He swam front crawl for 12 minutes. Then another 2x3 foot sign was held up telling him to switch to breaststroke for about two minutes. Then switch to backstroke. Another sign reminded him how to breathe so he wouldn't wreck his left shoulder. In the progression was a sign reminding him of divine mercy. "Whenever that sign came up it just warmed me. It made me feel like everything was going to be fine."

The swim wound on: 12 minutes freestyle, switch, don't forget to breathe, switch to breaststroke, backstroke, divine mercy, a flood of warmth. As he rolled onto his back over the night he tracked a satellite spinning overhead. When he returned to backstroke, he tracked what he thought was the same satellite. Every so often he slipped his hand into his Speedo bathing suit and warmed his fingers as he peed into the Lake.

After starting in the warmth of the day, John found the cold harder to fight off. His mind began to tell him that yes indeed, he was cold. The heated Gatorade poured from a thermos actually made him feel the cold more and he started to refuse it. He began to wonder if he should pull out. But he could still feel his fingertips, his fingers, his hands. "So, that means you're not pulling out," he says, "because you're not dying, you're not having hypothermia." Actually, he was fine, and recalls only about five hours of real cold. What he remembers far more clearly is that he was the swimmer out in Lake Huron in the middle of the night under the Gibbous moon with the glow of Sarnia's skyline in the distance. Satellites spun overhead. "It was a pleasure actually, a real pleasure."

His pacers lifted his spirits. Bob Weir, one of his swim masters, hopped in to swim with him; so did his daughter Robin, who was also a lifeguard. His wife Becky, a nurse, served as chief medical person and cook. The crew on the sailboat and a 45-foot floating hotel of a powerboat kept the food going steadily. Eventually, with the sunrise, John could see shore and his destination of Port Franks. The warmth of the sunrise was important to him, filling him with the sense that he was going to make it.

Some of that the warmth came from Campbell's Chunky Soup, spiked with dextrose, which he had been drinking on the hour throughout the swim. Becky called Campbell's and told them their product was helping fuel a swimmer's crossing of Huron. Perhaps they should make a commercial. The company didn't go for that, but they did send a box of the soup which he later donated to one of his charities. Then there were his maple leaf cookies for the crunch. "It was the cookies I longed for. I just loved that sense of something grinding between my teeth." Still, over the final hours he couldn't stand the taste of any of his foods and forced himself to eat and drink.

Twenty-six hours and 49 minutes, and 55 kilometres after he started, on September 1st, John waded ashore, walking about 20 metres up the beach to where his other daughter Stephanie had emerged through the waiting crowd to greet him. He waded into a media scrum, then called his father in Sarnia. He had raised $11,000 for various charities, including the London Crisis Pregnancy Centre, Birthright in Sarnia and London, Rehoboth Girls' Home of Refuge and Support for pregnant, unwed youth and the London Area Right-to-Life Association.

Supported by swim master Bob Weir (right), John Bulsza hugs his daughter Stephanie on the shores of Lake Huron. Photo courtesy John Bulsza.

John relished this rare moment of swimmer as celebrity. A man brought his son forward to meet the first man to swim across Lake Huron. Before he left the beach, now bundled in a toque and blankets, John retrieved the stone his team had carried from the American side for him, and deposited it on the Canadian shore. The stone symbolized the water, the beach, the Lake—in his own way he'd made the two sides connect.

Everyone dispersed, but John headed to Bryan Finlay's cottage to recover. As John sat on the guestroom bed, he watched with fascination as his leg muscles vibrated rapidly, shimmering like fish scales. Bryan told him that he probably didn't eat or hydrate enough over the swim and his body was, clinically, consuming itself. After arriving home in London, John headed to bed, where he slept for the next 12 hours. He was the first man to swim across Huron and had to teach the first day of the new school year in the morning. Already. "I couldn't believe it."

Years after his swim, John was back on the Great Lakes as a swim master. His definition of success on the Lakes is about figuring out the difference between reality and fantasy and then getting into the water. "Is this something the swimmer is meant to accomplish? Or, not. If it's truly a dream of yours then that's the beginning of success—you have to distinguish between the two."

Lake Erie

If you want to swim a Great Lake, how about Lake Erie? It's only the world's 10th largest lake and the shallowest of the five Great Lakes, dipping down into the Earth to a maximum depth of a mere 210 feet. Narrow, 387.8 kilometres east to west and 91.7 kilometres north to south, Erie heats rapidly in the summer. The fact that it's the warmest lake makes it an ideal, even accessible spot to start for Great Lakes swimmers. It means the swimmer can "get" a Lake. The "dare" to try a different stroke besides freestyle mostly happens on Erie: first backstroke swimmer, first breaststroke record, and an assortment of speed records have been set on Erie. Cellphone coverage is better over Erie without the gaps crossing teams find on Lake Ontario. So, what with all this warm, narrow, and shallow stuff, it may seem like Erie can be "easy," that the Lake can be had.

But not so fast. Erie delivers its own unique wave pattern with the accompanying winds. Swimmers can face choppy waves that are close together, large, powerful, delivering a continuous smack, smack, smack, regardless of the direction the swimmer is heading. It can be more difficult than swimming the heavy rollers of Lake Ontario. In Erie, the swimmer must go with the beat of the Lake, not his or her own pace.

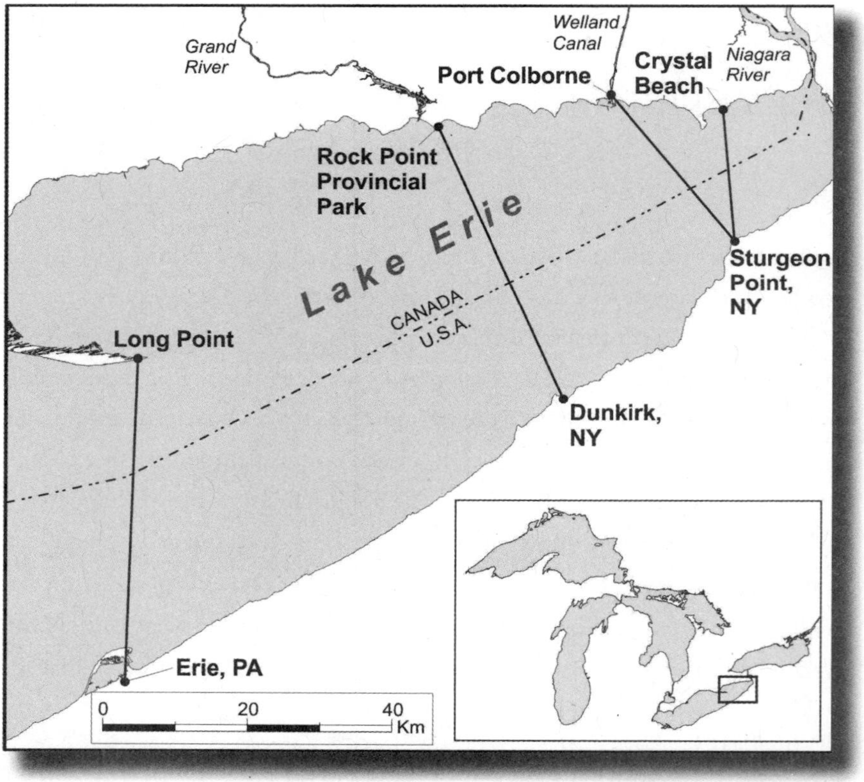

Routes on eastern Lake Erie. Map Credit: L.L. Lariviere—Laurentian University.

Ashley Cowan: first woman with a disability, 2001

A few weeks before Ashley Cowan started her swim across Lake Erie, she finally told her mother, Shurlene. It's hard to keep surprises from Shurlene, so imagine how she felt in August 2001 when they were discussing back-to-school shopping. Ashley, then 15, told her she had to miss her first day of Grade 10 in Toronto. "She thought I was just skipping but I had an actual legit reason why I wasn't going."

Some of it, this not telling her mother, was the fact of being a teenager, Ashley laughs years after the fact. But it was more. She wanted to make sure the swim was going to happen for real. It was getting late in the season for open-water swimming and there had already been a few postponements. Ashley didn't want her mother disappointed. But her main motivation was to prove she could swim Erie, that she could prove anyone wrong who told her she couldn't.

Ashley's coach Vicki Keith told her she had to get her guardian's approval. Shurlene's partner had signed the permission forms. Once Ashley passed her trial swim, she told her mother she would swim Erie. At first Shurlene didn't believe any of it, Ashley recalls. "She couldn't believe we were able to keep this from her, that she didn't know anything."

Ashley would swim 19.2 kilometres across Lake Erie on September 7, 2001, from Sturgeon Point, NY to Crystal Beach, ON. It took 14 hours, 20 minutes. She would claim two records: the youngest swimmer to cross Erie and the first female swimmer with a disability to cross a Great Lake.

When Ashley Cowan was 15 months she contracted meningitis and died in the desperate rush to the hospital. She was revived but in order to save her life, doctors amputated both arms and both legs beneath the joint. There was a point in all the medical conversations that Shurlene was told that really, her daughter wouldn't have much quality of life. With her baby comatose, Shurlene turned on the TV to shatter the silence of the hospital room. When Sesame Street came on, Ashley turned to watch it. Two weeks later she wanted to go home.

By age five, wearing her prosthetic legs, Ashley was figure skating and swimming. Eventually she dropped the skating. The commuting between the west end of Toronto for skating and the east end in Scarborough for swimming at Variety Village, was too much. She loved swimming more. "I just felt that when I was in the water that's where I was supposed to be."

In one of her motivational TEDX speeches (Keith), Vicki Keith tells the wider story of goal-setting and how Ashley came to her: Ashley was then nine. She came on her own to the pool and practically skipped down the pool deck on her stumps, with $100 tucked under her arm to pay Vicki. "There's something really wonderful about Ashley," Vicki says. "She just exuded that energy, that positivity. She didn't know there were any limitations in her life. She knew how to get what she needed to be successful and that is who walked onto my pool deck." Ashley had decided to swim across Lake Ontario and Vicki was going to be her coach. She swam for Vicki, her stroke looking like front crawl right off the top, her arms spinning like a wind-up toy. She had no endurance. She stopped after half a length.

Vicki hesitated. Not hard to see why: Ashley had just told her she was going to swim across Lake Ontario and here she couldn't swim half the length of a 25-metre pool. Vicki wondered how that was going to happen, but since Vicki doesn't believe anything is impossible, she sought the next best step. Ashley went with a group of swimmers at her level where she could learn how to swim. "She did that very quickly because she had no intention of swimming with anybody but me." Two weeks later she was moved to Vicki's group. At age nine Ashley qualified for the Canadian national swimming championships as a para swimmer.

While there were obvious limitations, Ashley was a natural in the water: she had buoyancy and good core strength which, combined, helped keep her at the surface. Her arms went to the elbow, and while it's the forearm that applies pressure to the water, Ashley's spinning windmill-like stroke worked, 68 strokes per minute on average.

The dream of swimming a Great Lake, however, moved to the back burner: it was a realistic goal, but not at that time. Ashley competed for Variety Village's swim team. When she was 15, Ashley missed the qualifying standard for the 2000 Paralympics in Australia by less than two-tenths of a second. Then Vicki reminded her of her goal to cross a Great Lake. "She needed to know in her heart that she had worth, value, that she could do something unique and special."

Ashley trained for Erie and, quite simply it seems, did it. Over the training she did question herself. The thing she loved most about swimming was the team aspect, the sociability and the travel. There were opportunities swimming gave her that would not have presented themselves to her on her own. But the preparation to swim a Great Lake was lonely, a solo pursuit. She wondered if she was prepared enough. The doubt centred on the fact that Erie, despite its place among the other Great Lakes, was still a big lake. "At least with the pool I saw the end. In the Lake, you can't see the end and I'm petrified of dark water, seaweed, and fish," she laughs.

The team organized the swim with the best chances for success. With Erie being smaller, they estimated she'd complete it in fewer than 20 hours. They needed a clear forecast: no lightning or thunder looming. They planned to start on the side of the Lake with the favourable winds and swim in that direction, ideally towards Canada from the U.S. side, but they were prepared to go the other way if necessary. If they'd had to change, it was only a two hour drive to the other side, Vicki says.

Late on September 6th Ashley headed out with Vicki, serving as her coach, and her swim master, John Munro. En route to the hotel the trailer towing the Zodiac support boats had a flat and the team was stuck on the side of the highway; by the time help came and everything was fixed, it was nearly 11:00 p.m. They were to be up by 5:30 a.m. to get to the launch of the swim. Vicki told her to get some sleep as soon as they got to the hotel but Ashley was restless, lying there, wondering, "If I was actually going to make it; all those thoughts were going through my head. At one point I thought, 'Oh my God, Ashley. What did you get yourself into?' Then I passed out."

That morning, no one was happy. It seemed that only the crew believed Ashley would make it across Erie. They had encouraged so many people to come down. Only three showed up. Some even seemed embarrassed for what appeared to be an impossible goal for a person with this level of disability, Keith reflects. "Yet," she adds, "Ashley wasn't being subjected to it. She had chosen, and drove the swim the entire way." Vicki called a media friend prior to the departure. He was one of three people at the start, plus her crew. But when Ashley was halfway across people started to realize it was possible, to believe she could do this. "That's when we started to have planes, helicopters come over. Media called continually. The phone never stopped after that."

But before that, as she waited at the launch site for the boats to get set up, Ashley exorcised her boredom by spinning around on a golf cart. When she stepped into the water at 9:00 a.m. on her stumps and started swimming, she panicked in the weeds that seemed to be so tall. "They were going to start touching me!" Vicki calmly directed her away into the open water, and Ashley took off. Vicki told her to slow her pace.

As she neared the halfway point, Ashley was tiring and mentally had to settle herself into the long second half of the crossing. "But we made it fun." Some firefighters came out on the boat. Tongue twisters passed some of the time: the crew had to learn the tongue twister Ashley had just taught them by the time she stopped for her next break. When she was starving and her energy drink hadn't been filling her up, she noticed how her crew was eating cookies, lunch, real food. "Over here, people." She called out that she wanted a share of the feast. Vicki started dropping pieces of lunch meat and ham into her mouth, "so I felt like a seal," Ashley recalls with a chuckle.

Eventually, she began to negotiate with Shurlene, who was positioned ahead in one of the boats. "If I finish this lake swim, can I have a new wardrobe?" Shurlene agreed. Another hour or so: "'Mom. If I finish this swim can I get a tattoo?' 'Yes dear, you can.' I'm thinking: 'Sweet deal,' so I started swimming again." Later, she requested new shoes for her artificial legs. Of course you can. Just keep swimming.

As the swim moved into night, into the cool evening air, Ashley was chilled and the swim was now hard. She began to tell everyone she wanted out. She would cry to her mother; Shurlene would tell her okay, just swim to the boat, all the while the boat was still moving forward. "I realized what she was doing, and then I was mad. I didn't want to talk to anybody." She told them to leave her alone.

About 4.8 kilometres from shore, she looked to Vicki in the dark night and told her she couldn't do it anymore.

"What are you talking about?" Vicki asked her. She looked at her swimmer and told her they were so close now.

"You're lying," Ashley responded, continuing forward.

"She was still swimming while she was complaining," Vicki recalls. She noted that Ashley was swimming a mere foot from her kayak. "Not once does she reach over to touch the kayak." If she does, the swim is over. "What she's saying isn't 'I want to stop.' She's saying 'I'm tired. I don't want to be here anymore.' She's asking me to pull her out so she can be mad at me later." The crew continued to cheer and encourage; Ashley continued to swim and complain. Vicki asked her to listen, did she hear that? She told Vicki, "I'm in the water, I can't hear." Vicki told her to lift her head out and listen. Then Ashley could hear them, the people on the shore, cheering, clapping. Vicki smiles. "She was like, 'That's shore!' and she began to sprint."

"My whole thought process was focused on one thing: 'Oh my god! Shore!' I just started swimming like there was no tomorrow. I got to the beach, but no one was allowed to touch me until I was completely out of the water." Her legs were so water logged she crawled up the boat ramp. As paramedics approached with a backboard and neck brace she told them she wasn't broken. "They all got a laugh out of that one." She declined a bottle of water, reminding everyone she'd had enough fresh water for the time being. All she wanted was McDonalds. "I just wanted whatever was NOT healthy for me at that point. I had been watching my diet and my food with the training."

The time: 14 hours, 20 minutes, 23 and two-tenths of a second. Ashley says, "That's a long time to be in water." Her swim came 47 years to the day after Marilyn's Lake Ontario crossing in 1954. "That made me feel weird, and warm and fuzzy, too. There was a lot to take in: that it actually happened; that it wasn't a dream anymore; that I actually did it." Along with being the first woman with a disability to swim Lake Erie, she was the youngest swimmer to do so, period, until 2008. "It was amazing. I didn't do it for anybody else. I did it for myself. I wanted to prove to myself that I could do it."

Afterwards, she did some interviews, then went home with her grandparents. When they couldn't find an open McDonald's, they bought submarine sandwiches. She had two bites, went to the washroom, then passed out in the back seat of the car. She was up a few hours later to do a radio interview, where the interviewer told her to be a bit more cheery. "I was like, no. I've had no sleep. I will try but there is no guarantee."

The interviews continued over the next few days, but were interrupted when the first plane hit the Twin Towers in New York, NY. It was 9/11 after all. Then the second plane hit. They were at the CBC in Toronto for the last of a round of interviews that morning. "At that point I knew I had to get Ashley home to her mom," Vicki recalls.

Vicki says there was awe and inspiration for Ashley's swim. The media may have turned its attention to the terrorist attacks of 9/11 and the ensuing wars, but at a more personal level, for months afterward, there were notes and emails to Ashley. "Parents were contacting her saying you know I now have hope for my child. Whole lives were changed by that one event when people realized that if she could do that imagine what they could do."

That fall Vicki Keith and John Munro moved to Kingston and continued their work with swimmers with a disability. The crossing had been their last hurrah together with Ashley. She tried to keep swimming but it seemed like she had accomplished everything she had wanted in her sport; it was no longer fun. "If it's something I want to do then by all means my heart and soul are into it. When I am being told I have to do it it's not fun for me anymore." She swam for about another year but the family had moved north to Bradford and again the commuting was too demanding. She started hanging out with friends and family, then hit a rough patch. "I thought I was a big, bad teenager and I left home," she laughs. "I found out the hard way. It's not so bad at home. Stay home."

She met Chad McCormick and they started dating. They married in 2007 when she was 21. She does not know what it's like to have her limbs because she was so young when the meningitis took them. She remembers none of it. She figures she is meant to be here, that there must be a reason, or she would have died. "So, I live every day as if it's my last. I always love, I always trust. Sometimes trusting gets you screwed over. I take chances because you never know otherwise if you're ever going to have that chance."

And as for that tattoo, the promise made out on Lake Erie if Ashley swam through another hour? Shurlene made good on her promises: new shoes, new clothes and, with the tattoo, a warning. It would be on her body for the rest of her life. Ashley sports a tattoo of a shooting star on her right shoulder. The star was her goal, the lines, all the obstacles she has had to overcome.

If she returns to Lake Erie she reminisces about the fact that she did it. That it's something she has forever. She has been widely quoted as saying anything is possible if you believe in yourself, yet it took her Erie swim for Ashley to believe that for herself, for real, to make it more than words strung together. "I'm hoping the next girl out there or little boy who think they can't do anything with their lives because they have a disability, will see what I've accomplished and know that's not the case."

Ashley Cowan, first woman with a disability.
Photo courtesy Ashley Cowan.

Paula Jongerden: to the Long Point Biosphere, 2002

Paula Jongerden was swimming for all this, all this ... nothingness.

On the choppy surface of Lake Erie the lights from her escort boats shone through the water. By now the layers of lanolin she had applied had worn off. Her nurse's hands were stark white just ahead of her in the night waters of Erie.

She was swimming north over supposedly impossible currents towards the Long Point World Biosphere Reserve, which was the heart of her environmental efforts. She had dedicated her swim and her fundraising efforts for this sandy 40-kilometre long sand spit in Erie, home to migrating birds and their list-obsessed watchers and thousands upon thousands of monarch butterflies on a layover en route to winter in Mexico.

Long Point is also a graveyard for ships and Paula was beginning to mull that over in her mind. What lies beneath? She would never see any wrecks, in fact there was nothing through the shimmer of lights from the boats above, only her eerily white hands stroking forward and back. "I had to shut my eyes for awhile except when I turned to breathe. It was really kind of freaky."

She had to think hard about what she was doing and who was counting on her. "You can make it to a mile off shore, but it makes all the difference if you make it to shore."

When Paula Jongerden, a mother of three, swam Lake Erie at age 49, she was the oldest woman to complete any swim of the Great Lakes (Solo Swims).

Over August 21-22, 2002, she completed her crossing in 23 hours, 36 minutes for a 43.6 kilometre swim from Presque Isle State Park in Erie, PA to Long Point, ON.

When she was young Paula was an age-group swimmer with the Brantford Aquatic Club in southern Ontario and like so many swimmers across the province, retired from the sport when she entered high school and found other things to do. She grew up—"sort of, I guess"—became a nurse, had Sarah, Emily, and Charlotte with her then-husband Harry and worked her shifts at various hospitals in southern Ontario before wrapping up her career in the ER at West Haldimand General Hospital in Hagersville, interestingly a place some Lake Erie swimmers have visited after their crossings and attempts. She, however, hardly ever swam.

In 2001, at age 48, Paula noticed how grown up Emily seemed and made an effort to reconnect. They took a scuba diving course together at the local YMCA where a hard truth left Paula cold. She barely passed the standard for her SCUBA certification. What the heck? She attempted the diving requirement of 16 lengths—in a tiny 18-metre pool, no less—and she was "just about dead." She returned to the pool.

As she trained, she noted another swimmer, an older gentleman in his 60s who faithfully put in his mile every day. With his encouragement, she worked her endurance back up and finally completed a mile. He patted her on the back. "In retrospect now it doesn't seem much, but it *is* actually to do that small step," she says. "So I thought I'm going to try two miles." She swam that second mile, then went home to announce to her family that she had swum two miles and could probably swim across Lake Erie. They all laughed.

For Paula, and she bets that for a lot of others who do these kind of marathons, it's the challenge in the face of people who say you can't. "You want a goal. It's nice to think about being in shape for sure, but the goal of swimming across the Lake is really what drives you to get swimming every day." There's no forgetting this is a Great Lake, but as her coach told her, if you can swim two kilometres, you can do four. And if you can do four, then you can do 10. "He said it's just a little bit further," she laughs. "I think that two kilometres is nothing to shake a stick at, right?"

When Paula made the decision to swim across Lake Erie, she had been retired from swimming for 35 years. When she found her coach Alan Fairweather in Guelph (who had overseen Kim Middleton's transformation from runner to marathon swimmer extraordinaire), she really only had about six and a half months to train for her crossing of Erie.

Yet there were many strands weaving the fabric of her motivation. Some of the drive to just go and do the Lake came from a general, lingering despair over the 9/11 attacks a few short months before she decided to cross Erie. "You think 'life is short; let's live the best we can;' that got me going on the swim. I read a phrase once—live your life as an exclamation, not an explanation—I always liked that. Yeah. No dress rehearsals."

Paula was an emergency room nurse. She knows the turns life can take. "You never know what's going to happen to you. I think that I wanted to do Erie that year because I thought what if I get sick or something." Indeed she had started back in the pool in the first place because she recalled how her father, Peter Howell, had died of heart disease when he was 55. He had driven her to swim workouts as a youngster, feeding her corn syrup for energy. Her mother, Norma Mary (nee Mars) Howell, had died of cancer when she was only 59. Norma had volunteered at the Brantford Y teaching youngsters with disabilities to swim, just like her own heroine, Marilyn Bell. Of course her mother had spoken "forever" of Marilyn Bell and Paula already thought that was a "neat" feat. She knew she could swim, had the drive. "I'm nuts when I come to do things."

And then there was the Long Point World Biosphere Reserve, floating out there in Erie, protected now but needing attention. In her effort to find something for herself now that the girls were adults, she had found it online: this UNESCO program right in her own backyard. The environment is the basis of everything, she says. "I know people swim the Great Lakes for many worthwhile reasons but I think that everything is related to our environment as well as genetics. As far as important causes go, that's huge," she says. "When I did it for the biosphere reserve it was my vehicle to say look at all these good projects and good partners. If I could leave this world believing that in some small way I have helped this cause, I would be truly happy."

But swimming a Great Lake? Why not display environmental pictures or, as Paula answers to the question, have a cookie sale? "I thought that was something we'd be doing. But a swim is a lot bigger than a bake sale. Marathons were in then, and still are. A marathon sounded like something that would attract attention."

When she prepared for Erie she wasn't out to minimize the effort it would take. She went into it not really knowing that these kind of marathon swims need more than seven months training. She didn't want to tell anyone but she needed to fundraise. She continued to work the fulltime shift work of nurses while swimming 15 hours a week in preparation to cross Erie. She often worked all night then went to swim before going to bed. "You stay up all night when you're swimming anyways but I just wanted to see how my system worked as well. It was fine. I always felt better after I swam—unless it was a gruelling shift."

Over the course of the heavy training her coach Alan found the right tools to motivate her. When things got hard at work, he would invoke a particularly challenging person Paula knew to remind her why she was putting in all this training in the pool. "There was this one girl . . . kind of a fuddy duddy, who sort of said, 'You shouldn't be doing that.'" During training Paula would complain and whine as many athletes do and Alan would say, tell me about so and so, and "that got me going again, past those walls that you get."

Paula's crossing of Erie was scheduled for August 17th-18th but was delayed in the face of 20 knot gusts, a small craft warning and looming thunderstorms. They boated out anyway, just around the edge of the inner bay at Port Dover into the main part of Erie, just for a peek—and turned around. No way: too stormy. Paula went home to watch the weather. The forecast had to hint at winds under 15 knots. She already had enough to deal with swimming north into the swirling currents around Long Point.

The night of August 20th would ultimately become the night before her swim. Instead of sleeping, Paula was out in her driveway talking to a firefighter she knew after a lightning storm set the power box beside her driveway ablaze. She couldn't know that in a few short hours the weather window would clear and she'd be back on the road to Erie, PA, to start swimming across a Great

Lake. "I didn't sleep that much before, which was crazy but you didn't know. This power box was on fire and it was exciting."

The morning of August 21st dawned beautiful. Over in Port Dover, ON bets were being placed in a local pub: would she make it? Would she drown? Would she quit? And perhaps at one point another question was, would she even start. With helicopters flying overhead, Paula's crew was out in the bay in their boats, transferring items, looking somewhat suspicious in that first, raw year after 9/11. Meanwhile on the beach Paula stood behind a towel to put on her suit and grease up with lanolin. An official on the beach strolled by and asked what they were all doing. As she hid behind the towel, she nonchalantly tossed out, "Oh, we're just going to go back to Canada and not claiming anything."

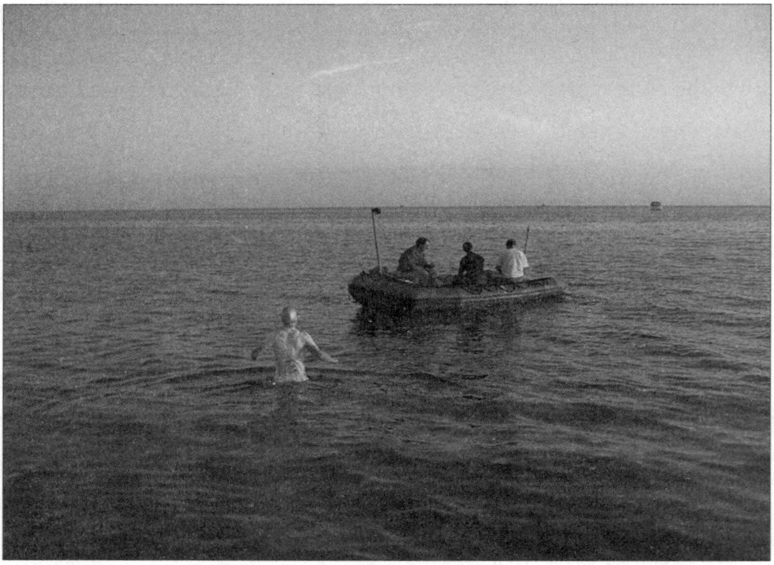

Lanolin-covered Paula Jongerden setting out from Erie, PA. Photo courtesy Paula Jongerden.

The swim launched at 7:01 a.m. Swim master Marilyn Korzekwa was pleased with the experienced crew, which included Dave McKellar at the helm of *Roller Coaster*, and Gary Copeland at the *Caramel*. Dave was also a paramedic. Kimber Jo Marshall was an ER nurse, George Hogan, Nick Wilson, Brian Craig, Harry Jongerden and Emily Jongerden were also on the crew.

There was ocean-sailing experience, no one was really prone to seasickness, and Paula's coach Alan was an experienced swim master with time overseeing swims on two Great Lakes, Lac St. Jean and the English Channel. Marilyn wrote in her report that the swim would not have succeeded without the assets which included the maturity and judgement of the entire crew.

Paula started optimistically enough and hoped to complete what would be a historic crossing in 18 hours or so. "I'm not a fast swimmer; short distances I can swim fast but as soon as I lose that adrenaline thing, I peter out." She estimates her speed at about two kilometres per hour, give or take, and didn't plan on breaking a speed record. As she stroked into the Lake in the early morning, Erie was beautiful. She thought about her parents. "I so wish they were alive in 2002."

As the day wore on and the waves tossed her about, her left shoulder began to hurt, and she felt nauseous. At 7:00 p.m., when she knew she wasn't yet halfway, she agreed to a course change to land at the closest point possible on Long Point. Nick Wilson, a local lifeguard, and swim master Marilyn hopped in to pace her.

The thing with a biosphere is that it's a reserve, protected space, developers kept at bay. All of which is fine except when swimming across a Great Lake at night to a point with no lights. Long Point could not be seen at night, unlike the Toronto skyline which is always lit up like a mall at Christmas. The team's biggest and brightest point was the *Roller Coaster,* which true to its name was riding in the two-metre waves and likely drifting. At one point, Dave McKellar checked his radar in the *Roller Coaster* and noted a freighter en route. After communicating with the crossing team, the freighter altered course to avoid the crossing. At about 3:40 a.m., the *Roller Coaster* weighed anchor so the team could verify depth readings. In the rocking waves and wind, the anchor rope wrapped around one of the propellers. With a flashlight in a plastic bag, a knife, and a lungful of air, Nick dove under the boat and managed to free the prop.

Overnight, Paula swam on, surfing waves reaching two metres, launched with a mighty boost from the sandbars beneath, her white hands reaching into nothingness. The winds crossed their path blowing in from the east. The crew in the Zodiacs rode Erie's distinct chop, its shorter waves compared to the high, rolling waters of, say, Huron. It was worse on the boats than in the water, though. Paula looked to her side and saw that her team was bent over into the wind and waves like mariners at sea; at one point a Zodiac reared up and formed the letter L on a wave. Paula spent the final hours swimming breaststroke to shore, fearful of being swamped if she continued swimming freestyle, with her face in the water. The team would tell Paula she was maybe five kilometres off shore, though she was actually further out and no one wanted to discourage her. Still, if they had been further out, Paula thinks that Marilyn would have ended the crossing attempt. The weather was bad and safety—for both crew and swimmer—is paramount.

As Paula drew closer to Long Point, Erie was shallow; eventually, after 4:00 a.m., she passed the *Roller Coaster* which could go no further in the shallow waters. Paula aligned herself with the waves as bits of pebbles and grit from the bottom misted her. She complained about the cold and the swim, her back and her shoulder. If she told them she was having chest pain, they would have pulled her out. "So I complained enough because I needed to," she says. She figures had she truly wanted out, she would have said the words she needed. A dose of Advil alleviated the pain in her shoulder.

Then, with the aid of a hand-held GPS in the Zodiac, after a long night, her progress became clear. As Marilyn writes in her swim report, "The sunrise saved the day and made it evident to everyone that they were almost there."

As Paula neared shore, truly swimming to the biosphere, Brian Craig asked Paula if she could see the cottonwood trees on the shore, "And that made me almost want to cry. I still get choked up. 'Can you see the cottonwoods, Paula, the trees on the point?'"

When she stood up, she could still feel the sandblasting Lake Erie had sprayed along her skin like miners spraying shotcrete beneath the surface. Her swim ended at 6:37 a.m. She had swum 43.6 kilometres (Solo Swims) for the first south to north, supposedly-impossible swim, and was the oldest woman at a mere 49 years, to have a SSO-ratified swim in any of the Great Lakes.

Her swim raised $10,000 and more awareness than money could buy for the Long Point Biosphere. Although the biosphere reserves around Ontario have since received somewhat real government money, at the time of her crossing, all the funding came from donations and memberships—and Paula's swim. Paula credits her crew with pulling her through those final hours. "They were all part of the team. I would have given up if I hadn't had this group. It's so much a team thing," Paula says.

Afterwards, headlines hailed the fact that Paula had "conquered" Erie, but she says Erie allowed her to pass; that it was her good fortune to have had the strength to go with the flow and do it. No one conquers Mother Nature, she says, "unless you spray poison or something, and she'll always get you back anyways, right? That's just the media; I guess it makes a good headline."

In 2004, Paula returned to the shores of Erie to see if her 2002 crossing had been a fluke. In 2003, she was raring to go again but Alan Fairweather told her to wait a year, that he was tired of having a cold bum, she laughs. In 2004, she was pulled out of Erie about 10 kilometres into her swim. The weather was plain bad for swimming and boating but she had no idea what was going on in the boats, tuned into the Beatles as she was on her swim music player. Up top, her escorts weren't visible in the high waves; nor was she making progress. If she stopped to say anything, or to feed, Erie would shoot her backwards about 50 metres, she recalls. "I was disappointed, though certainly not in myself. I know how much effort you put into it. It's not that you are over-estimating yourself when you go into a swim like that. I feel there's success in just getting into the water, getting that far."

She would never say someone failed because most of the time the weather stops the swim. She recalls hearing about Thie Convery's 2010 crossing of Erie. "She was very positive. That is such a great place to be in your head," Paula says. Paula herself would work on imaging, on telling herself she was going to walk out of Erie. "Those mind over matter things I really feel strongly about, the psychology of it being huge, huge, huge. Obviously you have to have some strength and be able to swim but it's huge the psychology of it. It can cause you not to swim. You have to say you're going to do it."

After 2004, that was it for Paula and Great Lake crossings. Maybe. Perhaps. She retired from nursing in May 2011 though she still works the occasional shift. She and her life partner, Brian Craig, are also partners in a canoe and kayak business affiliated with Long Point Eco-Adventures. They guide visitors down Big Creek in Norfolk County.

Paula and Brian often return to the spot where she finished in 2002 to gaze across Erie. "I get a lump in my throat and even as I'm saying this I'm getting a lump in my throat. You go down there because in some sort of spiritual way you're part of the Lake. I know the water empties itself every so many months but it's like I'm special to that Lake and it's special to me."

Lake Ontario 3

Colleen Shields' Unfinished Business: Lake Ontario in 2004, 2005, and 2006

Despite crossing Ontario in 1990, despite crossing Huron in 1993, something wasn't right for Colleen Shields. The niggling dissatisfaction didn't surface in her consciousness until 2004 and the 50th anniversary of Bell's historic Lake Ontario crossing. Colleen was one of 12 swimmers on a commemorative relay. When she exited the water at Marilyn Bell Waterfront Park, she knew she had "some unfinished business here," she says. "I was going to do it again, and do it right. Then I could retire and be totally satisfied." She swam that little last stretch of the Marilyn Bell relay in 2004 in 12.2C water, and it was a bracing dose of awareness—she hadn't done the 1990 swim properly. She hadn't had the proper respect for the Lake; she had lucked out. Looking back as a swim master, she felt that an aspect of her earlier self had been a hotshot.

Marilyn Bell was out there at the Lake cheering everyone on. "I thought to myself, how can I not? I've got to get in there." So, despite having already swum her leg of the relay, Colleen jumped into the water and began swimming that last three-quarters of a mile into Toronto. "It was the fasted I'd ever swum—it was so cold." When Colleen stopped at one point, Marilyn Korzekwa, another relay crosser, asked why. "I said 'I'm a little concerned about having a heart attack.' She said 'You would have had it already. Just keep swimming.'"

As it turned out, however, the cold water wasn't the danger for Colleen. As she came through the breakwall to complete the relay and touch at Marilyn

Bell Waterfront Park, she said, "Oh, wow!" Swim master Bob Weir looked at her and said, "Oh, God, you're going to go again."

In 2005 she went in tandem with her best friend, Nicole Mallette. They had organized everything. Their exhaustion was so visible that when their support crews arrived the night of the swim, their swim master John Scott said they were both too tired. They weren't going into the Lake, they were going to bed to sleep. They would go in the morning. It's something Colleen doesn't recommend since the swimmer will then finish at night. It can be cold. Depending on the air temperature, a chop can start. Sure enough, the choppy waves started for Colleen and Nicole. "We were maybe five miles from Toronto. I didn't have any energy to swim through that. John was in the water with me a lot on that swim." She told him she didn't feel well and he replied that he could tell. She was white, pasty. She grabbed his hand and got into the boat. She told everyone she was going the following year. "They said, 'We're all here for you.'" She promised she would make it in 2006.

And so, in 2006, she touched at Marilyn Bell Park in Toronto on a sparkling golden day. She swam a 51 kilometre-long crossing of Lake Ontario in 16 hours, 30 minutes on August 12th and 13th. She was 54 and had lowered her own personal record. She is not entirely sure why she was faster over a longer distance. "You have a certain sense of maturity. I feel that with that maturity come more chances for success." Through that swim, Shields raised $5,000 for Right to Play, which uses sport and play to help children in underprivileged countries—including First Nations in Canada.

Then she was training with a new swim coach and the ideas started brewing. What about Cindy Nicholas' record? It had come up during the 2006 crossing. "I thought that was a really nasty joke because I'd had a really bad night. I'd been sick a little bit with the boat fumes and there was a pretty bad chop going on." She had no idea she was moving that fast. Then she began discussing time with her then-coach at Etobicoke Masters. She analyzed it: perhaps the record wasn't about swimming faster. It was about taking shorter breaks between feedings. She was taking three to four minute breaks, chatting with her crew. If she could take only 30 second breaks, "I would so have the record."

Open water swimming has its challenges beyond being fit and mature enough to handle the distance, and Colleen was convinced that showing the Lake proper respect was a key element in her 2006 success. In 2006, she thought she was finished with Lake Ontario swims. "I don't think I could ever repeat what I did. I'm thrilled. I don't want to try and repeat. It's all good and it's done," she said then. And, people thought, right.

Five Lakes, One Swimmer—Part II

Paula Stephanson: no way are we going back to Superior, 1996-2009

In Great Lakes swimming, logistics have also proven challenging and are sometimes harder than the actual crossing. Organizing family, crew, food, the infrastructure needed to get across—not to mention the weather—have waylaid more than one crossing attempt. Paula Stephanson had done the training, the preparation and certainly put in the years to swim across all five Great Lakes. Turns out what she really needed was a $20 bill to complete a 13-year odyssey.

On August 21, 2009, Paula Stephanson, then 30, was being coated in sunscreen and lanolin oil cream to prevent chafing before setting out to swim from Chicago across Lake Michigan to Michigan City, 51 kilometres away. Some members of Chicago's Open Water Chicago, the city's open-water swim club and host of the Big Shoulders Race, had come down to Chicago's magnificent waterfront to cheer her on.

But now there was an issue. Paula wasn't sure exactly what happened—"I am just the swimmer." Her team had contacted the coast guard and let it be known she was starting this swim. Her escort Zodiac waited off the beach. It was too obvious something was going on here and an official was saying they needed permission to leave the beach. "I'm hearing all this. I don't know what to do," Paula says.

It was about the last thing Paula needed to hear. When Michigan was completed she would be the second person ever to swim all five Lakes, after Vicki Keith. Whereas Vicki had done her five in two months in 1988, for Variety Village, Paula was instead closing a chapter in her life before marriage, children, and a fulltime career in education. She had already put back the start date of the swim as she and her family struggled to secure the requisite support boats for the crossing attempt. She had moved out of her home in Ottawa and back to Belleville on Lake Ontario, essentially ditching her fiancé Andrew Duggan, so she could train in a Great Lake with her mother beside her in a boat. And now she was being told she couldn't leave the beach.

A member of Open Water Chicago stepped in and asked who they needed to call. He called for permission but couldn't get the administrator. Paula was slick and goopy with sunscreen, stuff under her armpits for chafing, the support boats were off shore. No one on shore knew what to do. Then the Open Water Chicago member shook the official's hand and said, where does your jurisdiction end? How far are you allowed to monitor? He was told: "If you went past those rocks there, technically it's not our jurisdiction."

Again, they shook hands. A friend turned to Paula: "I can't believe it. He just bribed him. You didn't see him shake the hand with money in it?"

Paula was completely oblivious. When they got around to the other side of the beach they were told that this is Chicago, of course you've got to bribe him. Even the captain on the sailboat further offshore had been on the radio saying they had to pay the official. There had been no way to let the team on shore know this, Paula recalls. With the $20 in hand so the official could take an early lunch and not see the departure, Paula didn't waste any time. She slipped down the rocks and into a picture-perfect Lake Michigan.

It was oh, so cold, a biting, numbing 13.3C and she told Bob Weir, her swim master, there was no way she could do 24 hours of this cold. Then, again, she was told not to worry, the thing with Michigan is the further she swam from shore, the warmer the water would become.

About five hours and 20 kilometres into the swim, Paula knew it was only a matter of time and her swim was going to end, the feeling growing with the rolling waves and grey sky moving in overhead. The Zodiac was rising on the waves beside her. The wind had changed direction, swooping around to the north from the west or behind her. Michigan turned "absolutely chaotic." Windows hadn't been closed in time so everything was wet on the sailboat.

In the water, Paula was managing better than her crew on the boat and in the Zodiac. The boat captain had never been out in conditions like this. The weather forecast said things were only going to get worse. Paula was aware of the chit chat going on, the fact they were only one-third of the way across, that unless the weather settled quickly, her swim was about to end. Her friend Kendra Cooke, who had paced Paula on Lakes Erie and Huron, was back to pace for Michigan. Kendra couldn't believe that Paula just accepted the word to end the swim like that. "Kendra, I could see it coming for the past two hours. We were lost in these waves."

With conditions worsening, the crews couldn't handle the crossing and if they couldn't support Paula properly, ensuring her safety and feeding her, the crossing had to be called off. Back to Chicago.

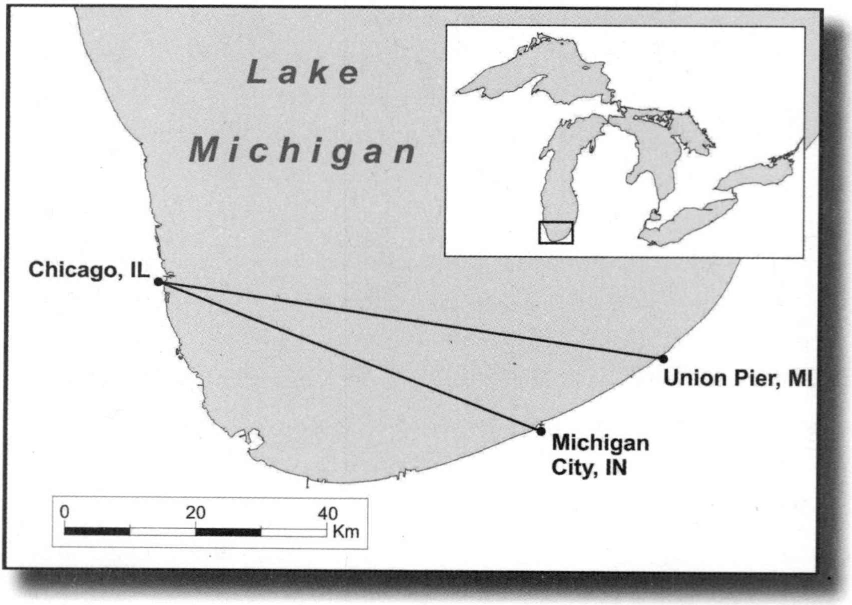

Two routes followed by two swimmers: Paula Stephanson took the southern route from Chicago, IL to Michigan City, IN, while Vicki Keith swam from Union Pier, MI to Chicago, IL. Map Credit: L.L. Lariviere—Laurentian University.

Paula spent the next day rehydrating, as she swallowed pain relievers and iced her body. Trying to rest, her mind jumped from worry to worry: would the boats be available for the second crossing attempt? How much money was this going to cost? Given that she had already swum for seven and a half hours, she wondered if she had anything left in the shoulder. On previous swims, she had only waited two or three hours to restart. "Things like that go through your mind, but if you don't try you're never going to know, so you just go for it."

Meanwhile, in another room her team was figuring out the logistics: when would the weather window open? Could they fit in the crossing? "I never really doubted I would get across the Lake. I didn't want to not get a chance to do it that summer. Everything was lined up, everyone was there. It's asking a lot of people to be on a crew. They're spending their own time and money and energy to help you get across," Paula says.

On the Sunday they were back at the beach in Chicago, this time hiding out in a car, greasing Paula up to protect her against the sun and any chafing. There was no lingering along Chicago's magnificent waterfront. Paula was told to make a dash for it, start swimming and not look back.

"When I got in the second time I knew I was slower." The first time she had been making amazing progress across Michigan. The second time was "oh my God, this is going to take forever," Paula recalls. "It's one of those things. You just keep plugging away. You've got to get in believing you'll make it to the other side or you never will."

There were other things to think about this time. On that first crossing attempt, helicopters had been flying back and forth over the same area, following a grid pattern. No one on her crossing told her but she would later learn that a boat had capsized, the boater was missing and presumed drowned. "They didn't want to tell me. But I knew, because I could see the helicopter. I knew they were looking for somebody. But I thought it was somebody alive."

Now on the second start, Paula knew the man had still not been found and was certainly dead. She spent a long, cold night counting down the hours until the dawn and saying she would never get into the Lake again if she ran into the body. She bumped her forehead on a water bottle in the pitch black night. "What is that?" she called to her crew. "Shine a light over here." A flashlight showed a water bottle. Paula shivers, what if it had been the man's head?

The crossing took a lot out of her and she did not make the same progress. The finish was choppy and her aching shoulders were ripped up some more.

She had hoped to break 24 hours for the crossing but finished in 25 hours, 38 minutes. She hadn't been going for time, though, and had not wanted to spend another summer training. She and Andrew had planned to marry in 2010 and that couldn't be postponed. When they were really struggling to find support boats, Bob suggested waiting. Paula wanted to close this chapter of her life. She didn't care about how much it cost to stay an extra day or so in Chicago. It would be worse to lose the money and time spent on training all summer of 2009. Now she was done, five Great Lakes, the second person to complete all five, solo, naked but for her suit, goggles, cap, and a massive support team.

Paula's journey to complete the Great Lakes began, as it does for most crossers, on Lake Ontario. She was 17 in 1996 and knew next to nothing about crossing the Lake, beyond the fact that Vicki Keith had done it four times. "As soon as I got it in my head I had to do it. It's something so different that many people can't do," Paula remembers. "I don't know why we do it. You put yourself through hell. The media was asking—my answer was always 'it's there to do.' I'm a determined person. I'm a swimmer. I heard about the challenge and thought I could do that."

Her mom knew Vicki Keith worked at Variety Village so she made a cold call and told Vicki Paula wanted to swim the Lake. Vicki directed them to Solo Swims of Ontario. Paula met with Bob Weir, who would be her swim master on all five crossings. After their first meeting, Bob had such confidence in her that he knew she was capable of swimming Lake Ontario.

Ontario was a rough crossing that August 16th in 1996, but at first Paula enjoyed the push from the Niagara River current. Then it was like crossing a line: one stroke the water was warm and the next, the temperature dropped, from 22.2C to 20C. "You think, well 20 isn't too bad. But when you drop four degrees so fast, it's shocking." At that point all she could think about was having to swim in water so cold. The night took its toll and her stroke rate dropped as she drew closer to Toronto. She touched at Marilyn Bell Park 22 hours, 30 minutes after starting. She had been naïve about how fast she could swim Lake Ontario. It was far more difficult than she had ever imagined, but no matter, she was done.

That was supposed to be it. Then her swim master, Bob Weir, an experienced lake crosser himself, stoked the fires and suggested she train to cross Lake

Erie. She laughed him off, but like moms of two or more children, Paula forgot about the pain, the intensity of the swim, and began training for another Lake.

On July 18-19, 1998 she completed the same crossing Bob had, becoming the first woman to swim the central part of Erie, from Dunkirk, NY to Rock Point Provincial Park, ON, a 43 km, 18-hour, 23 minute journey. She was 19. Erie was the most relaxing of her swims, despite having to be pulled three hours into the swim when poor weather forced her lead sailboat back into a safe harbour.

When it came to completing the five Great Lakes, Vicki Keith's situation was different than Paula's. Vicki devoted a whole summer to her Great Lakes crossings to raise money for Variety Village charities. On Paula's journey, her family was the core support group. Paula saw the size of the commitment to crossing a Great Lake and adjusted accordingly. It was especially a big commitment on her mother's part. For much of the summer, Eleanor Stephanson rode in the boat as Paula trained.

And Bob Weir tried to convince her to swim Erie and Huron in the same summer. Erie is warmer and it could be done sooner, and then Huron could be done later in the summer after the second largest Great Lake had time to warm up, relatively speaking. But Paula didn't know whether she could put her body through two Great Lakes in one season. "In reality, it would have been better, just a few more weeks of training. But because of the commitment of the whole family and what it takes to do the swims, it was easier on everybody to spread it out."

Still, the seed had been planted. By the time she finished her second year at Brock University in St. Catharine's, she was ready to challenge Lake Huron. August 12-13, 2000 could not come soon enough. Throughout her Great Lakes journey organizing boat support was always a major stress. For a time she doubted whether the swim would happen. And yet, in Huron she swam her fastest average speed, nearly 2.5 km an hour. She completed the same route as John Bulsza, the 55-kilometre crossing from Port Sanilac, MI to Port Franks, ON. She finished in 22 hours, 26 minutes, four hours faster than John. After that swim, Paula delighted and surprised onlookers by running to the finish, a 50-metre burst through the shallow water to touch the Port Franks side.

Looking at the five Great Lakes, Huron is situated in the middle, linked to the remaining two Lakes through the St. Mary's River and the Straits of Mackinac. She had done three Great Lakes and now it was expected that she would finish the remaining two. She felt like she had to, and after Huron she wanted to: "I wanted to be able to say I had done all five Great Lakes."

Life gets in the way, though. After Huron her father grew ill with cancer. His battle became the family focus until he passed in November 2003. By then Paula had to get away. She was finished at Brock, and in January 2005 she finally took off to Australia to complete her teaching degree. She didn't swim as she had in Canada. In Australia it wasn't like home where she could just hop into a master's swim practice. Instead, she took advantage of the ocean. While enjoying the surf she wrenched her right shoulder and tore ligaments and tendons. Every physiotherapist she visited told her to stop swimming. In 2006 she returned to Ottawa and began training to complete her Great Lakes journey. Only Superior and Michigan remained. Only.

Paula now had serious shoulder issues to contend with, not the kind a few weeks off could heal. In fact, in 2012, long after she had completed the five Lakes, surgery repaired her shoulder but she expects that it will never be the same.

But in 2007, with about one month before the crossing, she wasn't sure her shoulder would be able to handle Superior. Still, as she sought boats and did the out-of-water preparations, she figured, wryly, that if anything Superior would ice her shoulder the entire way, numbing the pain.

As always, Paula had to secure a decent-sized boat. On Superior that would be even more important. She located a potential boat at what she thought was a marina but it was actually a shipping business. The owner thought the idea of Paula swimming Superior was interesting enough to take one of his own boats out of service to support her crossing. The boat was massive, solid, over 15 metres long, and built to go out on Superior and greet the tankers.

Paula convinced her Brock teammate Melissa Brannagan, who had already completed a crossing of Lake Ontario, to come and see a crossing from a different perspective, as a pacer. She also brought her friend Jody Williams.

Paula was leaving from Port Wing, Wisconsin for Two Harbors, Minnesota. The theory at play is that the distance is short enough—in Lake Superior terms—that it can be completed in the relative warmth of daylight. The morning dawned beautiful on the Wisconsin side. As the sun rose and the team prepared for the crossing, Superior lay flat over its ancient blue depths, a beautiful calm. Paula thought that if Superior remained like this she could handle the cold water. "It was so nice and we were having such a good time."

After several hours of swimming alone in Superior, she requested a pacer. "I was freezing my ass off. I thought if I was this cold by myself somebody else should be in there suffering with me," she reflects, laughing. On one feeding, the team asked Paula how she was doing. "I can't feel my hands anymore," she said. "Should I wiggle my fingers or should I let them go numb?"

They told her to keep wiggling them. She had turned white, iridescent. "Superior is beautiful. It's so cold. It's not polluted the same way Erie and Ontario are. You see every stroke. I'd see my white hands." Eventually, though, white hands were only one of her worries. The crossing was not even halfway when Superior's legendary waves began to roll. Soon Paula's pacers wondered among themselves whether Paula would make it. They knew Paula was capable, but conditions were becoming so bad, Melissa recalls.

The water temperature barely nudged 15.5C. The team kept one pacer in the water with Paula at all times. Meanwhile, on the boat Paula's mother rubbed the hands and feet of the other swimmer to help her warm up. She would be barely warm again and it would be time to hop back in with Paula.

Her swim master Bob was concerned, to say the least. He would tell Paula that had they any other escort with them, like a smaller sailboat, he would have ended the crossing. But their support boat was meant for any weather and it hardly moved in Superior's roll. Bob had the boat positioned to one side to try and break the waves as he perched in the Zodiac and tried not to get knocked around. Eventually he would order everyone but Paula onto the large boat. She kept on swimming. Bob would have received a ferocious argument from Paula had they pulled out. She had spent the swim preparing to tell Bob there was no way he could pull it because she simply was not coming back to try it again. "We never had that discussion, but oh, that was in my head."

Beyond the high elbows of her pacers, Paula didn't see much. She was so drained from the effort of swimming in the bitter cold and waves that it was simply easiest to follow her pacers. At times it looked like their support boat would slide down the waves right on top of them.

Once the team was close to shore, the boat couldn't go in any closer, so it peeled off and headed towards Two Harbors in a slightly different direction. The final two hours Paula stroked her way in to shore. Alone.

As they stood on shore Melissa and Jody couldn't see Paula at some points; the waves were too high. But finally Paula could see the shore in the intervals between waves, and she aimed for it.

Despite the number of times over the swim that she'd told herself "I need to make this," Paula was surprised at the toll the cold was taking, at how miserable her normally effervescent self felt about being so cold. Years later she reflects on the experience: "Obviously you're proud of yourself. Superior is the one most people are amazed by because they can't believe you were in water that cold."

Melissa Brannagan says, "If it hadn't been for Paula and wanting to see her succeed so much it would have been really difficult to keep getting back into that water." Years after the crossing, Melissa remains inspired by Paula's swim. "I have no idea where she found the mental strength to get through that." Melissa would never take away anything from a crossing of Lake Ontario or Lake Erie. She pauses, a swimmer's long, steady exhale. "They're all very difficult things to do. I have no doubt, after being there and seeing that. Yet it takes a very special person to take on Lake Superior."

Paula crawled out of Superior and sat on a rock. She completed the 32-kilometre crossing in 13 hours, 15 minutes. The team threw blankets around her, took some pictures to mark the occasion and then took Paula, shivering and convulsing, to warm up at their hotel.

Later the team ate at a nearby restaurant. The waitress noticed they'd been there for a few days, this big group who didn't look like regular vacationers. She asked what they were doing. Someone said Paula had just swum across Lake Superior. The waitress begged to differ, saying she couldn't believe it, that adults don't go in Lake Superior. Even only children run in and out. Two weeks earlier, she told the team, a guy had gone out in a kayak and rolled over. He couldn't get back into the boat and died of hypothermia. "This is what we know of Superior."

For Paula, it was tougher to explain that her swim was different, that she was always moving. "The key is you have to produce more heat than is being sucked out of you. You can go in cold water that you can't survive in as long as you're moving," Paula says.

Then there was Michigan. In 2009, two years after she crossed Superior, and 13 years after crossing Lake Ontario, she would finally finish her journey.

As a teacher living in Ottawa, a few hours from any of the Great Lakes, Paula still feels a connection to the water. She has a gold necklace bearing charms in the shape of each Lake, inscribed with the date she crossed them. "It's very neat. For a long time it only had the three charms on it. People would look at it and they could never quite guess what it was. 'Is that an animal? Is that a bird?'" Once a 12-year-old boy asked her, "Why do you have the Great Lakes on your necklace?" Why indeed. "Now that I have all five on it, it's far more obvious. People ask 'Is that the Great Lakes?'"

Paula Stephanson, 17, was only a year older than Marilyn Bell, her heroine, when she swam her first Great Lake in 1996. Photo courtesy Andrew and Paula Duggan Collection.

And indeed it is. And more. "It's not just the Great Lakes. Because of what I went through with each one there's still a sense that they're pretty ferocious. I don't think you ever conquer those Lakes. You cross the Lakes. I don't want to say you're lucky because it has nothing to do with luck. It's determination. But, I think the Lake is still so in charge. If it chooses—you may be a fantastic swimmer—but you're not going to get across it."

That being said, the right mindset remains one of total belief until the swimmer crawls out on the other side, white, seasick, frozen solid, never wanting to see hot chocolate again. Paula's approach to her swims was straightforward: there is no way out; you have to make it across. "A lot of people think 'Oh I'm going to give it a shot and see what happens.' It's the mindset, it's all about the mindset. You've got to believe. There is no other option. The second you doubt yourself, or say 'Well, as long as it stays warm, I'm going to make it,' it will mess with your head. You really have to be as mentally tough as you are physically."

Lake Ontario 4

Virtually Solo and Unclothed: Colleen Shields, 2010

Swimmers learn about the Great Lakes at the most intimate of levels: coated in sunscreen and lanolin for chafing and some measure of insulation, they might as well swim naked for all they are protected from the elements. To ensure the swim is legal, the required bathing suits are subject to current FINA rules, the world governing body of swimming. Since Marilyn Bell proved it was possible, swimmers have come forward, not in numbers, but in power, and, as Marilyn herself says with the heart of a marathoner, virtually solo and unclothed—looking far off to the horizon, over the curve of the earth.

Most swimmers tackling the traditional route on Lake Ontario enter the spongy, dicey Queen's Royal Beach in Niagara-on-the-Lake, with much anticipation and sheer relief, then swim north to Toronto. The clock starts running the moment the swimmer's toenail touches the Lake. But it's a weird thing. In Ontario, and elsewhere across Canada, people swim in "the lake" at the cottage, camp or city beach. It's a summer ritual.

So, at first the 2010 Lake Ontario crossing of swimmer Colleen Shields seems so normal to me, even as she shoots across towards Toronto with a mighty heave-ho from the Niagara River current. I'm in Colleen's support boat, and as the sun shifts in the west, we pass some of her Zodiac crew leaping into Lake Ontario, for all the world like vacationers. So normal ... as Colleen heads north—out into the lake, beyond the normal zone. The sun descends. Hours pass. The weather holds. She's still swimming. The sailboat escort bobs out ahead. Colleen swims on—stroke, stroke, breathe, stroke, stroke, breathe—in a rhythm that is at once hypnotic and never-altering, into the inky darkness. Toronto does not appear to be getting any closer, except that by night time it's easier to distinguish the buildings along the waterfront. Swim master Bob Weir jokes that the Colleen needs a bit of drama out there.

Waking from a fitful sleep, too chilled to shiver, I thank heavens I packed extra socks and pull them on in the dark. This was the part of a Great Lakes crossing that I didn't really understand until this moment. Just up ahead, fuzzy green glow sticks reflect on the black Lake from her bathing cap—Colleen Shields, 58 years old, is still swimming. It's about 4:00 a.m., though time is irrelevant except in context. At this point, only the time to get into Toronto and Marilyn Bell Park matters. Will she make it in time, before a forecast storm? Will Colleen take time off her previous best of 16 hours? She's still seriously swimming. It's not her first time out here: she has crossed Lake Ontario twice previously, in 1990 and 2006. But she's back again, viewing the time record, but mainly trying to wrap up some unfinished business with Lake Ontario.

The August sky shines clearly above, even brighter than the tantalizing lights of Toronto. The Zodiac GPS registers boat speed, lake depth, air temperature, her route north into Toronto—both the direct route and the one the team has drawn over the hours of this swim. Above, the sky reflects how it's also possible to navigate by the stars: Orion's Belt, the Big and Little Dippers. Colleen swims on, topless now. She stripped her bathing suit partway down since the straps were digging into her aching shoulders. Her stroke rate has slowed. Shaun Chisholm, a Toronto firefighter who crossed in 2008 and is an assistant swim master on this crossing, has hopped in to get her through the darkest part of the night. Shaun is freezing in there. Colleen stays warm, as she always does on these marathon swims. She draws ever nearer to Toronto. After enduring cold and weather over the past two summers, now it seems she has Mother Nature and Lake Ontario working in her favour.

Then around about 5:00 a.m. the waves begin a telltale knock on the transoms of the boats. Lake Ontario is waking. The drama that Bob Weir thought Colleen's story needed, back when a complete swim seemed certain, is about to kick in.

And so it does, rolling waves, wind out of the west that shifts the landing from Marilyn Bell Park east to Leslie Street Spit, then pushes the team further east, Colleen swimming in a zigzag vain attempt to overcome the other formidable challenge to landing in Toronto: the Humber River current that pours into the Lake and seems to capture the swimmer in a perpetually swirling pool. Even an experienced open-water swimmer can feel uncomfortable out here, wondering where the lifejackets are and what exactly that was brushing over the legs. Just the current or something else in Lake Ontario's waters?

With Lake Ontario rolling in with the wind, the swim master calls Colleen's crossing attempt off. She's helped aboard, and the team of boats zips into the oh-so-close shore. Colleen tosses her swimsuit into the Lake in a gesture symbolic, defiant, and promising. I'll be back for you. On shore, the marine unit of the Toronto Police wonders who the "idiots" are who have been out on the Lake in those rolling waves. Later that afternoon the storm whose advance guard ended Colleen's crossing rolls into southern Ontario, rain and wind playing havoc with the traffic on the super highway running east-west through Toronto.

In late 2011, Solo Swims of Ontario has redone the plaque at Niagara-on-the-Lake that recognizes all the traditional route crossings of Lake Ontario. Colleen and I are driving the ETR 407 highway towards Niagara-on-the-Lake and we're talking about that crossing attempt in 2010. "So now I've got to finish my business again." She pauses. "If anyone had told me I'd be thinking of crossing Lake Ontario again at 60 years of age I would have said you're nuts." She laughs. But really, though, it is cool to be 60 and to show women in her age group—not to mention younger—"that you can achieve greatness if you want it badly enough."

She can't pinpoint why people keep coming back for more of Lake Ontario. Certainly she has a thing for it. There is something about the Lake, yes, she agrees. "For me, I really just want to finish it. That will be it. I don't want to be swimming the Lake at 70." Of course, that's what they were saying back in 1990 when Colleen was nearly 40. Though that would be cool to be 70 and swimming Lake Ontario. But for Colleen, at least for now, being 60-plus will be cool enough, thank you. "I don't know, yeah, some people are done with it with an attempt and they haven't made it and they don't come back. But I wonder, how badly did you want it? I was very lucky my very first time coming across because I didn't train for it. I was pretty cocky about it." She thought she could cross the Lake if she wanted. It's an attitude that should have prevented a crossing. "Mother Nature should have thrown all kinds of stuff at me then, not now. I had no respect for the Lake or anything." Her late friend, the swimmer Rick Wood, would tell her that she had to become one with the Lake, that before any crossing the swimmer must go down and talk to the Lake and ask permission to come across. "And I do that now. I'm Irish; of course I'm superstitious."

Youngest on the Traditional Route: Annaleise Carr, 2012

There were water snakes in the old Welland Canal in June 2012. More of a problem was the cold water: 16.6C in the sun with a brisk spring breeze. But like the other, all older swimmers, Annaleise Carr hopped into the waters for the open-water session at the Solo Swims of Ontario swimmers' workshop.

There's a strong case to be made that it was here in the waters of the Welland Canal that any doubts about her application to swim across Lake Ontario were erased that Saturday in June, long before the 2012 open-water swimming season had really begun. Until then it was fair to ask whether this 14-year-old's application was serious. No one had really heard much about the age-group swimmer from the Norfolk Hammerheads in Simcoe, one of the dozens of small towns sprinkled across the southwestern reaches of Ontario.

At four-foot-ten Annaleise Carr is built like a gymnast who specializes in the explosive power events of floor exercise and vault. And yet, over the lunch and following swim in the canal at the Welland International Flatwater Centre anticipation grew. The team supporting her was organized and energetic, with many members giving up their Saturday to attend the sessions on safety, hypothermia, and flotilla formation.

And it was obvious over the five kilometre swim that afternoon that she loved open water; in fact she prefers it to the pool. Her stroke was smooth, her body nicely positioned high in the water as the swimmers and their teams moved 2.5 kilometres along the canal to the 406 bridge and back. Three strokes, breathe on the left, three strokes, breathe on the right, steady for 2.5 k down to the railway bridge, then back to the Flatwater Centre dock. Her pacers hopped in to practise with her and she was openly smiling and waving. Afterwards she was dressed in her sweats, hanging with the other kids on the dock; at home she would go on Facebook to connect with other teens she'd met that day.

In the heady, overwhelming weeks following her historic swim across Lake Ontario, that Saturday in June felt like forever ago. But here were all the components of her story and the roots of her success: a happy-go-lucky 14-year-old teen who loves to swim and who wanted to do something good with that ability. The rest was up to Lake Ontario.

On August 19, 2012, Annaleise Carr of Simcoe became the youngest person to swim across Lake Ontario. At 14, the valedictorian at Walsh Public School crossed the traditional route from Niagara-on-the-Lake to Marilyn Bell Waterfront Park in Toronto, a 51 kilometre swim. She raised over $250,000 for Camp Trillium, which provides outdoor recreation to children surviving cancer, and to their families. The only indication of her struggle lay in her time: 26 hours, 40 minutes, 54.2 seconds. That swim landed her in the exclusive 24-hour club, for open-water swimmers whose marathon ran at least 24 hours.

In the summer of 2011 Annaleise, a competitive swimmer since she was four, was a member of the North Shore Runners/Swimmers. They swam a 10-kilometre race to raise money for Camp Trillium. Before the event, they visited the camp so they would know exactly what and why they were raising money. They ended up raising $15,000.

Annaleise wanted to do more for the Camp. She was too young to volunteer so she and her sister Larissa started tossing fundraising ideas around. They knew about Marilyn Bell and thought her swim was, "really cool." With Larissa's support she decided to swim across Lake Ontario to raise money for Camp Trillium.

First, they had to convince their parents. Annaleise and Larissa plotted out the entire conversation, then one night before Christmas they informed their parents over dinner. Debbie and Jeff said no. "They spent a month trying to talk me out of it," Annaleise recalls. "They were surprised. They knew the cause I was doing it for was really good."

The girls continued to mention it. The swim-running group talked about it and, naturally, ran with it, Debbie Carr recalls. It took a month to convince her parents, yet as they looked into it, read the rules and saw the support she would have, they came around. Solo Swims has stringent requirements for the team. The safety of all—both swimmer and team—is paramount. In fact a big problem for lots of aspirants is meeting the requirements, long before dipping a toe for a crossing. Annaleise's parents concluded that if their daughter could meet the organization's requirements, she'd be ok. "We decided she's going to be safe, she's going to be well watched, well looked after." Then they watched as the commitment in time and money grew. The North Shore teammates stepped up and wanted to help. In February 2012, the crew started to come together. The Carrs thought that perhaps this was actually possible. "She had a lot of good people that supported her."

Not that anyone was going to talk Annaleise out of it: she knew the kids, the leaders at Camp Trillium. A child at her school had passed away from cancer. All that stayed with her. And Annaleise's Radical Crossing was launched, with the goal of raising $30,000 for Camp Trillium.

As the story emerged that she was going to attempt the Lake, the comments began: she was too small, too young. She never knew what to say to those comments; she knew only that her family, friends and coach believed in her. She tuned out the negativity and approached her coach, Hammerheads' head coach Lisa Anderson Georgiev for guidance.

There were many days over the summer of 2012 where she and Lisa would go to the beach, run and swim and talk about the mental aspect of the swim. Lisa knew well from talking to other coaches and Lake swimmers that the mental aspect of a marathon swim was the hardest. For Annaleise it was so different from the usual distance racing of age-group swimming: "it's a competition between you and the Lake," Annaleise says.

Early in the training process Lisa told Annaleise that any swimmer she coaches could physically swim for 15-26 hours. "Most coaches would tell you that: a competitive swimmer training 20 hours a week could physically do it." But the brain was another matter. Could a youngster's brain suffer the emotional time in the water, deprived of conversation and the busy visual world, experiencing nothing but a dark lake? "Especially with a teenager, how are you going to handle it? You have to have visual stimulation."

So they selected visualization, which is in fact a prize tool in any athlete's toolbox. Together coach and athlete created two movies for Annaleise to direct in her mind, and she worked at them as she trained, attached to a tether cord pulled taut in the pool, sculling and stroking for hours. The first focused on the physical conclusion of the swim. With her parents, she visited Marilyn Bell Waterfront Park in Toronto to get an idea of what it looked like. They saw the wall she would touch to conclude the swim, the ladder she hoped to use to climb out. She learned to compose the picture, putting her parents and her siblings Larissa, McKenna and Ayden on the wall; she learned to occupy her mind for long periods of time.

During training, she would break and eat every 15 minutes and discuss the picture in her head with Lisa. They would add more details, more faces, "even though at that time we were thinking only family and crew members were going to be there. We started to add in crew members, my husband, my kids, some of the ground crew she runs with," Lisa recalls. Annaleise filled her mind with visuals of her successful finish at Marilyn Bell Waterfront Park. "If all you're focused on is seeing that wall happening then you're able to forget about all the stuff in between."

Camp Trillium was the focus of the second movie: featuring Annaleise walking up the camp road with a big cheque. She saw the camp sign, the road, the faces of the people she had met the previous summer. "That picture is just as important, especially because a lot of people will push themselves further for others than they will for themselves," Lisa says.

As a hot July warmed Lake Ontario and summer rolled into August, weather delayed the start of Annaleise's crossing on August 17th. She was relieved. The night before she was scheduled to depart she had slept poorly, barely getting four hours. With the delay, she had an extra night and slept a full 11 hours. On August 18th they had a late check-out at their hotel and lingered, gathering to pray in the room. Before setting out for the swim's departure point, Annaleise ate pancakes and chicken breasts, a 4-1 ratio of carbohydrates and protein that sounds disgusting but coach Lisa knew it would stick to her ribs. An hour before they were to set out, Jeff Carr and swim master John Bulsza checked the weather forecast. It seemed fine; in fact, they even dared to think it was going to be in their favour: one-foot waves that seemed to suggest a push towards Toronto.

When Annaleise pulled up to Queen's Royal Beach Park at Niagara-on-the-Lake, a crowd of over 400 was there to greet her. Now she was nervous. As she strode carefully over the dubious shoreline and into Lake Ontario, her nerves eased and she was relieved. "It was nice to start swimming and not worry about everyone behind me."

In Annaleise's Carr swim it was her coach Lisa who would handle the technical aspect, the actual coaching and talking to Annaleise. If need be Lisa had to remind her athlete of the plan they had discussed and devised. Swims on Lake Ontario work best when one person is dealing with the swimmer and only that coach can talk about what is happening; or not talk about it. John Bulsza, the swim master, had crossed Lake Huron and now he was assigned to Annaleise's swim. The Solo Swims rules are tight on safety. The hardest part perhaps for the swimmer says no pacers can accompany swimmers for the first six hours, or at dark when they are alone and naked in the Lake in only a swimsuit and lanolin for warmth and to deal with chafing. That meant Annaleise would be alone from the start of the swim until sunrise.

All the technology that could be brought to bear came into play: in the effort to avoid hypothermia, she swallowed a radio pill that allowed her core temperature to be read. The pill takes a reported four hours to get into the stomach. It stayed long enough to complete the crossing. John Bulsza took regular readings on the pill and reported back to Mark Ghesquiere, the team's doctor. A SPOT tracking GPS system meant anyone online could follow her course across Lake Ontario and estimate her arrival on the Toronto side.

The rest was up to Lake Ontario, and Annaleise.

For the first two hours Annaleise swam steadily, stopping only to sip water and drinks to maintain her electrolytes. Lisa maintained eye contact to see how she was faring. All seemed well, they were laughing, having the time of their lives.

After those first two hours, with Annaleise having cleared the Niagara sandbar, the food came out. Again more science. The sandwiches were tiny, but these were no ordinary baby shower crust-less snacks. A crosser's snack isn't food—it's fuel. Lisa had prepared a secret blend of protein and oils. She won't divulge all the ingredients but the bite-size morsels included peanut butter, and hemp seed, a package of potassium, protein and carbohydrates that was easy to chew, before quickly resuming swimming. Every 20 minutes Annaleise fueled. Her menu included jello and cottage cheese, all in proper combination of protein and carbohydrates.

Lisa is a proponent of Shawn Achor's *The Happiness Advantage* and its seven principles for success and performance. In short, a happy athlete will perform better. Out on Lake Ontario that meant Lisa couldn't feed Annaleise, who was still just 14, a bland, boring diet. That meant there was chocolate in the nutritional mix. "Chocolate makes everyone happy. You get a smile. It's proven with positive psychology that food and happiness will keep someone going. She's a happy, happy kid, happy swimmer, loves the water so you get the full formula of her picking a kid's charity, all the perfect storm that happened for her swim," Lisa adds. Later Annaleise would explain that chocolate doesn't taste good when there's the taste of hemp oil in her mouth.

They had pulled a solid crew together on the water: Dave Scott, Roddy Millea, Jeff McCurdy who was her junior lifeguard coach in Tillsonburg, Scot Brockbank of the North Shore Runners/Swimmers, her pacers: Scot Brockbank, Nancy Norton, and Chris Peters; the two 14-foot Zodiacs with leads Wayne Boswell and Wally Mummery. Captain Charles H. McInally provided two yachts, the *Sunrise* and the *Ceilidh*. Tracking the swim, just as in the olden days of the 70s when Cindy Nicholas completed her record-setting swim complete with the *Globe*'s Christie Blatchford reporting, this time *The Toronto Star* had an embedded reporter Tim Alamenciak who sent back regular on-location reports. And so Annaleise's Radical Crossing headed into the night, trying to take advantage of the supposedly calmer waters, the theory being that Lake Ontario is flatter at night.

That's the theory. It was fortunate that the team was well-organized; they needed to be a prepared and tight unit. After her crossing, Annaleise would reflect that Lake Ontario is unpredictable. Her coach, an avid boater on Lake Erie, became nervous on Lake Ontario. As darkness fell, the favourable forecast was tossed out. The wind picked up. Lake water began to slosh over the sides of the Zodiac. Lisa held onto the ropes of the Zodiac to maintain her spot and didn't dare let Annaleise out of her sight. She watched her swimmer as the waves began to roll. Then there was rippling, and white on top. No one liked the look of things. Annaleise kept plugging away. She ate, but not a lot.

"Can you see my eyes," Lisa would ask.

"Oh yeah. I'm fine," she would reply.

They had practised surfing the waves while swimming off Long Point in Lake Erie, oddly enough on the day of a drowning on the Civic Holiday Weekend. Lisa knew Annaleise could handle the rolling and reminded her to swim like they had at Long Point.

As the weather deteriorated, Annaleise would eat, but was getting frustrated; Lisa could see that she wanted to have a conversation with her coach. Lisa didn't let her talk about it. They had agreed not to talk about being tired and cold. They could talk instead about getting to Marilyn Bell Park. They had prepared for the weather physically, but not mentally. "It's a contradiction I understand; as much as we talked about the water and trained for it." In crew meetings they had discussed the chance that the happy Annaleise they all knew might not be the one they saw out on the Lake, Lisa reflects. Perhaps if the crossing happened in 15 hours that would be the case. But the chances of that were slim; as always, it hinged on an unpredictable Lake with a short weather window.

In addition to the 1.5 metre waves, during the night a tanker went by, stirring up water and, as they had done to so many other Ontario crossers, leaving Annaleise bitterly cold. It was crossing her mind that she should get out. The forecast turned out to be wildly inaccurate. The waves were pushing her back towards Niagara-on-the-Lake. About halfway through the long night, everything seemed to be coming at once. They were 10 hours into the swim and only 21 kilometres across. The waves came fast and hard. "It was crazy," Annaleise reflects. "And no one was expecting it."

Still, she never asked to get out. She continued to play the movies, not letting her brain entertain the perfectly sane and rational thought of getting into a warm bed—she kept going. But she was hardly taking on any calories, and she was not making the progress they had hoped. It was increasingly hard to believe they had once spoken of Annaleise breaking the time of Jade

Scognamillo, who in 2009 became the youngest swimmer to cross Lake Ontario's traditional route in 19 hours, 59 minutes. Recognizing her own desperation, Lisa retreated to one of the guide boats to regroup.

The most desperate moments came, appropriately, before the sun came up. They were trying to conserve Annaleise's energy; the waves were moving her backwards and sideways. She wanted daylight, and a pacer for company. Her coach tried to get her to scull and conserve energy. Lisa said: "Honey, I'm going to remember this night my entire life, whether you get to the wall or not. If you want to get there you need to swim only when I tell you to swim and you need to do exactly what we have practised."

They played the movies again: who did Annaleise want to see at the wall? They put the people on the wall at Marilyn Bell Park and pictured them there. In the meantime, Lisa was calculating the distance and time still to go and estimating they were in for a long haul. They had estimated 16 hours for the swim: now it looked like at least another 12. Mentally they had not prepared for this.

Annaleise began asking for the sun. She didn't ask how much further or if she could get out, just when she would see the sun. Lisa could see the yellow crack on the eastern horizon that said the sun was on its way, that she could actually see it being higher up in the Zodiac. When the sun rose Lake Ontario filled with light, coming alive after a long, rough night. For Annaleise this would be the highlight, that best time on the crossing, aside from the finish. The crew and swimmer stopped to take it in. "The sun was so pretty. Everyone just sat there for a second and watched it. I can remember that really well," Annaleise says.

For Lisa, though, Annaleise didn't look great. Lisa went to her own place of desperation, watching her swimmer stop smiling, take off her goggles, try to make eye contact. She was beaten physically by the waves. With daylight, it was safer to put more swimmers in the Lake. Her pacers hopped in: Nancy Norton, then Scot Brockbank and Chris Peters. Annaleise didn't come around. These were now desperate hours; Lisa hated the way she looked. She even debated taking Annaleise out, but they stuck to the plan to bear with it. Annaleise was rallying from time to time, but mostly floating. All night, Lisa talked; at one point it seemed like a solid hour with everyone staring. "My God! I can't believe she can keep talking." Rob, in the lead kayak, hugged and praised her.

Her pacers later reported how hard it was to see Annaleise like this. They encouraged her to eat. She had to get her calories up. "Otherwise, I was probably going to have to pull her out. There was a lot of begging," Lisa says. By 10:00 on Sunday morning the crew began feeding her updates on the fundraising. An anonymous $10,000 donation came in as she swam and raised everyone's spirits. Annaleise felt stronger when she heard of the donation.

For Lisa, things really came around on that swim around mid-afternoon. On a fuel stop Lisa said: "You should eat more."

"You're just trying to make me fat," Annaleise replied.

What? The tone, the words, the back-talk. This was good.

Later they went through the safety questions, prepared in advance to indicate whether hypothermia was addling her brain. Lisa asked one about the swim team. Annaleise answered it, then before Lisa could continue, Annaleise told her the next question, what the answer would be and then onto the next question. All of which Lisa interpreted as enough with this ridiculousness and let's keep swimming.

Lisa thought, "Hey, there she is." Her swimmer was back and her head was back to playing the mental game so vital on a Lake crossing. Lisa turned to the swim master, John Bulsza and said "I guess we're going to Marilyn Bell Park."

"I knew then there'd be no looking back," Lisa says. "She was taking food fully, totally following directions."

When Annaleise's stroke began to tire and droop, Lisa asked for patterns to remind her how to be efficient. Her freestyle stroke diminishes when she's tired but she's a solid butterflier so they worked a pattern: eight strokes full butterfly (now this is well over 18 hours into a marathon swim), eight strokes full freestyle or front crawl, down to seven each, six, and so on—the patterning designed to keep her brain busy, to remind her about stroke efficiency.

Annaleise was swimming the butterfly, a draining stroke, but hey, whatever works. This was a mental reminder, getting her back up and reminding her muscles how to swim front crawl or freestyle.

Tracking Annaleise's swim online felt like looking at a cluster of grapes for the overnight period when there was so little progress. Her trail heading north to Toronto had showed her struggling to stay on course eight hours into the swim. With 21 kilometres done, winds drove the crossing team one kilometre east of its desired course; she was making an estimated 1.5 km per hour with an estimated finish time of 31 hours.

Then, as the waves dropped on Lake Ontario and she began to pick it up again, her line moved. Her ETA into Toronto changed. A solid 16 hours into the crossing, she was swimming two kilometres per hour and now it was going to be a 26.5 hour crossing. By 6:15 p.m. she had completed 46.9 kilometres with a mere 5.5 kilometres to go. It was the same spot where Greg Willoughby had been pulled out unconscious in 2011, a point of oh-so-close and yet Toronto remains so far.

With about a kilometre left in the crossing she could hear the cheering on shore; her story had been picked up on the national media. The cheering spurred her to shore. The crowd and lights blinded her. She told Lisa she couldn't see because it was so bright. Lisa shone a flashlight down the water to give her a line on the water and tried to get her to follow Rob in the kayak. She reached for the ladder at the wall on the waterfront side of Marilyn Bell Park. Someone yelled at her to touch the wall; she slapped it to make it official. The swim ended at 8:58 p.m., exactly 26 hours, 40 minutes, 54.2 seconds after it had started.

She would remember most of this finish, despite her fatigue. Rather than climb the ladder, Annaleise swam back to Lisa, and coach and swimmer hugged. Lisa took her hand and asked, "What are you doing?" Everyone was beyond ecstatic. Lisa sent her back to the ladder. Annaleise went, but looked back—and it dawned on her coach: her swimmer needed food, and fast: "That's what she's trying to tell me. She's starving."

The plan had been to have land crew team members hop in the water and push her up the ladder but that wasn't necessary; she climbed out under her own power. At the top of the ladder, the movie that had been looping in her head was now reality: her co-conspirator and sister, Larissa, who had helped her hatch this plan so long ago now in November 2011, reached to hug her first; then their parents. "Then they let go," Annaleise recalls, "and I'm saying to myself, 'Oh my goodness, don't let go of me or I'll fall over. Going from horizontal to standing up was so different after 27 hours."

Lisa tries to explain why people want to swim these Great Lakes, or at least why it's worthwhile to take a turn as a member of the crew. Lisa has four kids and loves her husband and family life. And yet, there on Toronto's waterfront, with the crowds cheering, the sky alight with media and floodlights, and flowers scattered on Lake Ontario's night-dark waters, it was like being lifted up.

"It is the most love I've ever felt. I don't mean necessarily for Annaleise. I mean for the whole event. The most thankful I've ever been for something succeeding was when she touched that wall."

Ultimately Lake Ontario took its toll, but Annaleise was resilient: taken to Sick Kids Hospital, she was released after half an hour. Her core temperature had held steady, never dropping below 36.6C the entire crossing. Her legs ached from the beating Lake Ontario had administered. They had cramped on the crossing and were worn out from her kicking hard to shake it out. "The soreness was the worst part. That night everything was really, really sore." Even her jaw ached, which was bad: "I'd been in the water for 27 hours; I needed to talk."

She was more tired than she had ever been. The next day she was connected by phone to a delighted Marilyn Bell Di Lascio. They compared notes. Like Marilyn, Annaleise's upper shoulders and her entire core muscles were sore, as if she had done hundreds of sit-ups in a row, hard and fast. The two record holders spoke for over half an hour. "It was pretty cool," Annaleise says.

She was feted and celebrated in the global neighbourhood of the Internet. Attempts were made to get her to dance with Ellen DeGeneres on her talk show; a school three big Canadian provinces away in Calgary, Alberta, paid for her to come and speak; her hometown gave her a parade and named the pool after her on Annaleise Carr Day in Simcoe. Understandably she was overwhelmed. In the end, the $30,000 goal for Camp Trillium was mere pennies; by the time school started in September, the swim had raised over $250,000 for the camp. "It's crazy. I don't even know what to think about it," she says.

She doesn't think luck was involved in the success of her crossing: instead she credits her team, the devoted group at North Shore Runners/Swimmers. "If I didn't have the people I had on my crew I don't think I would have made it." They had cheered her on, told jokes, even provided some "bad singing," Annaleise laughs. "I don't know what they were singing but I know it made me want to swim faster."

She had not thought about post-swim; this crossing was always about raising the money. "I had no idea what to expect. But I didn't expect anything that happened, like just nothing." Getting the Lake and getting the fundraising went hand in hand. Perhaps she could not have had one without the other but what she feared was letting people down if she didn't complete the crossing. Debbie and Jeff reassured her that what she was doing was amazing and that no one would be let down. "That was the thing that crossed my mind when I thought about getting out. I would let Camp Trillium down. I'd let all those people waiting on the other side down."

In the days after the swim, there was some discussion that 14-year-olds should not be doing this. Lisa doesn't see age limits on athleticism or ability and maintains Annaleise was always treated like a 14-year-old. If she was tired, they played waterpolo instead of swimming lengths; or they'd do visualization. There are athletes who are pushed and while Lisa agrees there are other ways to fundraise, "in this particular case you have a happy young girl who is passionate about swimming, who loves it, who knew she could do that and help someone."

Annaleise revisited Marilyn Bell Park in Toronto with her father Jeff shortly after the crossing. As she looked at the Lake, blue, shimmering, with a far horizon, she told her father she was crazy. "He's like, 'Yeah, I know.'" Sometimes it has sunk in, that yes, she has swum across Lake Ontario. "But sometimes I can't believe I actually did that. Everyone says that I won't really understand what I did until I'm older."

Annaleise Carr, powering into the sun.
Photo courtesy Dr. Mark Ghesguiere.

Part Two

From All Walks of Life ... They Swam

A Host of Not-So-Regular Folks

Loreen Passfield Jablonski, Lake Ontario, 1979

Loreen Passfield Jablonski wanted Lake Ontario, but in the three summers she attempted to swim the Lake she never waited for the perfect moment. She found other things to do, the kind of swims that cemented her reputation as among the best marathon swimmers in the world. Loreen is the first to say she's better off in the water. Go to the gym and do workouts. Not fun. Go for a run? No thanks. Nothing compares to swimming. "To spend five or six hours a day training you have to love it. It's not something you can force yourself to do. You wouldn't make yourself do it if it's not fun." For Loreen, swimming was fun, something she could do for hours in cold and warm water, salt or fresh.

From 1975 to 1979 Loreen was ranked in the top five by the World Professional Marathon Swimming Federation, first in the world in 1978 and 1979. Of the 20 races she entered over her career on the world circuit, she always finished in the top 10. She has "conquered" the Nile River, the English Channel, Capri, and Lac St. Jean. At the Lac St. Jean World Championship she was the first Canadian and only the third woman to finish the course that year. In 1978 Loreen swam the English Channel in nine hours, two minutes.

Lake Ontario, however, became her personal foe, a "she" who beat her up twice before Loreen swam across completely. When Loreen completed her swim of Ontario on September 2, 1979, she said, "she didn't beat me again, but she tried" ("Loreen conquers...").

Loreen was part of a remarkable era in Canadian marathon swimming. "There were a lot of great swimmers out there at the time. We were all from the same area in Toronto and we were all doing the same things. It was a lot of fun." They were like the second coming of the sport after Marilyn Bell and Winnie Roach Leuszler in the 50s: the cream of this lanolin-soaked crop included Loreen, Cindy Nicholas, Angela Kondrack, Kim Lumsdon, Kim Middleton, and Vicki Keith. No body of fresh or salt water seemed too much for them. Their decisions were about when to go for a swim, whether the weather would be kind to them this weekend or the following, would they swim the English Channel this summer. This was the stuff of legend for the local papers and their headlines.

Loreen's career ran parallel to that of Cindy Nicholas—they competed against each other—though Cindy was the more recognisable name of the two. In 1977 they were both among six finalists for the Lou Marsh Trophy, honouring Canada's athlete of the year. Naturally, the prize went to the hockey player, in this instance Guy Lafleur, a standout Montreal Canadiens forward who, interestingly, had never heard of the award before he won it (Guy Lafleur, Hockey, 1977).

Loreen wanted only to swim and achieve her goals. With her friend and trainer Pam Hrycyk accompanying her on most trips and in the boat for support, Loreen went swimming around the world. Like Cindy, she wanted Lake Ontario. Loreen grew up one block from the Lake, in Etobicoke, near Toronto. She developed her love of open-water swimming at the Victoria Harbour summer cottage near Midland, north of Toronto. At age nine she was 18th of 23 in the 4.8 kilometre "Cross Couchiching" race. She had little if any fear of open water and didn't mind cold water.

Back in this heyday of Lake Ontario swimmers, the 70s, the swims started at Youngstown and headed north to Toronto across Lake Ontario, the route made famous by Marilyn Bell in 1954. Once Cindy Nicholas set the women's record in 1974, Loreen had to try Ontario too. It was just a natural thing to do and it helped that Loreen's mother Elizabeth definitely remembered Marilyn Bell's swim. They felt they were familiar with Lake Ontario. "You don't realize how big a feat it is," Loreen says. "You just say, 'Okay, that's something I can do.'"

Lake Ontario would certainly let her know swimming the Lake was about more than being familiar. For three years Loreen and her team researched the weather, listening to the radio in these ancient days before 24-hour Weather Network and satellite forecasts, only to have the seemingly perfect weather turn. "A squall would come or something that was unforeseen." They researched the wind, how it might blow, when they should start a crossing. Most swims started at 1:00 a.m. because it was supposed to be calmer at night, she says. The wind blows up around four or five in the afternoon, "and that's always what happened. Just as you're coming near the end of the crossing."

In 1974, her first attempt in these pre-Solo Swims days started out with her crew in a motorized, 14 foot aluminum rowboat and Loreen in seven-foot-high waves. After eight hours out on the Lake, they were located and rescued by a boat unrelated to the crossing, which just happened to be heading into the safety of shore. Loreen says it was luck on everyone's part. "I don't even know how they found us. We were just out in the middle of the Lake. It was pretty scary." Loreen waited a year before trying again, only to have the second attempt called off because of weather.

In the meantime there were plenty of other bodies of water to try: chewing on Smarties, her sponsor, she swam for points in the Nile River in Egypt—hot and dirty—so she could claim the world marathon title. The English Channel also took a couple of attempts before, on August 28, 1978, she swam from England to France in nine hours and two minutes.

Lake Ontario is touted as one of the three most difficult marathon swims in the world and for Loreen it lived up to that in terms of providing enough of an opening to fit in a swim. Her third try started on September 1, 1979. It would be her final attempt, regardless of the outcome. By now she was 21 and the year had already taken a heavy toll. Just a few months earlier, in June, her father Alfred had died of heart failure. He was 63. She dedicated her swim to him.

Her departure from Youngstown was delayed more than two hours as she waited for the arrival of the requisite number of support boats. She had been provided with a 14-foot Zodiac, and a 10-foot one, but Solo Swims (created in 1975) required two 12-foot boats. When they showed up, delayed by Kim Lumsdon's attempt at a double crossing of Ontario, Loreen faced rough waters.

Overnight the water dipped to 16.6C and Loreen endured a time of doubting whether she would make it. Fortunately, the Lake began to warm up and reached a more reasonable 18.3C.

With the passage of time it feels to Loreen as if most of her swims have blended together; for the Ontario crossing, though, she remembers exactly where she was in terms of time and space. Lake Ontario was relatively calm for most of the crossing with only a mild chop and roll near the end. The distance always feels like it's not getting closer, especially from the water, from the swimmer's eye view, she says. "That's probably the most frustrating part, seeing the same thing. You think 'I'm not even moving. Yes, you are. No I'm not. I'm in the same spot.'" The swimmer senses the forward movement, "but you just can't see the progress when you're that small in a big lake and there's that much distance. Until you're really close and you look up and you go, 'Oh yeah. I'm close.'" She reached the Canadian National Exhibition grounds at 3:41p.m. with the CNE airshow soaring above and a British Airways Concorde taking centre stage as she was helped onto dry land.

Her time of 15 hours, 43 minutes remains one of the fastest to date and well below the average of 18-20 hours. "My goal was to be the fastest. It was always the waves or the weather that interfered, and always at the very end." On this crossing three-foot waves and a stubborn easterly wind conspired against her. "You always want to be the best. You want to be the fastest, that's your goal. I wanted to beat the top person. It didn't work out."

Still, she was pleased, relieved. The swim closed her marathon swimming career. She couldn't do it anymore. The swimming was hard but the mental effort drained her over the 15, 16, 17 hour swims. "It's a long time, so your mind has got to want to do it." She is glad she never had to deal with a third failed crossing attempt on Ontario, never had to decide whether to stop without having finished the Lake.

After retirement she married Paul, had two daughters. She was a nurse for over 25 years and became deeply involved with horseback riding, and, of course, the Barrie Colts of the Ontario Hockey League where she and Paul are season ticket holders. When the list of accomplishments is read back to her years later, she is content, even proud. "I did it for myself, because I loved it. I didn't want to be in the media's eye. I think if I was a different type of personality I could have done a lot more with it and brought more attention to marathon swimming."

Swimming across a Great Lake is a big accomplishment, but she also sees it from a non-swimmer's perspective. "If you just go up to somebody and say 'Oh, I just swam across Lake Ontario,' they're like 'Right. Really?' Nobody will believe you. They're like, 'There's no way.'"

Loreen laughs about what they did in the 70s in marathon swimming. What were they thinking? They were in a little boat in the middle of the night on Lake Ontario. "Pretty scary. I think of what my mom must have thought: 'Here's my daughter. I'm just putting her out in the lake.'" She laughs. "I wouldn't do that with my kids now."

Jocelyn (Muir) Saunders, Lake Ontario, 1981

Usually it takes an awful lot to get Jocelyn Saunders angry. But in this case she was mad as hell, and it was awful.

On Mother's Day 2001, Jocelyn Saunders sat on the road nearly 64 kilometres from her home in Wilmington, Delaware. Her right knee was shattered into 21 pieces. Her bike was hanging from the telephone wires overhead. She had landed only inches from a guardrail, fully conscious and yelling.

Moments earlier the triathlete—who had swum across Lake Ontario at age 15—had been riding and wondering whether she should turn right to take a shorter loop, or go longer. She thought that since it was Mother's Day, her husband Blair could make dinner for the family, including their two young children, Brooke and Brett. She'd take a longer Mother's Day ride.

As she headed down a slight hill a car approached from the other direction, pulling up fast, trying to make the turn before the oncoming car, just behind Jocelyn. The turning vehicle didn't see her, nor did it signal, she says. Accelerating into the left turn, the vehicle slammed into Jocelyn. Her knee hit the front of the car. She landed on the other side. Her bike shot into the sky. Remarkably she did not black out. She was fortunate she crashed where she did. She could practically touch the guardrail. Had her head hit at the speed she was travelling she figures she would be a different person. If she had been alive at all. "I think that it was odd how I landed on my left hip but it probably saved my life because my head, for some reason, didn't go into the guardrail."

Fortunately, a firefighter was next on the scene, had witnessed the entire accident and stopped. "He figured that I would be dead because of the speed and because they hit me directly," she recalls. She was starting to touch her knee. He covered her leg, keeping all the pieces together. "He saved my knee, which was pretty amazing. He managed the situation really well."

Her injuries were significant: spinal injuries required back surgery. There was fluid in her abdomen, making the lean triathlete look pregnant. Emergency abdominal surgery followed. There was a head injury. She had to learn to walk again, climb stairs, shower by herself. In the early days of recovery, just eating made her sweat. If she made it to the kitchen for breakfast and back to bed, rising to shower later in the afternoon—that was a good day.

Then there was the pain. Medication after her surgeries made her sick. She would think, she was only 35 and there were so many years ahead to live, every day, with this level of pain. "Yeah, the pain was a very difficult thing. Sometimes it was frustrating learning how to do things that should be so easy. All of a sudden you're not even walking right."

Jocelyn was so far away from a happier time. On September 5, 1981, when she was 15 years old, Jocelyn (nee Muir) Saunders swam across Lake Ontario in 15 hours, 55 minutes. Hers was the third-fastest crossing until 2006; she was the youngest swimmer to complete the Lake's traditional route until 2009.

At age 14 Jocelyn was spending much of her summer at Camp Ak-O-Mak, a girls' swim and sports camp north of Toronto in the Muskoka region of Ontario. Ak-O-Mak is also an official open-water training site, according to the International Swimming Hall of Fame. The dining hall walls are lined with photos of the names of great marathon and open-water swimmers who have trained or visited: Cliff Lumsdon, Colleen Shields, Diana Nyad, their photographs fading above the one electrical outlet able to handle the charger for the IPods and MP3 players of today's modern young swim campers.

At Camp Ak-O-Mak in 1980, Jocelyn had fallen in love with open-water swimming; she completed a 29 kilometre swim and figured she could cross Lake Ontario. She wanted it, she went for it. The camp's legendary coach Buck Dawson came on board, as did another employee, Bob Duenkel. On the boat were Cliff and Joan Lumsdon. Bob relished the simplicity of the swim and its planning. Before he died in 2008, Buck Dawson told Jocelyn she had the worst conditions. The Lake rolled 2.4 metre waves under Jocelyn, conditions that today either keep a crew on shore watching the forecast for another opportunity, or have the swimmer pulled out.

Still, she went ahead and touched the Toronto side after 15 hours, 55 minutes. There had been navigation errors to contend with, along with the horrendous conditions. "I wasn't that far off Cindy Nicholas' time. I never looked at that as being a failure. I was the youngest one to do it and I did it to the best of my ability. I never looked back." She finished her interviews with the media and drove home in her boyfriend's white truck.

But not so fast. Her coaches looked at her time and her ability in the open water and talked about world marathon championships. In 1982 she became the world marathon champion, and eventually held five world records. In 1986 she became the first person to swim the waters of Burrard Inlet beneath the Lions' Gate Bridge in Vancouver. During that 1986 swim she thought about doing another big swim, this time around Lake Ontario. In 1987, at 21 years old, she swam seven hours a day for 60 days—521 nautical miles—which set the record for the longest international marathon at the time, and raised $250,000 for the Multiple Sclerosis Society. She was in bed around 10:00 at night; all things considered it wasn't early. But it was fun. "I was with all my best friends. We had a good time."

That Lake Ontario tour was a once in a lifetime experience made all the better because some of her best friends went along with her. "You just don't get those chances. I'll never have an experience quite like that again. And it's pretty amazing when we drive by the lake every summer on the way to camp. It's kind of neat looking at it and thinking I actually swam around that."

After university Jocelyn discovered triathlon, qualifying to compete in the Hawaii Ironman world championships after only seven weeks of training. Laughing, she doesn't recommend that. "I made all kinds of mistakes the first time, but you learn. Then you continue." She worked as a massage therapist with the Canadian cycling and triathlon teams, then married Olympic cyclist Blair Saunders and the two Canadians moved to the U.S. She competed as a professional triathlete for seven years. In 2000 she won the Great Floridian

Ironman. She was the U.S. amateur sprint distance triathlon champion. Then 2001 rolled around and her season ended on the pavement in Chester County, Pennsylvania along the popular 88.5 kilometre cycling route.

Remarkably, in 2002, Jocelyn returned to triathlon. She loved it after all, and triathlon was fun to do. Why not continue? As she says, it's easy to have an excuse; it's harder to not back out. "I mean everybody would have understood if I never raced again but I didn't want to have any excuses for why." She didn't want to be that person who says I can't do these things anymore. "I wanted to relearn how to do everything again."

Now a triathlon and swim coach in Delaware, Jocelyn won't let the accident define her. Most people are enthralled with the tale and her comeback. Kicking back after a rousing lunch in the Ak-O-Mak dining hall, Jocelyn pauses between her summertime duties as head coach and athletic director. Sitting appropriately in a Muskoka chair, a couple of chocolate bars nearby, she traces the roots of her Lake Ontario swim to here, in Muskoka in the annual 14.4 kilometre swim to Magnetawan. After swimming to town she swam back to camp. Lake Ontario wasn't much more than that.

Jocelyn Saunders at Camp Ak-O-Mak. Photo courtesy Jocelyn Saunders.

That being said, swimming Lake Ontario is perhaps a bigger deal now than it was when she was 15. In April 2012 her brother James died suddenly. Lake Ontario offered a measure of relief and perspective on her grief. Arriving in Toronto for the funeral, she looked at the Lake glittering out there and was reminded again how big Ontario is, how she was able to swim the Lake, and how she would get over her brother's death. "I don't say that lightly. I said at his reception that once we all finish grieving, we should all live better. That's what I want to do. I think the Lake helps me in life situations like that."

Marilyn Korzekwa, Lake Ontario, 1983, 1984

The sight of Lake Ontario is a powerful one for Marilyn Korzekwa. Driving by any body of water and Marilyn will want to get out of her vehicle, dive in and swim across. She would rather swim than drive around or take a bridge across. The bridge over Lac de Deux Montagnes coming into Montreal is one such spot; so is Silver Lake on Highway 7 north of Kingston. And she could go on about how much she loves and respects Lake Ontario. "The idea for me is that water is like a mode of personal transport or a pathway. Sort of like a hiking trail to a hiker or the open road to a motorcyclist. I look at bodies of water on a map and dream about crossing them."

In 2011, Marilyn Korzekwa, a psychiatrist in Hamilton and a mother of three grown sons, became the oldest Canadian woman to swim another pathway. At age 53, she swam the English Channel, on August 21st, 35 kilometres from England to France in 16 hours, 40 minutes. It was a swim that blossomed over 20 years of long summer nights swimming with, or perched on a Zodiac beside, a swimmer crossing the Great Lakes.

Marilyn has swum across Lake Ontario twice and was the first Canadian to swim the north to south route. She serves as a swim master with Solo Swims and is often the first point of contact for would-be lake crossers. Sometimes SSO president Greg Taylor wonders how they would manage without her. She has supervised over 16 crossing attempts: ten on Lake Ontario, the rest on Lakes Erie, Simcoe and Couchiching, the latter two lakes located north of

Toronto. With the power to end a swim attempt regardless of where the swimmer may be on the crossing, she has attended at least ten "unsuccessful but safe attempts."

By 1984 Marilyn Korzekwa had become the first Canadian to swim Lake Ontario in both directions. In 1983, she swam the traditional south-to-north route in 21 hours, 29 minutes; in 1984 she made it in the other direction, swimming from Toronto south to Port Dalhousie. In 1974, American marathon swimmer Diana Nyad had been the first to do the north-to-south crossing. Swimming against mingling currents, Marilyn Korzekwa completed that swim in 21 hours.

Irene Korzekwa used to deny it but now she proudly says that her daughter Marilyn was named after Marilyn Bell. Irene was sick in bed with the flu and had tuned into the entire radio broadcast of Bell's 20 hour, 55-minute crossing. In her mind the name Marilyn now meant endurance and strength, so in 1957 when she had her daughter, Marilyn it was.

Having grown up with the name of a Canadian swimming icon, and living by Lake Ontario, it was perhaps inevitable she would swim the Lake. She was watching another swimmer train for a Lake Ontario crossing when she realized she could swim the same pace times. The next year she asked that swimmer, Elizabeth Plank, who had actually never completed the Lake Ontario crossing attempt, to be her coach.

In September 1981 Korzekwa's first attempt was literally lost in the fog. These were still the ancient days of compass and charts navigation; GPS didn't yet exist as it does currently. It was just coming on the market, she recalls. She estimates the crossing team was perhaps eight kilometres from shore when they started drifting... but perhaps not. Who knew? When the Coast Guard located them, the team was 16 kilometres off shore. "We were probably drifting past Toronto the whole time. I could give you a whole course on navigation and the errors that navigators make because they're not used to navigating at such slow speeds. But now we have GPS so people get off at the most by a kilometre or so. In those days it was worse."

She was back in 1983 and completed the crossing, powering against a head wind and nasty chop. "My crappy kick really slows me down with the chop. I had to lift my neck up over the chop to see where I was going." After the swim she couldn't move her neck. "People had to hold the phone up to my ear for the first few days after that swim."

She would find inspiration in her pacer and friend Libby Brown, who said she would swim the whole rest of the distance with her, even though they both knew Libby had never swum that far. "I thought this was a huge commitment and I couldn't let her down."

Marilyn's walls of fatigue rolled in at odd, three-hour intervals, around the 14th, 17th, and 20th hours. "When I realized that it did get somewhat better after a wall, I was better able to convince myself not to stop during the next wall. Marathon runners have it easy only going through one wall!" By 1984, she had learned not to give in to the fatigue. "I had realised you make it a million times worse by stopping and indulging in these challenges."

The object is not to think, to space out as fast as possible. Time goes faster that way. These days it takes about an hour before she gets into the zone. That hour is filled with completely understandable questions: "What am I getting myself into? How long is this going to take?" and any other details that were left onshore. Then they all shut off.

After the first swim, her mother organized a thank-you party for the crew and invited Gus Ryder, Marilyn Bell's legendary coach. Ryder gave Korzekwa a Lakeshore trophy and club patch. She had once learned swimming from Ryder at his pool. "I have a terrible kick and at some point Gus Ryder was looking at my stroke. He said I would never learn to swim because I couldn't learn to kick."

When she finished successfully, everyone asked what was next. "That's the reporters' favourite question." She told them she wanted to swim Lake Ontario the other way. To that point only Diana Nyad had swum north to south. "She was American so I could be the first Canadian. That's a record I'll always keep," Marilyn says. "I love Lake Ontario. I thought this way I would be done with the Lake. I'll do it one direction and then the other."

Although both successful crossings were hard there were highs—long, pleasant stretches of swimming that were enjoyable, that swimmers know, the stretches of swimming the easy place between water molecules. Then there were the extreme lows, where she would be sinking mentally into the depths of the Great Lake and it was impossible to take another stroke. "The south-to-north traditional way gives you a real boost from the Niagara River current. You're halfway across in one-third of the time and you think you're doing great. Then the really hard work starts," she says.

For 1984 she sang from a memorized list of songs as she powered south and her crew navigated towards Port Dalhousie to avoid the Niagara Current. "You can probably avoid the current by swimming into the Welland Canal area but then you're aiming straight for the canal and the shipping." Then they discovered a different, yet nasty current swirling out of Port Dalhousie. She fought the current to the end. "It was long but I was in better shape."

After she finished, she warmed up and rehydrated at the St. Catharine's General Hospital. Company was coming so she headed home to clean her apartment before, finally, going to bed.

Again the media asked what she would do next. The English Channel? Other legendary swims around the world, like the Catalina Channel in California? As if Lake Ontario was not enough. "But I kept coming back to Lake Ontario and how much I love Lake Ontario itself because I grew up around the shores of it."

Thoughts of swimming across the English Channel lingered, but then she met her husband. She had always told swimmers there are three things in life: swimming, work or school, and social life. "You can only do two of three," she laughs. "So I discovered social life and swimming kind of took a back burner."

In 1985 she became a swim master, tasked with overseeing swimmers aspiring to swim across a Great Lake. Why? "Because it's there!" She laughs. "Lake Ontario is like the Mount Everest of swimming, right? Because it's a challenge. Because I love swimming."

The Great Lakes are an irresistible challenge; "they are inland seas." Swimmers do sense the size as they cross, that there is indeed a lot of water to be found here. "I hate looking at the bottom so I love it when I'm right in the middle of Lake Ontario and I can imagine there's 600 feet down there. I don't ever have to look at the bottom," she laughs. "Some people are freaked out about that mind you."

The pride in accomplishment that comes with swimming a Great Lake is so satisfying that it becomes a feeling that feeds the need to swim. Marilyn would have loved to swim in the Olympics, but didn't have the body to win medals or even be in the top ten in the world in anything, she reflects. "With this kind of accomplishment I can say few people in the world could have done it."

After her crossings, she focused on her career and her family, reduced her swimming expectations. As her family grew, she found more time to herself, and began ramping up her training, overcoming her discomfort with chlorine and crowded masters' lanes. She's a lake swimmer after all.

In August 2010, she was an assistant swim master on Colleen Shields' Lake Ontario crossing attempt. Weeks after that unsuccessful attempt, Korzekwa began thinking about emerging from retirement and taking up the Channel crossing challenge she had entertained after her 1984 swim of Lake Ontario. Among others, she was inspired by people like Shields who, at 58, had "breezed" across the lake until the weather turned against her, mere kilometres off Toronto. Now she had a firm answer to all those reporters' boring questions. Yes, she would swim the English Channel. In the summer of 2011. And she would raise money for the Good Shepherd Centres of Hamilton, which help some of her patients.

In training she had sworn to herself that she would inspire her teammates to believe that she could swim the English Channel. She wanted to prove she had the guts, the endurance. She would sprint the final sets of workouts and lowered the time in each set. She changed lanes in the pool to swim in the faster lanes and get less rest between sets. She swam butterfly, the most draining of strokes, whenever possible. For two months, she came in at least an hour early to start her own workout. Then she joined her masters' practice.

On August 21, 2011, she sprinted through the tidal current and came ashore in France, 16 hours, 40 minutes after she had left England. She had only known for the last 500 metres of the 35 kilometre swim that she would make it. She proceeded to throw up until her stomach was empty; she shivered for three hours before warmth crept back into her body. After five hours and handfuls of antacids she was able to keep water down. Her right wrist had troubled her throughout the swim. It would remain full of fluid for several days. Still, she could lift her arms the next day. She had hurt worse after her first crossing of Lake Ontario.

So, which swim was tougher? How can anyone really compare? Inland sea versus a Channel in the Ocean? Salt versus fresh? Still, comparisons of two of the greatest marathon swims are inevitable. Lake Ontario turned out to be the toughest swim physically. The English Channel, with the salt water she swallowed and the anxiety she felt with every stroke, called upon all her mental reserves. "I used everything I ever learned in 20 years of marathon swimming, coaching and observing of swims to get across the Channel," she wrote after her swim. "Not a swim for beginners."

All greased up and somewhere to go: Marilyn Korzekwa, then a medical student, prepares to cross Lake Ontario. Photo courtesy Marilyn Korzekwa collection.

Kim Middleton, Lake Ontario, 1985, 1993, 1994; Lake Erie (double) 1988

Kim Middleton was precisely that, a beginner, when she took to the pool and asked Alan Fairweather, the aquatics supervisor at the pool at the University of Guelph, what he thought. Be honest. Think I can swim Lake Ontario like Marilyn Bell?

She was but a recent convert to swimming after stress fractures in her legs had ended her running career. She was told to take up swimming to stay in shape. After a few lengths, Alan said, "Kim, to be really honest, you couldn't swim a mile of any lake like that."

She asked him to work with her. "I just got this crazy idea I'm going to try this." Kim and Alan still laugh over all this and well they should. When she retired from marathon swimming in 1994, Kim Middleton was 35 and she had swum across Lake Ontario three times, completed the first double crossing of Erie in 1988, the first marathon swim of Lake Simcoe, and in 1989 the English Channel—among others. Swimming had become her Olympics.

As a young teen Kim had been a promising runner in Toronto, dreaming of racing in the 1976 Olympics as a 100 and 200 metre sprinter. But there were roadblocks she couldn't clear en route to the Olympics. When Kim was five, her mother was diagnosed with manic depression and was in and out of hospital. Her father Maurice raised the three children as a single dad but Kim did her share keeping the family together, cooking, cleaning, while their mother struggled. Kim turned down a chance to qualify and move closer to the Olympic dream. "I withdrew from it because I felt such a heavy responsibility to my family." In 1998, Kim and her mother Jean would reconnect and enjoy a great relationship until Jean passed away in 2007.

Ultimately, stress fractures below her knees proved to be the catalyst for much healing and an Olympic dream for Kim. The injuries ended her running, so she took her doctor's advice and tried swimming. As she put in the mileage at the University of Guelph pool, her mind began to roam. She thought of Marilyn Bell and all those Lakeshore Swim Club athletes she had read about at a sports hall of fame. "Marilyn Bell was my heroine." Kim also lived along the Credit River and often went to stand with her father by a lighthouse at the end of the pier and watch the Credit spill into Lake Ontario. It was natural then that while she was swimming, Kim would wonder how Marilyn had done this, how she had gone so far, for so long.

In another compartment, swimming was becoming a way of coping. There were the demands of university added to the weight of her mother's on-going illness, the responsibility Kim had felt at home for so long. "I was quite a mess emotionally."

She talked about her swimming ideas with a professor who had competed in the Olympics in the 1930s. He told her to talk with Alan Fairweather, then the swim coach at Guelph. Alan said he'd work with her and measure her level of commitment. She swam with him for seven months. That summer she had to head off to Alberta to work; Alan thought he'd never see her again, that she'd find a guy, get married and stay out west. Kim was back after the summer. She worked her way up to a 12 hour swim in the pool, joined masters, and prepared for Lake Ontario. She connected to Marilyn Korzekwa on the evening of her crossing and began an instant, lifelong friendship.

On August 16, 1985, Kim launched her swim from Niagara-on-the-Lake at 10:00 p.m. (Mallick). Not ten minutes into the swim, she began to panic and flounder. It wasn't the fact of the night swimming since she had practised that. She didn't know, really, about the current, the push of the Niagara River and the clash with the sandbar when river meets Lake. How could she be so stupid? She couldn't do this. "And I was swimming like a bat out of hell."

Alan yelled at her to slow down and relax. She calmed herself, cleared the current and took off. The sun rise was magnificent. The Lake was like glass, only moderately cold at 17.7C. The final kilometres into Toronto remained a challenge, the Humber River all but stopping the swim in its tracks. Exhausted in the brutal current, shoulders in agony, she felt like she was going nowhere. She could see the CN Tower; her pacers came in to help her pick up her pace and spirits. At one point she began crying, knowing she was so close but not getting in. She told herself to stop, that her goggles were sealed and she wouldn't be able to see if she was going to keep filling her goggles with tears. "I was just frustrated because I was so tired." She kept an eye on her pacers. Telling herself she'd gone this far and couldn't stop now, inch by inch, she got to shore.

Boats in Toronto harbour had gathered and were honking, cheering her on and in: "It felt like I was gathering energy from I don't know where. I just had to tell myself mind over matter: you have to keep going here." Forgetting the pain, clearing the current, passing the breakwall, she sprinted to the finish in 18 hours, 34 minutes—and overall, it was amazing. And to top it off, the first person to reach her as she climbed the ramp at Ontario Place was her University of Guelph counsellor, Norm. Kim says she could not have completed her university degree without counselling. She had been suffering from a major depression for a few years of university.

Kim Middleton gets a bouquet from her father Maurice, something he did after each of her crossings. Photo courtesy Kim Middleton.

Kim continued to swim marathons, working throughout the year fulltime with adults who have mental challenges, and taking a leave of absence from work over the summer. In 1987 she became the first to swim Lake Simcoe north of Toronto and raised funds for handicapped associations in Guelph and Orillia.

Over her swims, Kim would raise over $100,000 for various causes, including two hospitals in Guelph and the Arthritis Society. It was an aspect of her swimming that Kim enjoyed. "I met a lot of amazing people. It was neat to have a personal goal and to be realizing you could be helping others by doing that."

The big swim for Kim was the English Channel. After her first crossing of Ontario in 1985, CNE officials arranged a telephone call between Kim and Marilyn Bell. "I was just blown away; I was so excited. She was so awesome to talk to," Kim says. Marilyn told her that she wasn't a marathon swimmer until she'd done the Channel. Marilyn had swum the Channel a year after her historic 1954 crossing of Lake Ontario. "It took me five years to get there, but that day I said to myself if she said that, then I'm going to get there," Kim says. In 1989 she completed the swim from England to France in 16:33.

But, why go back to Lake Ontario? In 1987 she watched Vicki Keith complete what was supposed to be impossible—a double crossing of Lake Ontario. It seemed like the ultimate marathon swim. By now, Kim had completed other marathon swims and understood how rare a feat it was. The famed American swimmer Diana Nyad had finished one crossing, the north to south, before exhaustion pulled her out on the way back to Toronto.

Kim would score her own double, becoming the first woman and the first Canadian to complete the double of Erie (Rowe). In August 1988 she waited nearly an entire weekend as thunderstorms and high waves rolled over Erie. The swim was supposed to launch Friday; they left Sunday, August 7th, with some crew members having to leave early and not join the crossing. Then a cold front cleared away the storms, leaving rolls of massive waves in its wake. Kim and her team discussed postponing the swim but Kim wanted to go ahead, knowing she was setting out in high waves with warm water and that she was mentally and physically prepared. Still, the waves never settled. "It was brutal."

Swimming to the American side was a reasonable crossing, however, as she rode the waves for much of it. On the way back a pacer was sick so he was unloaded and left behind with her swim master Marilyn Korzekwa's relatives in New York state.

On the turnaround of a double the rules allowed the swimmer a ten minute break on shore before resuming the crossing. Kim looked at the rough waters of Erie and decided that she just wanted to get back to the Canadian side. "I realized when I was going back everything was going to be against me." As she completed the first leg of her 35 kilometre double crossing, she told everyone to watch as she hit the land at Sturgeon Point, NY, because she was about to turn around and swim for home. She knew if she rested she'd look at Erie's rough waters and likely, wisely, decide to stay put. She swam against Erie the entire 18 kilometre journey back. "It was unbelievable." Still, the water temperatures were warm, and she was strong. Some members of her crew were "deathly ill" with seasickness but Kim's friend from Guelph, Susan Hardie, had stayed strong and she hopped in to pace Kim home. She touched at Crystal Beach after an 18 hour swim.

Lake Ontario proved to be another matter though, as Kim would make four attempts at the double crossing, but would never complete it. In 1994, she made two attempts before finally pulling the plug. On the first one the waves were so strong that they were flipping Kim upside down and her coach couldn't see her in the night portion of the crossing attempt. One of the Zodiac support boats flipped, and a motor caught fire on another escort boat. Crew safety is linked to swimmer safety on these crossings: sometimes the loss of one boat can be compensated for and the team can work around it. Not this time: the swim was cancelled with the waves keeping Kim from making much progress.

Her final attempt to complete the double of Lake Ontario began on July 30, 1994. Kim was across Lake Ontario and on her way back towards Toronto when, around the 76-kilometre mark, she suffered a severe asthma attack. Out in the middle of lake Ontario she could no longer breathe. Her team had to pull her out.

By this point she was losing interest, her motivation wavering. Swimming had been good to her, had taken her further than running. Yet there was a flip side: she developed cold-induced asthma. Swimming at night was difficult since she put out such effort getting through the second night on these double attempts. Cold water hurt. In 1986 in Lac St Jean, Quebec water temperatures dipped to 13.3C and Kim had to be pulled from the race due to cold-induced asthma. For the double crossing of Ontario, her biggest challenge, and ultimately her big fear, had become the cold. "Had I had been able to get 48 hours like Vicki did with warm temperatures, water and air, I probably could have done it. I believe."

As the sun set into Lake Ontario that second night, Kim felt the fear rising, her breathing became laboured. Once cold and unable to get warm enough, not even a blast of Ventolin could reverse her attack. The fact that she knew this would happen was a psychological aggravation which encouraged her asthma.

Out in the middle of Lake Ontario she looked at her situation and reminded herself she had already accomplished so much. "If you don't have the mental commitment, you just know you're not going to go anywhere with it." Life was changing, her priorities shifting. She was now 35. "I tried to make myself want to keep going. But after four attempts I felt like I really had given it my all. I felt like it was time to let go and move on. Things were changing. That was how it ended."

She was philosophical: she had the Channel, she had the historic first double crossing of Erie, and three crossings of Ontario. "I did the best I could. I have no regrets. I don't think when I'm retired I'll have to go back to the Lake and conquer that," she laughs.

Then there was the fact that people still remember what she did do. On an ordinary day in Guelph Kim visits the local thrift shop with a friend. As they talk with the clerk, her friend raises Kim's athletic achievements. Do you know who this is, her friend says, pointing to Kim: She swam Lake Ontario! A couple in the store overhear the conversation and are thrilled to get Kim's autograph. "I was so embarrassed," she laughs. "It was some 20 years ago."

Which is precisely her point. No one remembers the so-called failures, she says. "It's Kim, and she did the Lake. All they remember is the excitement of the first swim."

Kim transitioned easily into her career as a personal support worker for people with physical disabilities. Swimming was her path through depression and to prove that in some way she was worthy. Being that driven helped keep her focused, she says. She came to know that she didn't need to swim these massive, cold Lakes to prove anything, that "if I lay on my couch with my cats I was a worthy human being."

On the plaque at Niagara-on-the-Lake, Solo Swims credited Kim with two singles, giving her—in addition to the double of Lake Erie—three crossings of Lake Ontario, including two from north to south. That degree of success enabled her to let go of the uncompleted doubles, to retire graciously from marathon swimming, to say that stage of her life was over.

Bob Weir, Lake Ontario, 1989; Lake Erie, 1992

As Bob Weir learned, not everyone appreciates the effort to cross a Great Lake.

Bob Weir came to Great Lakes swimming having completed the unique feat of swimming across another Great Lake, Lake Winnipeg in Manitoba. The hazy line some 29 kilometres off to the finish on that Lake's horizon was not an end, but the beginning of a journey.

In 1954 he was the Manitoba boys' 11-12 champion in freestyle and breaststroke, but swims outside a pool captured his attention as well. It was the year of iconic Canadian marathon swims: Kathy McIntosh became the first to swim across Lake Winnipeg, with radio—and Bob—following her progress through the moody, ever-changing lake. He would later meet her and get her autograph. A few months later he learned of Marilyn Bell's historic crossing of Lake Ontario, and of Cliff Lumsdon, another marathon legend.

But for Bob, his goal was to be just like Kathy McIntosh, and swim across Lake Winnipeg. And at age 20, in 1963, his became the eighth completed crossing of the Lake, swimming from the west at Winnipeg Beach to Grand Beach in the east. At the time, his 9 hours, 57 minutes was the second fastest swim. In 1964, he became the first to swim across Lake Manitoba, a journey of 54.7 km in 24 hours, 17 minutes.

His marathon swimming career seemed to end in 1965, with a season on the world Professional Marathon Swimming Federation circuit. He swam four races and withdrew from another two after he contracted hepatitis. He wouldn't swim again for 20 years.

In 1987, he relaunched his swimming career as a masters swimmer and joined a Variety Village relay swim across Lake Ontario to raise money for a new pool. Various swimmers were needed to complete the night portion of the swim. The event brought together a pantheon of marathon swimming stars, including Marilyn Bell, Cliff Lumsdon, Cindy Nicholas and the then unknown Vicki Keith. Bob found his appetite again for solo swimming but decided to get a couple of more years of training under his belt before he would challenge Lake Ontario.

In 1989, he applied to swim "Marilyn's Lake" on August 4th-5th, leaving in the evening of the 4th. Over the summer he gained 23 pounds, blossoming from 167 to "a pregnant-looking" 190 in the five weeks of training.

After several delays due to weather, Bob looked at Lake Ontario on August 5th and the Lake was as flat as glass. The water temperature was 22C at Niagara-on-the-Lake. Should the swims have been cancelled? He checked the temperature 11 km from shore in Niagara and was vindicated. The water had dropped to 12.7C and would stay cold all the way to Toronto. By the Monday, the water temperature had dropped to 6C and he feared it wouldn't warm up in time for the following weekend. By the August 11th-13th weekend the water was back up to 12.7C. He swam at a meet in Winnipeg and then in the U.S. Long Course Masters Swimming Championships where he promptly picked up a cold, cough and congestion with a light fever. He began to wonder if he was supposed to swim Lake Ontario. Rick Wood, who swam for Etobicoke Masters, crossed Lake Ontario that summer, in 21 hours in water temperatures that held steady around 20 and 21C. Buoyed by Rick's efforts Bob aimed to leave Niagara-on-the-Lake on the night of August 23rd. But again his sneaking suspicion that Lake Ontario was working against him seemed to be borne out. Prior to departure, one boat opted out. The borrowed station wagon broke down en route numerous times before he finally took a cab from Stoney Creek the rest of the way to Niagara-on-the-Lake. They arrived after 10:00 p.m., three hours late. And now, on the dark on the shores of "Marilyn's Lake," he felt even more vulnerable, coated only in four kilograms of lanolin, one suit, a facecloth on his head under two bathing caps, and ear plugs wedged in tight. At 11:30 p.m., finally, the swim left Niagara-on-the-Lake.

Once clear of the Niagara sandbar he expected the chop on the lake to ease and to ride the Niagara River current, which can carry a swimmer 9.6 kilometres out into the lake in about two hours. He covered only three. The wind blew into his face from the north, pushing the waves to an average one to two metres and cresting often, he recalls, to 2.7 metres. By the end of the first hour of the crossing—which always seems the longest, he says—he felt like quitting and trying another time. "Then I thought, everyone is here. We're underway." Besides, the limited window of opportunity was closing; it was late August. "I knew I might not get another chance, so on I went."

As for the crew overseeing the swim, things weren't much better. His coach was seasick in the Zodiac, as were other crew members. Zodiac lights were breaking down, often leaving Bob to swim in darkness. Then the pilot boat shone its searchlight on him, blinding him totally. All attempts to clear his fogged goggles failed. His other goggles were available but since it seemed there was so much chaos he didn't stop to change. The Zodiacs struggled to maneuver in the waves and to keep their lights on. A Zodiac drove over him and then backed off instantly.

With the waves on either side, he couldn't alternate his breathing. "The first time a wave crested and white capped on top of me I thought I was at the end of Runway #9. I heard a mighty roar as if on the ocean."

At one point he was off course and headed for Hamilton, not Toronto. After two hours the water temperature dropped to 18.3C and stayed there. Into the fourth hour, his injured left shoulder was aching. Then his right shoulder called for attention. The waves subsided, eventually, to one metre and finally he began to make real progress, swimming 3.2 km an hour until noon. Around about 1:30 p.m., he hit the proverbial Wall. As well, the pain in his left arm was severe. The right arm had seized. He was struggling to lift them out of the water. He demanded to get out. He was still 16 kilometres from Toronto. "I couldn't contemplate doing the dog-paddle the remaining distance. I wanted out."

Bob was neither tired nor cold, merely broken mechanically. The begging and swearing continued. He turned around and swam breaststroke back towards the south. Bob continued with breaststroke amid cursing from the support team to get his arms going. Ignoring their curses, he lay on the water to stretch his arms. He sculled and repeated the stretching exercises. Then he was swimming again, his right arm functioning properly and his left arm dragging across the top of the water. A normal high-elbow stroke was too painful. "Nothing could stop me now. I felt invincible. I was going to make it," Bob recalls.

Still, his progress slowed. He could not turn his head to the right or it would put a terrifically painful strain on the left shoulder. He was asked where he wanted to finish and of course he said Marilyn Bell Park. But at around 4:30 p.m., his left shoulder gave out. He could only swim a version of dog-paddle, and then, a short time later, he knew they were going to finish instead at Leslie Street Spit, also on the shoreline but not where Marilyn Bell had finished. By now Bob was resigned to it and wanted to finish. The Spit, a protrusion of rock on the Toronto shoreline, was closer and his team figured he didn't have enough strength left to fight the Humber River current with one arm.

As he closed in on Toronto, his stroke had slowed to about 30-35 strokes per minute, way down from the regular 60 strokes per minute. "It felt like there was knife stuck in each shoulder. The pain was real. But I was not going to quit."

As the western sky set the Toronto skyline aglow in inspiring red, the waves and wind returned, this time hitting Bob broadside. They were mercifully, miraculously small, perhaps half a metre this time, mere ripples after what he had faced at the start of the swim. Knowing he would finish he started kicking his legs. Bringing the kick up into play gives the swimmer a glorious lift and an alignment in the water. He became aware of the blinking blue lights of his police escort. The Zodiac took off so his coach and swim master could greet him onshore when he finished. He followed the flashlight beam from the other Zodiac, the night air alive now with encouragement from the voices of his crew. "I was on a real high." He reached the red light but it was too dangerous to land. Coach Doug yelled, "In here, Bob."

Bob touched shore and stood up, raising his right fist in triumph. It was 9:38 p.m., 22 hours and 8 minutes after leaving Niagara. "I had conquered Marilyn's Lake." At the time it was the 23rd crossing. He was the sixth amateur male and the second oldest person to swim the lake. He was 46.

Through the Breakwall! Shaun Chisholm finishing at Marilyn Bell Park, Toronto, August 16, 2008. Photo courtesy Tony Chisholm.

Annaleise Carr heading over the horizon, into the sunset.
Photo courtesy Dr. Mark Ghesquiere.

Colleen Shields chasing the sunset.
Photo courtesy Laura E. Young.

Susanne Welbanks emerging from the night.
Photo courtesy Susanne Welbanks.

Susanne Welbanks swimming from dawn into daylight.
Photo courtesy Susanne Welbanks.

Rebekah Boscariol and her team measure the Toronto skyline.
Photo © 2011 Tommie Sue Montgomery.

Paula Stephanson in the elements on her way out of Chicago.
Photo courtesy Andy Duggan.

Madhu Nagaraja entering the water at night.
Photo courtesy Madhu Nagaraja.

Annaleise Carr finishing in the dark.
Photo courtesy Dr. Mark Ghesquiere.

Rob Kent being chased by the storm.
Photo courtesy Melanie Price.

Paula Stephanson finishing Lake Superior.
Photo courtesy Andy Duggan.

Paula Stephanson wrapped up after emerging from Michigan. Photo courtesy Andy Duggan.

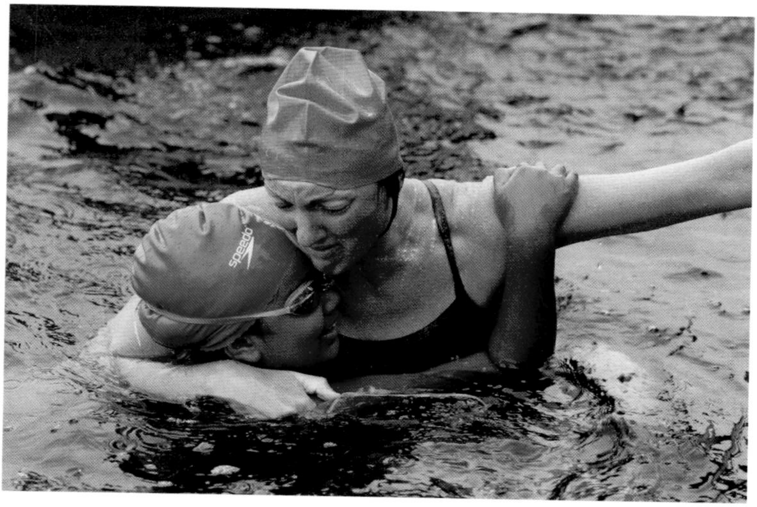

Christine Arsenault hugs her daughter after touching at Marilyn Bell Park. Photo by Peter Power/*The Globe and Mail*

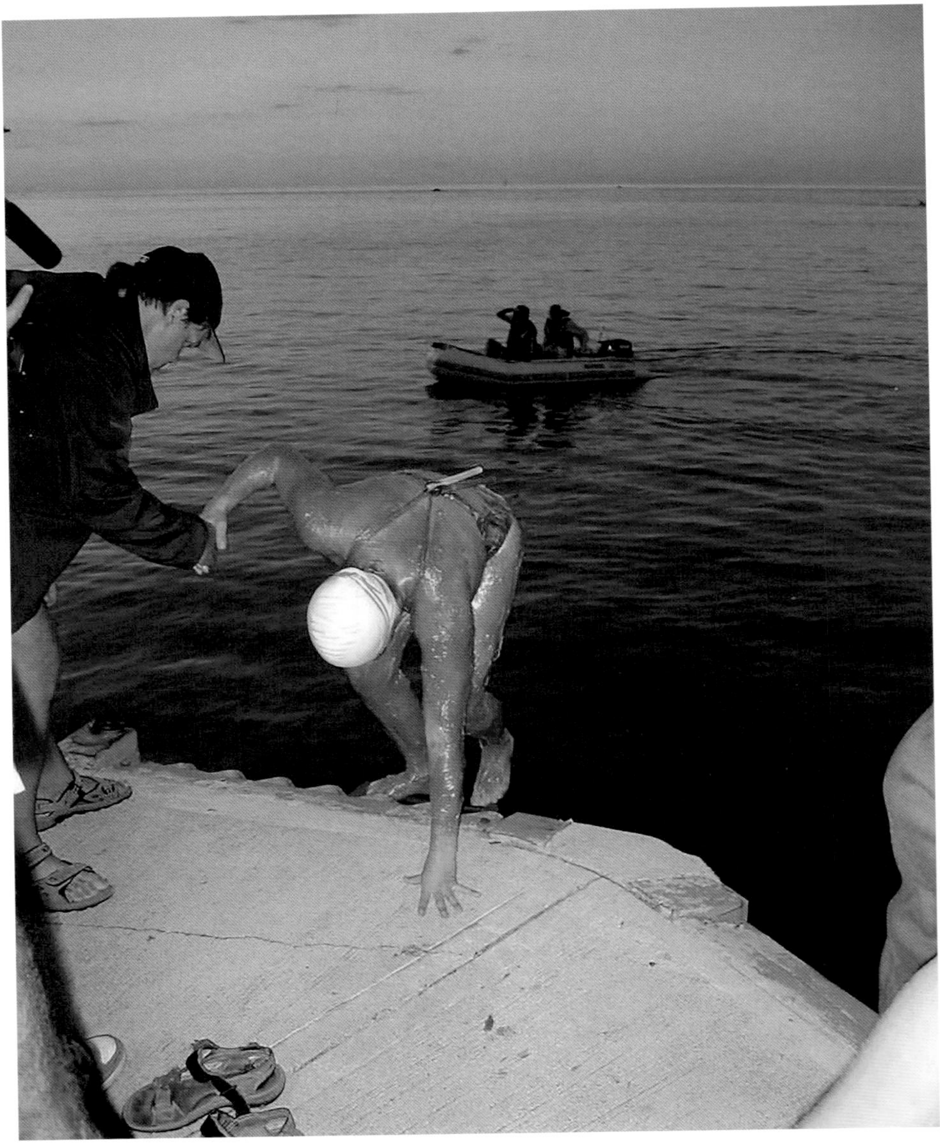

"You put your head down and go." Lanolin-covered Stephanie Hermans gets a hand down the ladder as she begins her swim from Niagara-on-the-Lake, August 10, 2007. Photo courtesy Stephanie Hermans.

Bob's story on Lake Ontario should end here, full of personal accomplishment and gratitude to his crew. He floated back into Lake Ontario to the Zodiac and without the strength to climb into the already overloaded boat, he hung off the side while the Zodiac towed him to the pilot boat. He was wrapped in towels and sleep bags. His swim made the late-night CTV news as he was lifted from the boat deck to a stretcher and into the ambulance, then whisked off to a Toronto-area hospital.

And there he lay. Where Marilyn Bell was wrapped in the warmth of the city, an entire province, arguably the country, Bob Weir lay on a bed, ignored. Under the blankets he was greasy with lingering lanolin. His pulse and blood pressure were normal. As he awaited the doctor, he told his parents to leave and come back in the morning with some clothes.

His shoulder pain became unbearable. The doctor took the blood pressure machine that paramedics had inadvertently left behind. "He said he needed one and he was going to keep it. I thought that was strange." The doctor checked his blood pressure and said he could go. Since Bob had no clothes, he asked if he could stay the night. The doctor said it was an emergency department and the rooms were for injured people. He could go.

Bob had no clothes or money and wasn't sure he could stand much longer. The doctor told him he should have thought about all that before the swim. Bob repeated his request to spend the night, perhaps in another part of the hospital. Again the doctor said he should have planned all this before the swim. Bob told him that a swimmer the previous weekend had actually stayed overnight at another Toronto hospital. By now it was 1:00 a.m. and Bob had the doctor call his parents, who were asleep. He had to leave a message. Fortunately his parents had heard the phone and called back. They were told to come and get him.

Bob was wheeled out into the admitting section. He reminded the doctor he needed a shot of Demerol for the shoulder pain. His request for a hot shower was refused. Eventually he was wheeled to a shower and, as Bob recalls, given a towel and soap as if it was at great personal expense.

He staggered into the shower and slumped into a chair on the verge of passing out. When he roused enough to turn on the tap, only a dribble of cold water sputtered out. There was no hot water. He wiped the lanolin "on a towel and on every hospital gown I could find." Slowly he emerged, wearing the clothes his father had brought. His dad returned with his prescriptions. They were home just before 3:00 a.m., with Bob "thanking" the hospital for its care: "May I never go there again."

Having swum Lake Ontario he wanted to give back to marathon swimmers, to encourage others and share in their own personal achievements. He became Solo Swims vice-president and later a swim master. He accompanied Rick Wood as he became the first Canadian male to swim a double of Lake Erie. Bob would swim Lake Erie in 1992.

In 1996, Bob Weir returned to Lake Ontario as swim master to Paula Stephanson. He would attend all her Great Lake swims over the 13 years it took her to complete and become the second person to swim all five.

Why do people want to swim the Great Lakes? Bob feels that for Lake Ontario, or any other large body of water, there's the obvious: the excitement, recognition, challenge, satisfaction. "Some of it is because I can and you cannot. Any way you look at it, these are all pinnacles, heights, the highest one can go. For some swimmers that is, Lake Ontario is the peak, a watery mountain of history, challenge, where Mother Nature rules. And simply, because it's there." Personal challenge is the most likely reason of all. "When one has the ability to do something, it is deeply rewarding, personally, to achieve a difficult physical task. Some people just like to test their bodies and take their minds to the limit. Can I absorb pain? How much? Can I mentally beat the Lake? Can I overcome nature? It's me against Mother Nature! I want to win!"

Patty Thompson, Lake Ontario, 1991

Patty Thompson was once asked how she could call herself a marathon swimmer when she had never swum Lake Ontario. It's okay to think "pardon me?" After all, at one swim banquet it took some time to introduce Patty Thompson: a 1964 Olympic finalist and Commonwealth Games medalist; the first Canadian female swimmer to break the five-minute barrier for the 400-metre freestyle; 19 provincial records in one year. After the 1964 Olympics her father Jimmy died and Patty retired temporarily from swimming to coach. When she returned, she joined the open-water, professional circuit. In 1970, she won all her professional swims from Hamilton to Rhode Island to Argentina, that one a 24-hour marathon. In 1971 she was inducted into the International Swimming Hall of Fame in Fort Lauderdale, Florida. She was a rare swimmer, an Olympian who became a world champion marathon swimmer. Welcome Patty Thompson! Indeed.

She came from solid swimming stock: her brother Robert competed at the 1972 Munich Olympics in waterpolo, and their father Jimmy was an Olympic bronze medallist in 1928, and won gold at the British Empire Games. In 1928 Jimmy was training to swim across Lake Ontario with legendary Canadian marathon swimmer George Young. Jimmy Thompson went on to create the Hamilton Aquatic Club where open water swimming was the norm for most of his swimmers, including Patty.

But not so fast. You call yourself a marathon swimmer? Since she had never swum Lake Ontario, she couldn't call herself a marathon swimmer.

In record time those comments got under Patty's skin. She knew she was a marathon swimmer and had the hardware to prove it. She was able to pay bills because of her winnings as a marathoner—in Canada. "Don't ever tell me I'm not a marathon swimmer, because I competed with some of the best marathon swimmers and went into races and a heck of a lot more competitions than people who swim Lake Ontario." So, despite the popular notion of marathon swimming being Great Lake swimming, she knew there was no basis to the challenge. Her credentials were solid. Yet, Patty also knew that in Canada the inevitable had arrived for her as a swimmer. It was her turn to challenge Lake Ontario. It had been a long time in coming.

A year or so after Marilyn Bell crossed in 1954, promoters who were looking for long-distance swimmers approached her father to see if Patty, then about age ten, would swim the Lake. She was offered a fur coat and a car, among other items. "I remembered them asking me would I like all of this. I could not drive a car but my father could." Her response was no, that she wanted to go to the Olympics which she felt was the greatest achievement an athlete could ever want. "I could swim Lake Ontario at any time in my life."

She went to the Tokyo Olympics on the 4x100 metre freestyle relay which finished 7th. She held no regrets about their finish. "That's the way it goes." When Patty returned her father was sick with cancer. She took over coaching. He died in 1965 at age 65. Patty was 19 and she desperately wanted to keep the club intact. Her dad had run it for some 35 years. Swim parents stepped up and backed her. They divided the club: waterpolo went one way and the swimmers went the other. A charter was written. Patty retired after a paid coach was hired.

She had harboured hopes of returning to amateur swimming but knew it was impossible with her finances and commitments. On the pro circuit, she made enough money to cover her expenses. Although the women competed with the men, the bulk of the prize money went to the men. "Say first place was $25,000. It went down from there. If I didn't get up in 6th place, I might as well just shoot myself in the foot. I was swimming 48 km for $3,000 bucks. The men would come out of that season maybe $125, $150-thousand richer." Still she made enough to pay her expenses and, in 1969, won enough races to defeat Judith de Nys of Holland for the title of world marathon swimming champion.

And so in 1989, that off-hand comment irked Patty. What got to her was the singular uniqueness of her record. She was a Canadian Olympian who also was a world champion marathon swimmer, a rarity. No one had a swimming record like that and so what the hell was this guy saying, she wondered. "I said, 'Freak, I'll do that damn Lake.'"

For Patty, people don't realize that a main reason the Lake can be crossed is because it's a solo swim. You can take 50 years if you like to come across the Lake; well, not exactly, but it's a matter of waiting for weather to change, she says. "As long as you're physically up to it and know what is happening, you'll make it. After all, you know if you're going to run into a storm. You should know. If you don't you're in big trouble."

Her first attempt on September 6, 1990 was launched though a storm was on its way. It seemed as though they had a wide enough window of opportunity through which to swim. On shore at Niagara-on-the-Lake they estimated that the storm would be somewhere behind them when she was about 15 miles out on Lake Ontario. In retrospect, with the way the swim went down, they should have waited another five hours in Niagara-on-the-Lake. But the atmosphere at the beach is always "let's get this going," she says. "You take the gamble. You could wait five hours and no storm. You just don't know. It's a guessing game."

Working with Cliff Lumsdon, they decided that if the waves rose over one metre, they were calling off the swim. By day, those waves are one thing. At night, it's totally different. For all that Lake Ontario crossings happen at the most crowded, brilliantly lit corner of the lake, night is still night. She was 24 kilometres, 6 hours, 45 minutes into the swim when it ended. The storm came in and changed the winds. "That's what Mother Nature is. That's fate. You either go or you don't go. You have a storm or you don't have a storm." An hour or so later, the lake was calm and the wind was coming from behind. Or would have been. Mother Nature is as she is, Patty says. "There's always something. If the water is cold, do you think it's going to get warm in a day? I don't think so."

On August 13, 1991 at the age of 45, she was back. The attempt began with a range of irritants: a storm was in the offing; her shoulder was a mess; her thumb had a pulled tendon. She figured if she could wrap the thumb before leaving shore that the problem would be solved. But they were in a hurry and she didn't bother. "When I saw the bad weather I realized this is not going to be nice." Her swim master, Colleen Shields, compared it to swimming with training paddles on the hands for the entire crossing.

For the media, it was an odd situation. Colleen had just set the record for being the oldest woman to swim Lake Ontario and here Patty was on track to beat that record. For Colleen it was awesome that Patty was chasing one of her records instead of Colleen going after all the ones Patty had set.

As the swim progressed Patty's shoulder was in massive pain. Her stroke rate dropped down to 60 per minute, from 68. At one point Colleen jumped in to have a chat: their parents, her mother, Patty's father had been part of the Hamilton Aquatic Club, just like Colleen. Colleen reminded Patty of the tough stock from which she was bred and told her she could do this Lake crossing. Patty swam breaststroke for the final two hours of the swim. She would rather have pulled out and returned in 1992. Maybe she could set a speed record, she mused. But Ted Roach, a member of her crew, told her she was going into shore, regardless. She estimated she was three hours late. "Once those waves are pounding you, you have no choice but to slow. You're being beaten up pretty bad, you're bruised badly and you're in a current."

Patty could hear her arm grinding. Linda Berry, her friend and coach, was a calm presence throughout the preparation and crossing and pointed the way into shore. With the winds they opted to land at Vicki Keith Point or the Leslie Street Spit, a rocky outcrop east of Marilyn Bell Park. Then, once she was through the staggering rush of the Humber current, Patty switched her stroke from freestyle to breaststroke, telling her team she was going to take her time. She felt bad for her crew sitting in the boat watching. "It's boring. It's so stupid, you know, and that's what I felt bad about. I didn't care about my shoulder going. It's just, 'Oh God. They have to wait another two hours before I get in.' It's a pain in the neck. Who wants to sit in a boat for two hours floundering around?"

So on August 14, 1991, at age 45, Patty Thompson became the oldest woman to swim across Lake Ontario. She completed her swim in 19 hours, 18 minutes. The age record was irrelevant. "Who would want that title?" she asks. She is just another swimmer who crossed Lake Ontario, end of story. She credited her crew, which included her main support Linda Berry and marathoners

Kim Lumsdon and Colleen Shields, for her success. "You're just swimming. You're just moving one arm over, then the other arm. They are the people controlling everything. End of story. They have the common sense to keep you going."

Shelagh Freedman, Lake Ontario, 1993

For Shelagh Freedman, Lake Ontario was all she knew. As soon as she had crossed her first lake, at age six, she only wanted to swim Lake Ontario. Her family would head to a cottage every summer near Tweed, another of Ontario's small communities. Every summer the big boys would swim the width of Big Gull Lake and Shelagh was the scrawny girl saying she could swim it too. Finally, the summer she was about to turn seven, she was allowed to try the crossing. She almost gave up. She had no goggles, no real swimming skills. "I wasn't that good a swimmer. I was all blue lips." But she made it, then said, "Yeah, and I can swim Lake Ontario."

Big Gull Lake was perhaps 400 metres wide at the point where they crossed. For a six-year-old it was far—a big challenge. A decade later when she was training for her Lake Ontario crossing, she would do laps of that 400-metre width. Her trial swim prior to the Ontario crossing was the length of Big Gull Lake. She believed her parents Ed and Mary Jane who had always told her that she could do anything she set her mind to and that meant swimming Lake Ontario. The rest of the year, living near the white faces of the Scarborough Bluffs in eastern Toronto, she would visit the cliffs and look out over Lake Ontario.

The Lake was what she knew in terms of big water. And for big dreams, she had turned to Terry Fox, the marathon runner and cancer survivor who had attempted to run across Canada, despite having one prosthetic leg, in 1980.

Terry later died after the cancer returned but he remains a hero. To Shelagh, his message about crossing territory and going after dreams was vital.

She spent years trying to find a way to make this goal happen. She dropped ballet. She became a competitive swimmer and worked as a parliamentary page at 13. She was talking about swimming and was subsequently introduced to Cindy Nicholas, then a sitting MPP, who still had the record for the fastest woman's crossing. Cindy directed her to Vicki Keith. Home sick one day, Shelagh found a V. Keith, in the phone book, took the plunge and dialed. Vicki's answering machine came on, but then Vicki actually picked up the phone... "Hi. I'm Shelagh Freedman. I'm 13 years old and I want to swim Lake Ontario," Shelagh told her.

Vicki was supportive from the get go. "She's a very powerful human being. I felt I'd connected with her," Shelagh recalls. Vicki was also the first person who didn't say Shelagh was crazy to dream about swimming Lake Ontario.

As much as Shelagh's parents told her to believe she could do anything, they also were hesitant about her goal to swim across the Lake. And there were more delays. The family moved west to Hamilton where Shelagh joined Hamilton Aquatic Club. Then a shoulder injury forced Shelagh to take a break from the sport. She was getting frustrated. She had never let go of the idea of swimming Lake Ontario and yet she just didn't seem to know how to make it happen.

But when she was 16, and working for Greenpeace, she decided to just start training to cross the Lake and let everything else fall into place. "The most important thing to do was train." Her work at Greenpeace made her want to clean up the Great Lakes. "I was just old enough at that point to realize it was going to happen if I made it happen." She ended up starting a charity called Free the Waters which raised money for environmental initiatives on the Great Lakes. Her mother located Project Paradise in Hamilton which worked towards cleaning up Cootes Paradise, a stretch of Hamilton Harbour behind McMaster University and near Shelagh's training venue.

Vicki Keith had put Shelagh in touch with Marilyn Korzekwa, who had swum the Lake in 1983 and 1984, and who became Shelagh's open-water coach. In 1992 Marilyn came over to explain what was involved in the crossing. "Parents want you to be safe. It was a very big deal when I had her come to the house because at this point in time my parents were still not very keen on the idea," says Shelagh.

It was still in Shelagh's mind that the distance was 32 kilometres, not 32 miles. She'd even managed to convince her parents that the distance was the shorter one. Marilyn told them the exact distance, nearly double what they had previously thought. "I didn't really tell anyone I didn't know that," Shelagh says. Still it didn't deter her. She had no idea what was involved and how long people could actually swim. Ignorance is bliss when you're 16. She figured people had done it so it could be done. The opposite shore was far, but however far, she'd have to swim. "I would have swum longer if I'd needed to."

The date was set for Friday, August 13th, 1993, selected to stand out over the summer. The team left Niagara-on-the-Lake at 9:00 p.m., in the dark. At first thunderstorms had loomed, but when they set out for Toronto the evening was beautiful. She was relieved and nervous. Above, the stars began to sparkle and shoot in the Perseid meteor shower that rolls across Ontario skies every summer around the middle of August. She was incredibly happy she was finally in the water with her boats and support intact. "This was it."

There is so much emphasis on the organizing that when the athlete is finally swimming across the Lake, it seems that suddenly there is a lot of time available. For Shelagh that time was going to be unpleasant. After the second hour, she started vomiting, and continued sporadically through to the next day.

Otherwise, overnight conditions were decent until a freighter went by and churned up the icy cold deeper layers of water. "You're swimming and the next stroke you take the water is way colder. But that only lasts a few kilometres." She made progress enough that the team started wondering out loud whether she might be on track to break Cindy Nicholas' speed record set in 1974. Shelagh wasn't thinking about that, wanting only to swim the Lake until she got it done. Still, some of her supporters were called to Marilyn Bell Park on the Toronto waterfront earlier than scheduled because her progress was good and she could arrive sooner than expected.

But then, she'd been vomiting a bit in the night, though it wasn't clear why. Nerves? Pollution? Something that hadn't sat well in her stomach? Fumes from the boats? The sore shoulder she'd begun complaining of? The day started well with a glorious sunrise but began to drag and her progress slowed. The team had predicted a crossing of 18 to 21 hours, maybe 24 at the most. Instead, she was heading into the second night of swimming and Toronto seemed no closer.

She switched to breaststroke and one-arm freestyle to manage pain in her right shoulder. She wondered how she'd ever thought swimming Lake Ontario was a good thing to do. "I wonder sometimes about people who go back and do it again. I don't get it at all." Even when she was three-quarters across the Lake, the last ten kilometres seemed to take as long as the other 42. She stopped talking and stared face to face with the cold reality that this had been a really dumb idea after all. "I think I had too much pride to admit that I was right. This is a terrible idea." Shelagh held fast, convincing herself that if she could just finish she would never need to do it again, that she had learned her lesson. She laughs about it now. She never thought of quitting but "I was just really mad at myself."

Coming into Toronto in the dark after a struggle with the Humber River current, she actually missed seeing the breakwall as she headed into the final few metres to Marilyn Bell Park. She saw people on the shore and wondered why they were all on the breakwall. A squad of Great Lakes crossers had come down to welcome her and swim her in. Vicki Keith was there, and John Scott, who had set the amateur record in 1992, and Carlos Costa who only a few weeks before Shelagh's swim had become the first swimmer with a disability to cross Lake Ontario. In the water were Marilyn Korzekwa and Colleen Shields, crossers as well. They joined her for a few strokes, then pulled back so she could swim the final metres alone.

Throughout the swim she consciously reminded herself to make sure she really and truly touched the wall. Before her swim she had a nightmare that could also have been interpreted as a premonition. She was arriving in Toronto at night, about to touch the wall to end the swim at Marilyn Bell Park. Then, still within her dream, she was waking up and saying, "Oh, good. I swam the Lake." Then her father said he didn't know how to tell her but though she had finished the swim, she had passed out before she touched the wall. No one was sure if she'd actually touched the wall to end the swim officially. "That is a bad dream," Shelagh says.

She smacked the wall at Marilyn Bell Park 26 hours, 3 minutes after leaving Niagara-on-the-Lake. At first she didn't realize the swim was over. As she struggled up the ladder, John and her father Ed helped, mindful of her aching shoulders. Dizziness set in. "There was no elation of wow, I swam Lake Ontario. It was, 'Wow. I've touched; now I can stop swimming.'" At some level she knew she had crossed successfully but it takes time to realize what it all means. "It's really more a quiet sense of self-satisfaction, for me anyway."

She was lucky on her swim to a certain extent but figures the swimmer also needs to be committed to continuing with the swim until it's finished. Sometimes the Lake won't allow the crossing, tossing out thunder, huge waves, freezing water close to Toronto, she reflects. "But I think on every swim there's enough for you to quit with good reason. And, well, you just can't."

When Shelagh was preparing for her crossing of Lake Ontario she was so caught up in the swim, in raising money, in trying to accomplish her goals that she figures she was clueless about seeing how that kind of drive can inspire others. "At the end of the day that's worth a lot more. You can see it every time you're on a swim. People are inspired by the person's determination to just keep going when it seems like any reasonable person would stop."

As obscure as swimming a Great Lake is, especially compared to marathon running, it's a clearly defined goal. Swimmers train in a certain way; they need good weather and good boats. "You start here and you swim there. Often goals people have are not so clear-cut and it makes them much harder to accomplish."

For Shelagh, people want to see what they're made of or to test their limits; the idea is hard to put aside once it's been planted and sees the light of day. "The only way to put it aside is to actually do it. I don't really know why it seemed like a good idea to me. If I didn't grow up on Lake Ontario it probably would have been a different Lake or a mountain. Then it became something I thought I could do. The only way to cross it off the list was to do it."

Nicole Mallette, Lake Ontario, 1997

Nicole Mallette had actually given up her dream of swimming across Lake Ontario, thanks to 3-100ths of a second. It's hardly time to even think, to do anything beyond start the blink of an eye. But for Nicole Mallette, that blip, that trimmed fingernail of time, ended her competitive swimming career.

Nicole grew up swimming in the Ontario heartland during an unequalled and likely never to be repeated period in Canadian swimming history. Alex Baumann, Victor Davis, Anne Ottenbrite—legends of Canadian swimming, Olympic champions, world record holders, all mingling with the rest of the cream of Canadian swimming at meets across the province. Amid this excellence, Mallette trained in Barrie then moved north to the Northern Ontario Aquatic Club in the four and a half lane-wide, 25-metre R.G. Dow Pool in Copper Cliff. She would refine her strokes there, often swimming in nearby Sudbury with Baumann and the gang at Sudbury Laurentian Swim Club. By 15 she had moved to Burlington and was swimming for Hamilton Aquatic Club. She would achieve national ranking with a 2:28 in 200-metre backstroke.

Then she trained for the 1984 Olympics and came within 3-100ths of a second of racing in the Games in her speciality. Six months prior to the Trials she had been sick with mono and not at her best. Devastated, she even declined the B Tour to Hawaii; she didn't want the reminders. She could not watch the Olympic swim program, even as Alex Baumann claimed gold in the 200- and 400-metre individual medley.

Next she abandoned another dream of her swimming career: swimming across Lake Ontario to challenge her swimming ability and her strength of mind over matter. At that point it felt to her like swimming was done. She was 18. "I had trained all my young life only to fail. So for many years I gave up on the Lake Ontario crossing. I was no longer going to be the youngest swimmer to cross," she says. "So why try?"

A decade later, though, she happened to be swimming with Colleen Shields at Etobicoke Masters. She mentioned Colleen to her mother, Murline, who promptly said, "Colleen swam across Lake Ontario." Instantly Nicole was recharged with the idea of completing the crossing. Colleen promised to train her, if she was interested. "It was her knowledge, her experience, and her excitement when she talked about her crossing that got my juices flowing again and wanting the challenge."

At this point, Shields had already completed two lakes: Lake Ontario in 1990 and Lake Huron in 1993, and had served as swim master on John Scott's amateur record-setting crossings in 1992 and 1994.

In 1995 Nicole's first crossing attempt was upset with stomach and weather issues. After eight hours, it was over. Colleen Shields, now serving as swim master, circled Nicole three times in the support Zodiac boat like an odd grey shark before Nicole would touch her hand to end the swim. "It was the hardest thing to do. I didn't want to give up and let my team down," Nicole says.

Nicole thought she was ready but she wasn't. Colleen wanted her to fail so she could learn what it meant to succeed. "I was not ready with my foods or my mind. It was the best decision that could have been made because it made me stronger and more determined to prove to everyone that I was capable of crossing." There were people who doubted her ability to complete it, she adds. "What better way to pump someone up than by saying they can't?"

The cold temperatures in 1996 called off the swim, so by the time 1997 rolled around, Nicole couldn't think of anything else but her third crack at the 51-kilometre crossing. She changed her diet to gain some weight. She had heard people say that she didn't have enough fat on her body, that the cold lake water would stop her before anything else.

Inch by inch she trained to handle water colder than 17C. Then there was also the dark. As a child, Nicole shivered beside a babysitter who read her Peter Benchley's *Jaws*. After that, night swimming wasn't happening; Nicole couldn't even swim in her own backyard pool after sundown. "You may laugh but it was terrifying as a child," she recalls. Deep in the heart of Ontario's cottage country, too far for even an intrepid and severely hungry bull shark to swim up river, Nicole's hyperventilating could be heard from shore at night during training sessions. She was only swimming between two docks. She had to stop, Colleen told her, or she'd never get across Lake Ontario.

Colleen told Nicole she had a remedy from a friend in the U.S. Navy Seals who wore a special shark repellent while diving in the ocean. The "special cream" arrived in time. Colleen applied it just before Nicole entered the water at Niagara-on-the-Lake. "I was feeling more comfortable knowing I had this shark repellent and knew that I could now swim through the night with no fear." Later, the shark repellent was unmasked as blue food colouring mixed into Avon mask cream. "Whatever it took to get my mind properly set is what Colleen did. I still kid her about that to this day."

In 1997 decent weather boded well for the third attempt. The shark repellent was working: the night swim was the most enjoyable part, Nicole says. Lake Ontario dipped to 16C at one point. The water eventually warmed slightly, as if it had been set in the microwave for a reheat of 30 seconds or so. By this point, however, Nicole was so cold she didn't even notice. She knew this could happen and had set her mind to move forward, accepting what came her way, something she had learned on her 1995 crossing attempt and through long chats with Colleen. She landed at Leslie Street Spit or Vicki Keith Point after swimming for 16 hours, 10 minutes, despite chatting with her team on breaks.

Swimming a Great Lake is one of the best feelings, she says. The swimmers ride a wave; they know goals can be achieved. They know they are a select few who share the same success story. She was the 41st successful crossing since Marilyn Bell in 1954, the 18th woman, and holder, at the time, of the fourth fastest time for amateur women. Her Lake Ontario crossing remains her biggest and best achievement. Full stop. Every year she pulls out the video recording of her swim; still she chokes up. "I feel my pain and my reward at the same time."

Terri-Lynn Langdon, Lake Erie, 2002

Ashley Cowan's 2001 swim inspired many people, according to her coach Vicki Keith. Her teammate Terri-Lynn Langdon, who has a form of cerebral palsy, was now determined to swim Erie in 2002. Seven years earlier Terri-Lynn had nearly drowned in a river in Newfoundland while on vacation. Many people would have ended their swimming right then and there, choosing perhaps to deal with it later in life, or maybe just spend the rest of their lives wading ankle deep in the lake on a hot day. She joined the competitive swim team at Variety Village, coached by Vicki Keith. CP continued to affect her hand-eye coordination. In the pool she often smacked her hand into the wall as she perceived the wall to be further away than it was. Terri-Lynn is also petite, and jokes that even soaking wet she weighs 90 pounds on a good day. Her size also affected her ability to manage in cold water, which would then aggravate her CP even further.

But Ashley's success stuck with Terri-Lynn. She thought it was also within her to swim a Great Lake: once she set her mind to something she knew she would see it through. She had also put that swimming hole incident into perspective and was fine with open-water swimming. "I wasn't going to get freaked out."

As she prepared Terri-Lynn heard comments that she was going to drown out there in Erie's warm depths. A few unnamed charities turned down the opportunity to support her crossing attempt. Eventually the Ontario Federation for Cerebral Palsy came onboard to support her. Still, even the OFCP had to double check. About one week before her crossing attempt someone called to ensure she actually knew how to swim. "That was a real question. I said, 'Well, if I don't know how to swim I'm in trouble at this point.' How do you respond to that, really?"

Years after her swim she reflects that sometimes expectations of someone with a physical disability were lower. That phone call galvanized her and clarified things: regardless of what happened on Erie, she would show that indeed, people with CP can swim. No wonder few knew that she had a bout with pneumonia in the weeks leading up to the crossing of Erie. She kept it very quiet. There had already been enough negativity.

Terri-Lynn slipped into Erie at Sturgeon Point, NY at 7:20 a.m., aiming to finish before it got dark. The start was delayed slightly when the lead boat skipper was late arriving but once Terri-Lynn began to swim, she knew it would be okay. The water was warm, a balmy 23C, and it stayed that way throughout the crossing. She didn't worry about Environment Canada warnings about swimming when there's a danger of bacteria being produced in really warm water. For this crossing and this swimmer, warm water was like a gift from Erie.

Vicki had warned her that marathon swims could be boring and to a large extent that would be true for Terri-Lynn. As the swim progressed, Terri-Lynn began to hallucinate that rocks in the middle of the Lake were blocking her path. She stopped swimming, telling her crew she couldn't go on because, there was a wall in the way. They told her to test her theory and touch the rocks. When she did, the rocks were no longer there. "That was kind of cool and a little bit scary." As the sun began to set, the winds shifted to the east and ramped up the waves to just under one foot. Even over the final two hours of the swim, as the wind shifted to the north and Erie's chop increased a touch more, Terri-Lynn's progress didn't falter. She finished at 8:15 p.m., as the sun settled in the western sky. She was the fifth person to swim the eastern side of Erie. She met her goal of finishing in daylight, 12 hours and 55 minutes for 19.2 kilometres to Crystal Beach, Ontario. Vicki told her she swam a lot further because she'd gone off course a couple of times. She raised over $10,000 for the OFCP.

As Terri-Lynn came ashore, she could see the brilliant bouquet of balloons that a family member had brought down to greet her. "I was pretty excited that quite a few people were on the beach." She was happy and years after her swim laughs at how she felt like she could have swum more. She finished the swim with the "mother of all sunburns" on her shoulders. Somehow they had forgotten to slap on the sunscreen prior to leaving. Her muscles were tired but she was otherwise unscathed. Paramedics checking her out after the race told her that her heart rate measured as if she hadn't exercised at all. She felt great and was more than alert enough to note the good genes of the paramedics checking her over after the crossing. She still felt like she could do more. There had never been any doubt: she knew she could swim Erie. "I know that sounds really cocky or maybe that sounds like the place a youth is coming from." Two days later, the muscle pain set in.

Terri-Lynn is now a social worker in Toronto with her own private counselling services. She doesn't use the word failure in Great Lakes swimming, regardless of the outcome; instead the key to completing a Great Lake swim lies in being prepared in all aspects, mentally, physically, emotionally, she says. "Because I'm a woman with a disability, there have always been lesser expectations, as if people with disabilities are not as expected to have a successful career, or to attend university, or to succeed in sports, particularly if their disability is physical."

Still, swimming a Great Lake is something that anyone can point to and say simply that it's hard and amazing. Regardless of ability. "In terms of how it ended, I feel that was beautiful."

Gregg Taylor,
Lake Ontario, 2003

Over 19 hours, during a hot, humid August 13-14, 2003, Gregg Taylor of Brantford, Ontario, became the youngest man, age 19 years and 218 days, to swim across Lake Ontario. It was his first attempt, a swim that featured two other peak performances: the Perseid Meteor Shower, and the Northeast Blackout that shut down electrical power to 50 million North Americans.

Gregg had been swimming for Brantford Aquatic Club for eight years by the time he reached the shores of Lake Ontario and the splendour of Queen's Royal Beach Park in Niagara-on-the-Lake. He was a touch bulkier than the other guys in the club, but he was a good distance swimmer. Perhaps distance swimming was the avenue to try, not the mere warm up of the 1,500-metres in the pool, but open water swimming. For Gregg, swimming came naturally. He had played hockey, and was on his high school football team. He worked at the pool next door to the school. Swimming: naturally convenient and relaxing. All pain from the day disappeared. "I think a lot of swimmers probably find that," he laughs.

His mother Christine (Murray) Taylor was a former national-level swimmer who talked about Marilyn Bell and Vicki Keith and their epic swims. His father, also Greg (only one "g" at the end), added that if he was going to do a Great Lake crossing, why not do "'the Grand one. Do Lake Ontario.' He was telling me that Lake Ontario was supposedly the third hardest lake in the world to swim," Gregg recalls.

If distance, water temperature, and a narrow weather window aren't enough, the currents of Lake Ontario offer their own unique challenge. If there's a heavy downpour a few days before the swim, the Humber River at the Toronto end will swell and shoot out a current that can slow the swimmer down to a snail's pace—and that's if you're lucky and it doesn't stop you dead. "It can be very much a pain in the butt," Gregg says.

Still, the challenge was also the allure. There was the exclusive membership: so few have gone across—he would be 43rd. "More people attempt Mount Everest in a year than have ever done Lake Ontario. There was that stature to it, too."

He convinced his coach Hans Witola that he was serious; they would train two years straight for Lake Ontario. His Great Lakes swim would be in honour of his great uncle Clifford. Every summer the family would visit his cottage in Sturgeon Falls on Lake Nipissing in Northern Ontario. They would boat, fish, swim. "He was from a very different background. He grew up during the depression. Sometimes up there at the cottage spaghetti was on the menu; if you didn't eat it for supper, sure enough it was your breakfast. Whatever you took, you had to eat. Whatever you started, you had to finish. That became the motto for my lake swim." Clifford passed away from cancer. Gregg also knew others in his family, and of course outside it, who had suffered from cancer. His swim would raise $25,000 for the Canadian Cancer Society.

Two years before his swim Gregg weighed 180 pounds, perhaps 20 pounds overweight, he says. When coach Hans realized Gregg was serious about the Lake crossing, he worked up a schedule to add weight training. Gregg's life narrowed, focused into a routine of get up, run five km, swim for 90 minutes, go to school, swim another 90 minutes after school, do an hour of weights, run five km. Bed. Despite maintaining the training regimen, at times it seemed like the swim would fail to launch. Two weeks prior to the scheduled departure, one of the sailboat captains suffered a heart attack and had to pull out. Gregg's parents raced around Niagara-on-the-Lake yacht club and found Terry and Ruth, who would ultimately guide the swim across in their sailboat. As they headed to Niagara, protesting truckers blocked the highway. "It didn't seem like it was going to happen at the time."

But then, suddenly, it had all come together. Passing the time before the departure, Gregg hopped into the pool at the Reef Winery where he was staying prior to the swim. His father arrived to find him swimming. At 9:06 p.m., they left Queen's Royal Beach Park, and Gregg followed the sailboat, staring at a bright spotlight for the next five hours. Another spotlight from one of the Zodiacs revealed a black mark on Gregg's arm. "I wondered, 'What the hell is that?'" Rolling over onto his back he saw the leech, ripped it off and kept going.

Stroking along at about five kilometres an hour, which included the three-kilometre per hour push from the Niagara River current, Gregg cruised across Lake Ontario. In the middle of the lake as he stopped to feed Gregg rolled over and stared up. The Perseid Meteor Shower was putting on a magnificent show. Hundreds of them were shooting—an awe-inspiring sight so different from what people see on land. The lights of Toronto lay ahead, bathing the night city in an orange glow; behind and to the south sparkled the lights of Niagara and Youngstown, in the United States. "It was one of the most peaceful things I've seen in my life," Gregg recalls. In the middle of Lake Ontario, in the busiest part of Canada, there is no light pollution. "You wouldn't believe the amount of stars you can see." Lake Ontario was like a sheet of glass. "At that point the swim was amazing."

The cold water brought up from a passing tanker provided a rousing wake-up call. "Here I am swimming along, and 'Holy Crap!'" His voice actually pitches higher here. Gregg was lucky; it took little time to cross the patch of cold back into relatively warmer water.

At one point, as many swimmers have been, Gregg was on pace to break the speed record. Then he hit the Humber River current. He figures it was a dead stop for about five hours. He slowed to perhaps less than one kilometre per hour. Of course there had been a heavy rain the day before which had increased the output from the Humber. For five long hours he slogged away. Over on the *Moonwind,* his crew Terry and Ruth charted a course looking for the quickest way through. And then they were through it, picking up speed again, Toronto again drawing closer. "We were in sight. Just go for the gold. Just go."

As they drew closer they all noticed that the large windmill on the waterfront had stopped spinning, something it hardly ever did. "What the hell?" they wondered, but Gregg swam on.

Nearing the breakwall at Toronto, about one kilometre from shore, Gregg was certain he would finish. A police escort moved to stop jet skis from jetting over to say hello. Gregg could hear the cheers. At 4:29 p.m., he touched the wall at Marilyn Bell Park in Toronto, 19 hours, 23 minutes after starting. It wasn't a world record but he had cracked the 20-hour barrier. He had been stuck in the damn current for hours.

The afternoon finish time was more than just a time to note for the record books, however. As Gregg headed to hospital for a check-up, the team noticed how people were using glow sticks to direct Toronto rush hour traffic. At the hospital, the situation was chaotic from car accidents. With everything running on back-up generators it was dim in the hospital and hot. The crossing had arrived in the crazy first minutes of the infamous 2003 Northeast Blackout which took out electricity to over 50 million North Americans.

Before the swim, Gregg laughs, he had bet his mother he wouldn't complain once. "I still have that $100." Besides, he didn't want to let anyone down. Coach Hans had trained him for two years, his pacers had been going out with him in cold water since May. The swim felt too big to fail.

Years later, Gregg was on a construction job waiting out the rain. There wasn't much for the team of bricklayers to do but get out of it and shoot the breeze. Talk turned to things they'd done. Gregg Taylor heard about all his boss's motorcycle riding. Gregg asked, "Yeah, and did you hear about that crazy little guy who swam across Lake Ontario in 2003? That was me."

While it doesn't hurt to have a swim like that on your résumé, this was the first time he'd mentioned it to his boss. In fact it's a swim he doesn't usually put out there on his sleeve. "I just keep the memory in my head," Gregg says. Being the youngest man to swim the Lake was a nice little record to have, but records are made to be broken. "If somebody else goes and breaks it I'll be there cheering him on."

Melissa Brannagan, Lake Ontario, 2005

For an athlete a moment of perfection can come with clarity, noting every detail from the face of the official judging the turn, to the sound the water makes as it rushes between bathing cap, goggle strap and ears. But that's in a pool, or an arena, where the situation is as controlled as possible and the athlete has practised for every contingency. But, what would a perfect swim be on Lake Ontario? Indeed, on any Great Lake? Is there even such a thing? Conditions, timing, elements, and all those other factors, like luck, have to join the athlete's pursuit of goals and dreams. The distance is long; the swim will go through the night. On average it takes 18-22 hours to complete the 51 kilometres of a Lake Ontario traditional crossing. Can a team plan for everything to go right?

Often Melissa Brannagan's swim is held up as the textbook crossing, but she would be among the first to say her crossing, August 9-10, 2005, was never as easy as it looks on paper. For most swimmers, the workload prior to the crossing is as intense, if not more so, than the actual training.

Melissa was in her final year of varsity swimming, the team captain with a new coach, and preparing to cross a Great Lake. She struggled to find the appropriate support boats mandatory for the crossing. Then, joy. Two weeks beforehand, she finally found a powerboat. The boater was a virtual stranger, a friend of a friend. The evening prior to her crossing attempt, on August 8th, though, he emailed Melissa to say his boat had lost an engine and the boat was no longer functional for crossing a Great Lake. There were fewer than 24 hours to go and Melissa was in tears. The email continued: the man had solicited someone from his boat club to loan a boat. She had her boat.

A few weeks after her crossing Melissa learned the rest of the story. The man was so upset that his boat had died and that he might have ruined Melissa's crossing attempt that he had walked up and down the docks at his boat club trying to find a replacement, repeating her story over and over, how she was swimming the Lake and raising money for Sick Kids Foundation.

Eventually he approached one boater and repeated her story. The man said take the boat, whatever you need. "I'd go along on the swim if I possibly could but my daughter is in Sick Kids right now. Take anything," Melissa recalls. "It was just one of those reminders that, oh, man, that's the important part of it all. You know, the Sick Kids people were there when I arrived on shore. I got a letter from the foundation president and whatnot. You don't realize the impact you're having on people until it's in your face like that." It's a story Melissa didn't have to handle before the swim. The day was already so difficult, harder than swimming at least 51 kilometres north to Toronto: the stress, the nerves, the continuous roller coaster of emotions on the day before the swim. "A couple of my pacers were around and of course my best friend at the time was there. They were trying to keep me calm and you know there's just so much going through your mind."

Melissa was 23 when she swam across Lake Ontario. She was a latecomer to swimming who packed a lot into a short, eight-year career. She had started swimming at 14 as a way to help her soccer. She tried running first, then fell in love with swimming and being at the pool, thanks to her coach Steve Gombai.

Swimming ultimately helped her soccer, but by then it was perhaps too late. Her focus began shifting to the pool. Steve likes to tell the story, perhaps a local legend now, that had the team been making cuts, they might not have kept the rookie swimmer. After all she was joining the sport at a time when a lot of youngsters quit. "It took a little bit of work to get to the level I wanted," Melissa says, "but I fell in love with the pool the minute I started racing."

At first she swam for Herb de Bray at Brock University in St. Catharine's, and dabbled around the top 20 in the OUA. She was never a racer; her pace in training was as fast as her race pace. She seemed to struggle with the transition to racing and the need to take her speed and pace up several notches.

At the beginning of that final varsity swim season in 2004-05, Melissa was looking ahead, thinking about doing something else. About 18 months earlier Meloday Salfi, the mother of one of her best friends, Lisa, had died of cancer. The family had been an inspiration to Melissa, who felt she had never been able to convey that to them.

Paula Stephanson, also a Brock student, would swim across all five Great Lakes over a 13-year timeframe. Paula was a few years ahead of Melissa and had completed the first chunk (three lakes) of her Great Lake swimming by the time the two were teammates. Of course Melissa knew the stories and even roomed with Paula. She thought it was such a cool accomplishment. The more she thought about it, the more she thought she should do this: what a way to end her swimming career and do something for the family who had been so good to her growing up.

Still, she told hardly anyone for the longest time, beyond her best friend and team manager, Lynsey Rivest, and Peter Bradstreet, the new swim coach at Brock. Then as the months went on and training grew serious, Melissa started to tell people and solicit the help needed. There wasn't much of a reason to keep quiet, she says; it's just that the amount of planning and preparation was overwhelming. She needed to put certain things in place before she was willing to announce her intention to swim. The cost with Solo Swims was a lot for a university student in her fourth year. "I just wanted to make sure I was as committed to it as I thought I was."

She was also training for OUA championships and was captain of her team. She needed to set the Lake Ontario crossing in the back of her mind and focus on the short but intense varsity season. When the OUA season ended in mid-February she took a week off, then went back to the pool.

Her approach was methodical, to say the least, a fact that had to do with her crossing coach, Peter, who is a planner. She knew that when she chose him. Even though they had been working together for less than a year by that point, Melissa says she really responded to his coaching style. "He's a planner and he taught me that if you're going to do something, you're going to do it 100 percent. He's very quiet; a kind of in the background type of person. But by picking him, I knew exactly how that swim was going to go."

Long before she would dive into Lake Ontario Melissa would know how virtually every minute would proceed. She would fuel every 15 minutes either with water or Gatorade and she would know what was on the menu to eat every half hour. She knew what Peter would say to her. She did not want to know certain details, like how far she had gone. "I didn't want to be discouraged or vice versa. I didn't want to bring the heart rate up too high and get too excited." She would not ask Peter how many kilometres remained. "I didn't want to know because I think that's part of the journey, too. You don't want to be overwhelmed by the fact that you've only swum halfway, that you've still got this much to go, and that you're feeling this tired." Of course, planning is never an exact science; it's all theory until the team is out on the Lake.

The swim was set for August 10th but launched a day early to avoid storms. She suffered through an upset stomach that prevented her from keeping food down. Her team adjusted but that's about as far as the flexibility and manoeuvring went. Only her coach was allowed to talk to her about the actual swim as it progressed.

"We were very firm with everyone on the swim—if they were coming with us they had to do it our way. Which was little bit harsh." Her father, Patrick, was in the boat beside her for the entire swim and he was only able to provide encouragement but nothing specific about time and distance to his own daughter.

Still, Melissa knows that was the way to swim. Every time she broke down, she focused on Peter, knew who was talking to her, and who was listening to her. "Of course, after he gave me whatever he needed to, people gave me encouragement and that was fine but it was more or less Peter and me when it came to what was going on in the water."

The strict planning was bound to offer clues. She was stopping to feed every 30 minutes, at the bottom and top of the hour. Between that, every 15 minutes, Peter tossed her a water bottle with a string attached. Melissa couldn't take in a large amount of food and water at the same time. She needed to break it up into shorter fuel stops. She kept track of her feedings to keep her mind occupied. At one point she came up for a feeding and asked, "Peter, is it 2:30 in the morning?" He replied, "Only you would be in the water for this long and know exactly what time it was."

Some swimmers and coaches have speculated that the trick to breaking Cindy Nicholas' 1974 women's record lies in how the feeding breaks are handled. For Melissa it depends on the individual swimmer. Besides, she was never out to set a record. Melissa's breaks lasted fewer than two minutes each. She would tread water, eat, get going. Sometimes she would chew and swallow her food while swimming. On the 15 and 45-minute water breaks, she barely broke stroke to drink. Some people are capable of feeding once an hour. Her swim master Marilyn Korzekwa was slightly against the break pattern, Melissa recalls, but that was how Melissa had to handle her own nutrition. She could not eat enough on one break.

In the final hours, she had been looking forward to the sunrise for it would mean she was close to Toronto. It's a moment so many Lake crossers relish, an unforgettable transition when the dark water is alive again, on fire with light. The sun never came. "It was one of those 'Oh man. I was so looking forward to that' moments." Instead, wedged between two storms, the sky was grey and crappy. The pacers, all teammates from Brock, were along to keep the experience positive. When the sun didn't come up and Melissa was discouraged coach Peter sent a pacer in. "What an uplifting moment to have one of those boys, who I'd swum with for years, come in the water with me. We laughed and we joked and we got on our way." At one point, all four men were swimming with her through the waves of water and discouragement. "I had no idea where I was going. But once they put the boys in my disposition turned. They were phenomenal. I always say I would never have made it through that last hour or so without them."

In the final kilometre the swim was slightly off course, about one kilometre closer to Toronto's Ontario Place than she needed to be, and 500 metres off shore, forcing Melissa to swim parallel to a shore she felt she could just reach out and touch. "Psychologically that was very difficult because to me I felt the swim was over. I was in Toronto. I could see the shore but I just couldn't swim to it."

Melissa was on pace to break Cindy's record when a storm hit. She figures that had she been any slower they would have pulled her out of the water, ending the swim before the finish. The waves were rolling in at 1.5 to 2 metres, making Melissa feel like she was swimming backwards. Some of that was fatigue, but in the final few hours conditions were deteriorating. They had estimated the swim to take 22 hours, though Peter, knowing how Melissa paced herself, thought she would be closer to 18. The team was thrilled, somewhat surprised even, with the time of 16 hours, 11 minutes. "Thank God we finished ahead of the pace we thought or we would have hit that storm." Two hours later, the looming storm hit Toronto.

Since the crossing, she has wondered whether she would have gone back had the swim ended so close to shore, due to weather. She and Peter had discussed the possibility of getting out of the Lake with an incomplete crossing. "He was trying to say to me that I need you to prepare yourself that if the conditions aren't good enough, we may have to pull you out of the water." She replied that if she had to then someone would be coming in to physically remove her. "I'm not just going to say I'm getting out of the water." She likes to say she would have tried it again in 2005, on the scheduled rain day.

Melissa's mother Vivian greeted her at the finish—she praises her parents for being the most supportive people on the planet—but Melissa didn't want to leave the Lake. "I could have been in that water forever."

Then there's her time, 16 hours, 11 minutes, about 1 hour off the all-time women's record. She was thrilled, but the time wasn't the important part of the swim. "I think that's why I didn't want to know as I was coming along. I didn't want to think to myself, 'Oh. I'm so close to the record, I'm going to get the record.' Then be discouraged. I think the success in this swim isn't so much in breaking the record. With the conditions and everything that goes on, you're never going to have a perfect swim."

Her motivation came from raising $8,500 for Sick Kids Foundation. One of her aunts, Ann-Marie Christian, worked at Sick Kids where there was a brand new research institute her funds could support. "I think one of the biggest things I learned about the swim was the impact you have on people without even realizing it. It was an in-your-face reminder."

The swim across Lake Ontario was great, but for Melissa it was just 16 hours out of a much longer ordeal. She also recalls the months of training and preparation, the physical and mental challenge. She could have not prepared anymore for it than she did. "Sometimes the failures come from things you can't control, right? The weather, the whatever. I think that if you look at the big picture, the success comes from the whole journey, not necessarily the time in the Lake."

Nothing compares to this moment: Melissa Brannagan touches the ladder at Marilyn Bell Park, Toronto, August 10, 2005. Photo courtesy Melissa Brannagan.

Samantha Whiteside, Lake Ontario, 2006

Eventually, that's how Samantha Whiteside, at 16 years old, reflected on her crossing of Lake Ontario. In 2006, she came agonizingly close to Cindy Nicholas' speed record. She swam the traditional route and raised over $52,000 for the Arthritis Society, to be directed towards juvenile arthritis, the condition she had suffered from herself as a child. Samantha swam the traditional route in 15:11:11—an amazing feat. There was never any doubt in her mind that she would complete the crossing. She wanted the record, and wanted to raise money for the children. And yet, this crossing became more than just completing the swim. Samantha's swim remains a study in how fine the line is between our definitions of success and failure. Her time over August 8-9, 2006 was insanely close, within 1 minute, 11 seconds, or a mere 71 seconds, of Nicholas' 1974 record.

The time, though, was battling with another fact, the colour Samantha was turning. As she crossed, her crew watched her feet turn from skin tone to a distinct shade of blue. Arriving at Marilyn Bell Park at the Toronto waterfront in a state of near hypothermia, Samantha finally touched the red ladder to end her swim. And now for the time on the clock: the swimmer turned immediately to see, a motion as natural and ingrained as breathing. As she crossed the Lake her crew had been telling her that she was really, really close—just keep going. So now Samantha turned and asked her coach Joni Maerten-Sanders for the final result. Joni replied: "We'll talk about it later."

Immediately Samantha felt a colder truth. She thought, I didn't do it. "When somebody tells you we'll talk about it later, you haven't done it." She doesn't recall when she started to process the fact. For days after the swim, the media was always asking how it felt to have come within seconds, over 51 kilometres and 34 years. "Well, obviously it doesn't feel too good.'"

In 2007 she dealt with missing the record by saying she would try again. "I turned around and said I'm going to beat the men's time. A lot of stuff happened for me in the second swim; the one I chose not to finish. I have regretted the decision ever since." She pulled out after five hours.

Samantha was two when she was diagnosed with juvenile arthritis. Water was her therapy, and through those times she developed a love of swimming. Her arthritis, fortunately, went into remission. The condition's effects were relatively mild. X-rays show that the bones on the second last toe on her left foot didn't grow properly. Samantha doesn't run as well as she could. "I was at the age where I was supposed to be learning that sort of thing and I wasn't able to," she says. "Something about my toe could have messed up my balance."

Over the summers she began to love open-water swimming, racing in events around Ontario, swimming at Camp Ak-O-Mak near Parry Sound on fun vacations. The stage was set at a ten kilometre open-water race in 2004 in the Olympic Basin in Montreal. She had been fast.

Afterwards Joni Maerten-Sanders was talking to Vicki Keith about that swim, how Samantha wasn't even tired. Vicki wondered if Sam could hold that kind of pace over a longer distance. If she could, then perhaps she could swim Lake Ontario and perhaps break Cindy Nicholas' world record for women. Joni happened to mention that to Sam and later they would joke that, oops, perhaps mentioning this possibility had been a mistake. "From there I thought swimming the Lake would be a cool thing to do."

In 2005 she was talking to Joni again, who told her if she was serious about Lake Ontario then she should go for mileage at Ak-O-Mak. Samantha took a few days to decide; part of her didn't want to make training all she did at Ak-O-Mak. She wanted to enjoy her last summer at camp. But on the third day she decided to go for it—she broke the Ak-O-Mak record of 80 kilometres, swimming 132 kilometres in the final ten days.

Joni also told Sam that she should fundraise, that many people swim for charity. Immediately she chose the Arthritis Society and recalled how sick she had been for several years. "I wanted to turn this around and help the kids who were suffering from it now. I knew what it was like; my family knew what it was like. We wanted to try and prevent more people from going through this."

She had her charity and her training; now, mentally, she was set. Her mindset for Lake Ontario was simply not to consider having bad weather. She trained for waves in Lake Huron and loved it, slicing through metre-high waves, half her body out of the water while the other half would be diving down. She practised for cold water in late April: family friends were opening their backyard pools so she could jump in. Her fundraising for arthritis continued to motivate her; after all, why swim if it wasn't to help her community? It was a perfect chance to raise awareness about a "heartbreaking" condition in children. "It gets so much news coverage when you do something like that. And, I think without the charity things would have been harder for me in the middle of the swim, or even when things were getting tough when I was training. I was able to think 'I'm going through this but I can swim. I have that chance. I have that opportunity and I need to make sure others have that opportunity too.'"

On August 8th, with "Sam Swims" shirts on the support crew, Samantha left Niagara-on-the-Lake under perfect conditions. The water was beautiful. She was confident in the dark. Much of the swim would go at night to take advantage of the calmer waters, in theory. They had left at 6:00 p.m., eventually finding a chop. The waves picked up, growing big enough to irritate her. "In my plan the water was going to be warm, there wasn't going to be any wind, I wasn't going to have any issues. It was going to work. So then it started getting windy. That bothered me." She shouted at Joni: "Just make the waves stop. I know you're causing them. I've had enough. It's not fun and games now; I'm done."

Joni told her she couldn't do anything about the wind.

Then the water temperature dropped. Lakers had gone by, churning up cold water from the depths of Ontario. Chill set in. Her feet began to feel like they were on fire. Coming closer to Toronto, the hallucinations began: she heard the voice of someone saying "Joni fell into the Lake."(Joni actually did fall partway in). But she would look and see Joni. She was there and wearing what seemed to be a spotted, dotted sweater. "I remember thinking like 'Wow, she changed her sweater. I don't know where she got it from. That's not the sweater she was wearing before.'" Next time Samantha looked Joni was wearing the Sam Swims sweater she had put on that day. Then she was back in polka dots. Sam found out later that she had been hallucinating but, at the same time, she thought it was cool: Joni keeps changing her sweaters. "It was so weird."

Coming into Toronto, Samantha was chilled to the bone. She touched the waterfront wall but doesn't recall climbing up the ladder, only that she had not set the record, not even tied it. She remembers seeing her mom. I was in extremely poor shape, she recalls. "Most people finish and talk to the crowd. I couldn't do that." She was put on a stretcher. A paramedic took her arm, told her she had great veins, that she would be fine. She was terrified of needles. "I was just, OH MY GOD! This is not going to go well." She argued, but had no energy left to fight. Before she knew it, the needle was in. The paramedic looked at her: "I'm done," he said.

It was a struggle to get a body temperature on Samantha at the water's edge. In the ambulance and definitely by the time the team had reached hospital, her temperature was rising and she was shivering painfully. Everything hurt. "I was just crying. My muscles hurt so much from the swim and from being so cold." Since at 16 she was technically a child, she was placed in a bed that was too small in the paediatric ward. Her feet hung over the end and her muscles tightened in a bent position. As an IV went in, staff had to try and push her muscles down. They wouldn't move. She was sent home a few hours later.

For 2007 she trained to break the record again. Her pool sets were so fast she'd turn to her coach in shock that she was moving faster than ever. She was winding up, tight, swimming faster and faster as the date for her crossing drew nearer. There was talk of not only breaking Nicholas' record but taking down the men's record, John Scott's phenomenal 14 hour 50 minute swim as an amateur, and even, in a really "go big" moment—John Kinsella's 1978 professional mark of 13 hours, 49 minutes. In preparation, Sam trained in Lake Erie, among other spots.

When the day came, conditions were fine. She left Niagara-on-the-Lake at 8:00 p.m. Five hours later she was done, swim over. Perhaps she had been so tightly wound up, that it all just came apart. "I had so many fears. I think I was just terrified." She panicked out in Lake Ontario. There was some speculation in the media that the death of a close friend had factored into her mindset. "I think I had a lot of feelings going into it that I should have talked about with people, but I brushed them off, thinking they weren't important. In hindsight, maybe they were and I should have."

She swam again at the University of Guelph, but by her second year she retired and put away another attempt on Lake Ontario. She wonders about it sometimes until logic snaps her out of it. The circumstances around her second swim will prevent her from trying again down the road, perhaps. "I don't think I could get to the middle of the swim and be okay." She channelled her drive into graduate school and took up canoeing, as she had during her summer swim camps at Ak-O-Mak. In July 2013, she returned to the Lake as part of the 'Because I am a Girl Relay Swim' which attempted to swim the 305-kilometre length of Lake Ontario. The relay encountered cold water and as Sam herself said, Lake Ontario threw everything it had at the team. The five swimmers completed 242 kilometres, still a record-setting swim.

The thing about swimming, any sport perhaps, is that it opens other opportunities, often unforeseen. In 2008 Samantha was chosen to attend the Olympic Youth Camp through the Canadian Olympic Committee. She was one of two Canadians among the 409 delegates from 205 nations and went to Beijing to greet the Canadian women's swim team as they were outfitted in their Olympic gear. She also attended various Olympic events, including the canoe/kayak slalom. Among other awards she received for her accomplishments, Samantha was named one of Canada's top 20 under 20 and Prime Minister Stephen Harper sent a commendation. In 2008 she also received a $5,000 UCBeyond scholarship, given to students who overcome health challenges.

Times change. Can a swim in 1974, one year prior to Solo Swims of Ontario being established, be compared to the uber-safety and regulations of 2006 and the current world of modern marathon swimming (which is now in the Olympics)? The Whiteside family disagreed with the issue of the record, though not her time. She had started swimming two minutes, 33 seconds after she entered the water. According to Solo Swims policy, the swim and the clock start running the minute the swimmer touches the water at the beach in Niagara-on-the-Lake. One toe in and the clock goes. Sam was in the water but not swimming and time was ticking. She says she didn't know the timer had started. "At one point, my coach looked and said, 'We're 2 minutes and 33 seconds in, you'd better get going.' It wasn't until after the crossing that those 2 minutes and 33 seconds mattered."

She defines her time as the fastest under the current regulations. The footnote is she missed the record. For most people, Sam says, success is in the finishing. "That in itself should be looked at as phenomenal because it is one of the hardest swims in the world."

She raised over $52,000 for the Arthritis Society on her two swims and toured to talk about the condition. "When you talk to kids they think that arthritis is something Grandma and Grandpa get. Even today, most people don't know that you can have arthritis as a child. So for me it was making people aware of that and what it can do." She was happy that the arthritis community had something huge to rally behind. "I'm really thankful to everyone in my community who supported me in all of this."

Stephanie Hermans, Lake Ontario, 2007

After pacing Gregg Taylor in 2003, and cheering him on, Stephanie Hermans was back on Lake Ontario in 2007. She knew early on that she would never get across the Lake like this. Minutes into her 51 kilometre crossing, Stephanie, then 21, realized that she had put on far too much lanolin.

Just before leaving Niagara-on-the-Lake for the swim to Toronto, Stephanie and her mom had applied about eight pounds of a ten pound tub of lanolin bought specifically for the occasion. The lanolin was supposed to add a measure of warmth and protect the swimmer from chafing. Wearing so much lanolin soaked and stretched her straps. Water was slipping down the front of her bathing suit and staying there. It was like she was wearing a parachute, one that was going to slow her down. This was no way to start the crossing. Fortunately the bag in which she had stuffed another suit was on her support boat. As the sun set in the west she stopped swimming, stripped naked, and pulled on the second suit, right there in the Lake. It's a feat that should have earned her a time bonus on the crossing.

On August 11, 2007, Stephanie completed the 49th official crossing of Lake Ontario, along the traditional route from Niagara-on-the-Lake to Marilyn Bell Park, in 18 hours, five minutes, 37 seconds—right on track, as she had been the entire time. It was a fitting and fast end to an 11 year career in competitive swimming.

Though Stephanie knew about Marilyn Bell and the other iconic female crossers, she had never considered swimming Lake Ontario. It wasn't until she swam as a pacer with her Brantford Aquatic Club teammate Gregg Taylor on his 2003 crossing that she first contemplated the swim. Like Gregg, she was a distance swimmer. Being a pacer on his crossing had been an incredible experience, so when the time came to end her swimming career, she turned to Lake Ontario.

In January 2007 she officially decided to swim across Lake Ontario. She had just been accepted into law school. This crossing would be the high note, the going out at the top of your game after 11 years in competitive swimming and spending the last four watching her times slow. "I figured once I was in law school I wouldn't have a chance to swim anymore."

When varsity ended that spring, she was back training with Brantford Aquatic and coach Hans Witola who had coached Gregg for his crossing in 2003. Although she wanted to draw the curtains on her competitive swimming career, it also made sense to raise money for juvenile diabetes. Her fraternal twin sister, Sarah, older by an astounding, agonizing 1 hour, 17 minutes, was diagnosed late, at age 17. She had just graduated from high school. It was a freak thing, Stephanie says. "Her pancreas stopped producing insulin and now she's dependent on insulin injections." Her swim would raise $10,000 for JD research.

That July Stephanie stepped into Lake Ontario to complete her mandatory trial swim for Solo Swims. The trial would be harder than her crossing, even though it was a mere five hour swim. The water temperature was a startling 13.3C, perhaps 13.8C (in the sun). She walked into the Lake and felt her feet freeze. As she started swimming, she had to stop to catch her breath. She knew if she could handle that cold then Lake Ontario should be no problem. "I think that was the best mental training I could have done for the swim." Lake Ontario was warmer on her crossing. "That's one of the biggest factors in a successful lake swim, the water temperature. It boosted my confidence."

Still, Lake Ontario decides things. She was set to leave on August 9th. The Lake was too rough. She went home to bed, thinking she was handling the pre-departure stress well. In the middle of the night she woke up vomiting bile. "I'd never had that before." She thought she wasn't showing or feeling anxious about the attempt, "but my body was stressed."

Friday, August 10th proved calmer but the bathing suit issue wasn't a perfect resolution. She hadn't cleaned off all the lanolin. Her straps still stretched enough that she was popping out of the suit on occasion. The swim was choppy and then all of a sudden her brothers were yelling frantically at her to stop. In the waves, and with minimal experience in Great Lake crossing, they struggled to control the Zodiac. Stephanie raised her head and the boat motor was right in front of her face. It could have been messy. Gregg Taylor recalls that for a moment it seemed she had lost her fingers in the prop.

"I didn't hit anything," she says. "But I couldn't see them. I was just head down and swimming. I looked up and, yeah, it was a close call. The waves made it difficult to manoeuvre the Zodiac. They got pushed out of the way."

Then the swim settled. For Stephanie there was no peeking at the stars, the night sky, the beauty of nature. She had turned her brain off. Through the night, alone in the Great Lake, she saw nothing beyond her hands, reaching ahead, pulling the water back to her feet; she was zoned out, just swimming. "You put your head down and go."

Every 30 minutes coach Hans blew his whistle and Stephanie rejoiced in the steady pace of the regular feedings. At one point she was convinced Hans was teasing her on the 30 minute break. "I kept seeing him, teasing me, pretending to blow the whistle. It wasn't time yet, but still, from the depths of Lake Ontario it seemed as if he was saying 'oh, it's break time. Ha, oh, no it's not.' It's one of those things in the swim that didn't make any sense. I guess I just wanted it to be time for break and it wasn't. I was convinced he was teasing me about that. He wouldn't do that." She sipped warm, orange Gatorade, occasionally ate a peach or a granola bar before swimming on.

As soon it was light her pacers began hopping in to swim with her. With the light and the support of her pacers, she quickened her pace, pulling off a negative split on the crossing. "I would say," she says slowly, "my swim was surprisingly straightforward, that I didn't really experience any particular challenges. Most people would agree that I was very upbeat during the whole swim."

Besides, this was fun. The trial swim had been so mentally draining, a five hour swim where she counted down every kilometre until she was done with the damn cold thing. Lake Ontario in August was much better. "There was so much support." The night was long, but once daylight rolled around her pacers could get in and keep her company. Even a sore shoulder didn't derail things. When her left shoulder ached at one point, she tried one arm butterfly to rest the arm but that didn't work. She was never a flier, anyway. She was given some Tylenol and the pain went away.

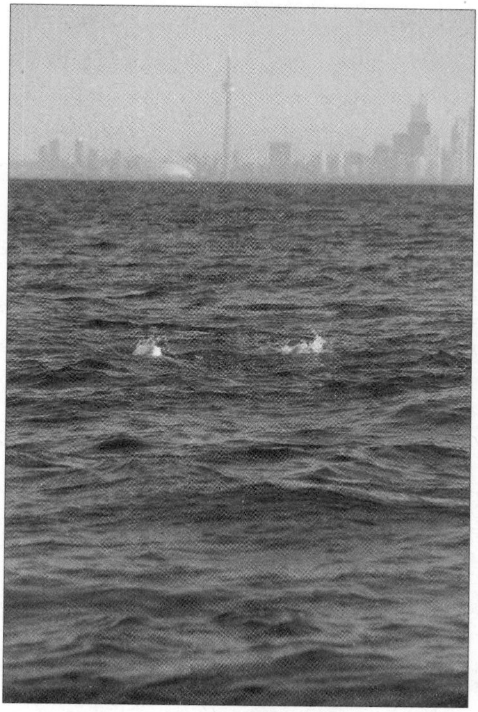

Stephanie Hermans with one of her pacers—and Toronto on the horizon. Photo courtesy Stephanie Hermans.

About eight kilometres from shore she thought that, wow, she was going to complete the swim, even though she was still a long way off. Then, finally, Toronto. Canada's largest city is visible the entire crossing, as if you could just reach out and pluck a building off the horizon. The city kept getting bigger but it was so far away for so long, she recalls. Then finally the team is at the breakwall, with about 80 metres left. "You're pretty much sprinting to the end because you're so close; it's just exhilarating."

Her time of 18 hours, 5 minutes was right on target. They had predicted between 16 and 20 hours. The early waves had slowed the crossing but she was focused more on finishing anyway, not on speed. Perhaps she'd try for the speed record if she did it again, but then again, there are so many things out of the swimmer's control, she says. "I was pretty happy with it."

And lucky. Though she hadn't thought of swimming across Lake Ontario before Gregg Taylor's crossing in 2003, she had followed the lake swims since. She felt for those swimmers whose swims had been ended by the Lake's turbulent weather, and relished her luck.

She replaced competitive swimming with social life and law school. It's hard for a competitive swimmer to see her times slow down over the years, the mind remembering what once was. If she was to attempt it again, she would want to break some sort of record. But there's risk inherent in that, in spending hours training only to have the weather and the Lake decide otherwise. "If you put yourself into that situation you can't control everything; I think it would be for me, hard to justify spending that much time when I don't have full control. I like to have control over my accomplishments. And that's one of the toughest things about Lake Ontario—you can train as hard as necessary and sometimes that's not enough."

The joy in the crossing came in having her battalion of friends and family together for the event. She has joked that her parents don't want her to try it again. Organizing the swim was demanding, but it brought them together. "I really liked that aspect of it. The swimming itself—you just shut your brain off and you just go. You don't think. You just swim."

Jay Serdula, Lake Ontario, 2008

For Jay Serdula, the following questions can cause confusion: how are you? How's it going? What's up?

But after the days of July 28-30, 2008 when Jay, then 35, swam across Lake Ontario in 41 hours, 1 minute, they were legitimate questions. The Kingston-based athlete and mathematician swam to raise awareness about Asperger's syndrome, a condition he was diagnosed with as an adult. For people with Asperger's, that "How's it going?" question is too vague, too literal. What does it mean? And, within social norms it's really more of a greeting, something you don't want anyone to answer for real. After his swim finished was perhaps the one time when Jay knew exactly what people meant by such a question. His mother Ann asked him the morning after his swim. He had lost his voice somewhere on the Lake and he was beyond tired, but he knew that this time the question was to be taken literally. The answer: tired. And eventually: elated.

Jay has written a detailed account of his Lake Ontario crossing and the preparation for it in his book *Ambition of an Aspie: A stroke by stroke account of one man's swim across Lake Ontario.*

A Nordic skier and triathlete with a master's degree in physical oceanography from Royal Military College, Jay was on a sabbatical from running and triathlons when he learned of Jenna Lambert's 2006 Lake Ontario crossing. Within a matter of days, maybe even that day, at least by the next, he had thought: "I want to do it."

One aspect of Jenna's swim stuck in Jay's mind. With cerebral palsy affecting her legs, Jenna, who is also from the Kingston area, doesn't use her legs to support her stroke. During fueling breaks on her Lake crossing she couldn't use her legs but instead tread water with one hand and took her food and drinks with the other. Though he isn't sure whether he would have been any less motivated had he heard of someone without cerebral palsy swimming the Lake, Jenna's experience planted the idea to attempt the swim firmly in his head.

Jay enjoyed being in the water, but didn't work especially hard to improve his swimming for triathlons. Once he began his plan to swim Lake Ontario, he talked with Vicki Keith and regularly sought her advice. He found a coach and a charity. He would swim for Asperger's syndrome. Knowing what he endured as a child, the misunderstanding of Asperger's, he thought this swim would raise awareness and contribute to research into the condition.

Asperger's is at the high functioning end of the autism range. The issue for Asperger's is social: the non-verbal forms of communication take longer to grasp. Things like vocal inflections and facial expressions require time and patience to teach and learn. Social norms and appropriate behaviours are tricky and take more time to learn if you have Asperger's. Jay says that sometimes when an Aspie is trying so hard to obey one rule, he'll often break another. They learn right from wrong by example and structure, clear rules.

For Jay, then, swimming across Lake Ontario actually made sense. With his form of Asperger's he must focus solely and entirely on a task, giving it all his time and attention and letting other aspects of his life lie fallow. Given two hours to finish an assignment might be too much for him, he says. Swimming across a Great Lake, with its years of time and preparation, now that is doable. "I think I actually succeeded at the swim because of my Apserger's syndrome, not in spite of it. I think an Aspie is less likely to undertake something this big. But once I make up my mind to do it, as an Aspie I'm more likely to succeed."

He discovered Kerry's Place Autism Services which helps people living with autism spectrum disorders with consultation, vocational training, respite, and residential supports. For Jay, having the KPAS cause was a major motivation. With all the training, sometimes an athlete is motivated and sometimes not, he says. "Each time I trained I was doing this for the children, and that would renew my desire." But thinking about what lay ahead would end his motivation for awhile.

But the training and eating were taking their toll on Jay; he knew he couldn't commit another year to this crossing attempt. Then he nearly failed his trial swim. His 12 kilometre swim in five hours, 41 minutes, as reported by Marilyn Korzekwa to Solo Swims, was a borderline pass. The extraneous circumstances weighed in his favour. There had been issues with a powerboat breakdown, GPS steerage troubles, and waves. His perseverance, the fact that in 16.6C water he wasn't hypothermic or fearful of the waves, tipped the scales in his favour. She warned his team that if he had waves on the crossing attempt and if it slowed his progress, the swim would be pulled.

With his trial passed—just—he launched his crossing of Lake Ontario on July 28, 2008. He resolved to keep stroking until he reached the other side of the Lake, regardless of how long it might take. He estimated the swim would take between 30 and 36 hours. About four hours into the crossing he took a

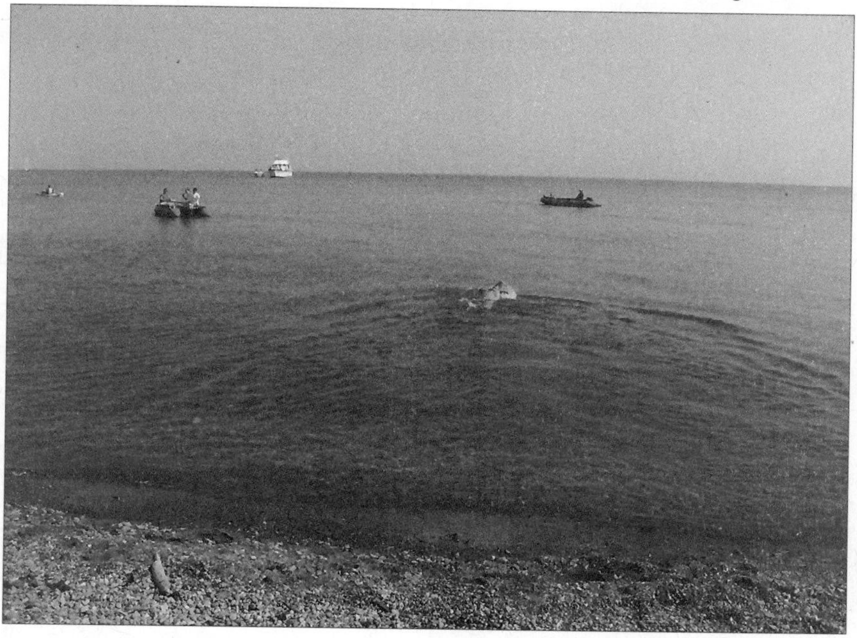

Jay Serdula setting out from Niagrara-on-the-Lake on his 41 hour odyssey. Photo courtesy of Jay Serdula.

look behind him as he took in food. He could no longer see Niagara-on-the-Lake. “That meant I was making progress.”

The crossing seemed straightforward, normal until the second night when it seemed he wasn't making sufficient progress. As darkness fell on that second night, he wanted to sleep. He was cold for the first time. He had been awake for 38 hours and swimming for 35.

By 9:00 p.m. on July 29th, Jay was still over 3.2 kilometres from shore with his arrival time still an estimated four hours away. He resolved to keep on swimming; then he felt the current the Humber River shoots into the Lake. He didn't understand the current it generated until he was in it. Toronto was agonizingly right there but never closer. At one point he asked his crew if Lake Ontario even had another side. He wasn't discouraged, though, just yet. His swim master Marilyn Korzekwa had forecast a 36-hour window for Jay to complete the crossing. Then she had her doubts. Then wind was a factor. She shifted the finish to Vicki Keith Point/Leslie Street Spit, which is six kilometres closer but still counts as a complete crossing for Solo Swims.

At first Jay remained encouraged; he had planned for this, and learned to deal with fatigue, muscle seizures. But then, after so long, he wanted out and told his team. His coach Pam replied as she had been instructed: “You'll be disappointed if you don't finish, really disappointed.” That was true. But he was struggling, like so many swimmers before and after him in the shooting Humber River current. “I thought, given that I may not make it, what's the point in even trying? Like that's what I say at the time, but I don't really mean it.”

As the second sunset spread slowly into the western horizon Jay's swim continued through the dark, and he went from mild to moderate hypothermia. He tried to stop sane and legitimate thoughts of quitting. Just after 10:00 p.m. Marilyn slipped into Lake Ontario to get an accurate reading of her swimmer's condition. He was slowing down but still responded to encouragement. His stroke began to fall apart in the final two hours. They were so near now. With a now famous 200 metres left, Marilyn offered to pull him. He shot off like a bullet and at the darkest point of the night, when it doesn't really matter what time it is—at 3:11 a.m., to be exact—he finally touched the rocks on the shore at the Leslie Street Spit.

He had been swimming for 41 hours and up for nearly two days straight. He didn't remember what he was feeling. But he did remember touching the Toronto side—at last.

When he awoke in the morning, five hours after finishing, he told his parents Ken and Ann that he had worked so hard but doubted he could go on much further. He knew he was in the hospital and that he had finished, but it hadn't sunk in.

For Marilyn Korzekwa, writing her report to Solo Swims, Jay is "an inspiration to all athletes, both disabled and able. He pushed himself further than I have ever seen a human being push themselves." She raised concerns with his hypothermia but speculated that he would not have been hypothermic had the weather been sunny. Having for swim master an accomplished marathon swimmer who was at ease in the dark lake and familiar with hypothermia also helped Jay. Finally, he swam 49.6 kilometres over the 45.3 kilometre course and joined the international 24 hour club for swimmers whose marathons go over 24 hours. Marilyn credited the crew with his success and their "'above the call of duty' endurance, patience, and enthusiasm."

As the family was driving home to Kingston along the busy 401 east Jay looked out the window to see Lake Ontario sparkling blue. "There's Lake Ontario," he said to himself. "That's the first time it actually clicked that I'd actually swum across it."

He says some people may wish they could wave a magic wand and get something done. "Half the fun of something is working for it. So the fact that I spent two years working towards that goal and finally made it, it was"—he pauses—"I'm trying to think of which word. I felt satisfied but that's an understatement. Overjoyed. Ecstatic."

As a mathematician he had to quantify how much his swim changed things for people with Asperger's. He felt that his swim instilled confidence in people. After the Lake, Jay wrote about his adventures and became a motivational speaker for a variety of community groups. He continues to sell his book. His swim had grown into so much more than a personal goal. Years after the fact he never imagined that he'd still be having an impact on the Asperger's community. "You never know what's around the corner."

Shaun Chisholm,
Lake Ontario, 2008

In a literal sense, that's how it was for Shaun Chisholm, a Toronto firefighter and father of two. Years before he swam to Toronto, Shaun was walking through the pretty town of Niagara-on-the-Lake viewing real estate with his father Tony who was looking to buy a home in the town. They found Queen's Royal Beach Park where Tony showed him the plaque near the beach that honours the Lake Ontario swimmers.

Shaun looked across to the Toronto skyline, reaching so much higher than that night Marilyn Bell stepped into Lake Ontario in 1954. It was still a long way. Although he knew about Marilyn's swim he had never really looked at the 'course.' "I just kept drifting back, thinking about that. 'Well, it's quite the challenge.'" He would later joke that if Tony bought a boat, Shaun would swim to Toronto.

Eventually the joke became real, involved dozens of people, and evolved into Swim for Kids. The swim in 2008 raised $27,344.82 for the Burn Unit at Sick Kids Hospital in Toronto. On August 15-16, 2008, Shaun, then 40, swam the traditional, 51-kilometre crossing of Lake Ontario in 19 hours, 23 minutes. He completed the 51st successful crossing on his first crack, despite strong headwinds and the gradual cooling, a numbing six degree drop of Lake Ontario as the swim progressed.

He had been swimming primarily for triathlon, though he found the most enjoyment and success on the swimming portion of a tri. Still, his sports were seasonal: swimming for winter, biking in the summer—chasing his wife Allison, also a firefighter.

Cycling remains his main sport, though he balks at the crashes, having seen the broken orbital sockets and the fractured femurs of riding friends who've crashed. He, Allison, and Tony spent a year with other friends preparing for Ironman Lake Placid. It was a social event, what he and his friends like to do: the party, the renting of the house, and the pre-riding of the course—now that was fun. "The race itself was actually a bit of a letdown. All the training leading up to the event—the whole year of preparation—is where I get most of my enjoyment."

But the training for a marathon swim across Lake Ontario took two years to evolve, compared to the relatively instant decision of a few friends and family members signing up for an Ironman. The idea to swim Lake Ontario came in that instant in Niagara but it took time to root and spring into action. He followed all the instructions of John Scott, the holder of the men's amateur records, who would become his swim master. John put it plainly, stripping away any notions that there was glamour involved.

Then the ball began to roll like waves on Lake Ontario. A firefighter colleague of Shaun had a sailboat and as they talked his colleague ramped up the encouragement, that they should make this swim a big charity event. Shaun followed his cue and so did others as people stepped up to take on the preparation. Tony was principally responsible for fundraising. Often the biggest hurdle for lake crossers, something that can be more challenging than the actual swim, is securing the proper boats to serve as escorts. It's a balancing act, juggling respect for the boat owner, the sailing rules, and boundaries. These Lake marathons can fall way out of the norm for the boat captains, he says. The weather can freak out the sailboat captains, leaving the Zodiac escorts to play a key role when the water roughens up. Fortunately Shaun secured two large boats early in the preparation which meant a potentially major headache was eliminated off the bat.

The charity aspect was a no-brainer for Shaun: the Toronto Sick Kids Hospital Burn Unit. No one accident on any shift over that time really stood out: burns are always bad, especially if children are involved. "The suffering and lengthy recovery caused by burns always weighs heavily on fire crews." He accumulated stories: one fire captain talked about a friend of his daughter who had been severely injured when some kids were goofing around with gasoline. The gas caught fire and the girl was so badly burned she was put in a coma to change her bandages. "Anyone that has been down to Sick Kids knows that there is no other place like it." A tour of the burn unit was organized for the team, "which was very positive since everyone knew what our fundraising would be helping." As the swim took on a life of its own, there were some especially bad calls in the winter of 2007, ahead of the swim. One fire involved an older woman and it seemed to really affect the emergency workers. It was the first time Shaun had seen paramedics incapacitated by what they were dealing with, "traumatized by the trauma. Some stories went around about a couple of really bad fires and it just trickles down. The worst part is it's always preventable."

On August 15, 2008, as Shaun made his final preparations, weather issues loomed in the distance. Shaun refused to get stressed, leaving the decisions to John Scott, his swim master, and the others on his team. "If they felt it was okay, then it was alright."

After applying the grease for chafing and the illusion that it might keep a thin layer of body heat from drifting away into a Great Lake, they left at 4:30 p.m., right on time, as Shaun tried to cover every potential detail. "I just didn't want anything, the preventable stuff, to stop the swim."

The first five hours of the swim went right into strong northerly headwinds. Water temperatures were, for a marathon open-water swimmer, a balmy 22.2C. But as the swim progressed and the sun sank into the west, the water began to cool, dipping eventually down to 16.6C. Shaun knew he could swim in water temperatures as low as 15.5C so no real worries just yet. Still, the cold began to creep into his fingers, up into his wrists, slowly into his arms, numbing, erasing feeling. "In the morning, after 12 hours of swimming, you are much less resistant to it. You can really, slowly feel the coldness going up your limbs." There was no room, however, for doubt.

Later he would describe the swim as a huge monster chasing him through the water. By 2008 blogging had replaced the embedded reporter of the 1970s, and the daily newspaper reports. Now everyone could follow right along, stroke by stroke. “There was all of the preparation and everyone’s expectations. There was no way I was going to let these people down. That’s basically what was motivating me across. And again it just boils down to mind over matter.”

By 7:00 a.m. he was approximately 10 kilometres off the massive Toronto shoreline. His seven-year-old son was brought out to cheer him on. And then, there he was: at noon he touched at Marilyn Bell Park to become the 51st successful crossing and the second oldest man to swim the Lake, at the tender age of 40.

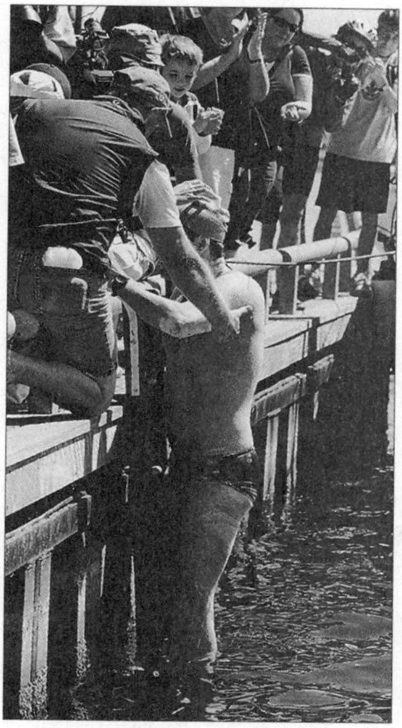

Shaun Chisholm climbs the red ladder. Photo courtesy of Tony Chisholm.

And John Scott was right: there was no glamour, only hard work and suffering. “There’s nothing like physical suffering to know and appreciate that you are truly alive,” Shaun says. “My time is completely irrelevant to me personally. Either the Lake allows you to cross or it doesn’t. It has very little to do with the swimmer.”

Still, people will do these crossings for the double challenge, the hard physical and mental work of training, and then the swim itself. Organizing everything is virtually as hard, something swimmers find out after they’ve committed, he reflects. “It is the challenge that I think is so appealing—pure mind over matter and not some idiotic ‘extreme’ sport that is simply life endangering.”

Shaun enjoyed his journey but it would be hard to duplicate that swim. Still, the experience wouldn’t let him go completely. The charity part continued to appeal, so he participated in the Severn River for Swim for a Cure, run by Deb Bang as a charity swim for breast cancer research. And he enjoyed the spirit of the Solo Swims community so much that he both joined the board and became a swim master.

Jade Scognamillo,
Lake Erie, 2008;
Lake Ontario, 2009

Jade Scognamillo flew across an ocean before she came to open-water swimming. She had not grown up around the Great Lakes or in the lake culture of Ontario in the summer. But she had been a swimmer. Born in Kent, England, she moved to Ontario in 2005 and began training in Vaughan, north of Toronto. Swimming was something she was familiar with, even in a new country. But she was beginning to question some things. Like why was she swimming seven times a week? Many swimmers find themselves at this point and often leave the pool, some for good. Yet she was loving swimming distance. She wondered how far she could go. How much further could she push herself? What would it be like when you just couldn't swim any further? Where would you be? Where would it end?

For Jade it ended on the rocky shore of Marilyn Bell Park in Toronto. In 2009 Jade Scognamillo, at 15, became the youngest person to swim the traditional route across Lake Ontario, 51 kilometres from Niagara-on-the-Lake. She edged Jocelyn Muir Saunders' age record from 1981. Actually, though, taking all routes into account, Natalie Lambert of Kingston was, at 14 in 2007, the youngest to swim the Lake, on the 54 kilometre route from Sackets Harbor, NY, to Confederation Park in Kingston. But if that isn't enough splitting of hairs on a Great Lake, Jade's swim cracked the 20-hour mark; she completed it in 19 hours, 59 minutes, 49 seconds. She was the only person to cross Lake Ontario that chilly summer of 2009.

The week before she swam the Lake she became a Canadian citizen.

At first she wanted to swim Ontario in 2008, as a 14 year old, but Solo Swims said she was too young. sso thought perhaps she could test her mettle first in Lake Erie, as a trial, and that would give her one Lake. Then perhaps she could try Ontario later that summer. Jade didn't feel like she could do both Lakes in the same season. So Ontario was set for 2009, and she went ahead with Erie. On July 12, 2008 she crossed south to north, from Sturgeon Point, NY, to Crystal Beach, Ontario, in five hours, 40 minutes, 35 seconds, setting records for both speed and age. She was 14. For Jade, her first Great Lake crossing turned out to be fun, almost a frolic.

The next year Jade would find Lake Ontario to be a very different body of water. She'd chosen Lake Ontario because it was traditional and she knew about Marilyn Bell. She picked Sick Kids Foundation for her charity because it was Canadian; that way she could honour her new country—and it also seemed to affect the most people, she adds. She found a shopping list of equipment needs at the hospital and an incubator was on it. It was a concrete item, not just more money thrown into a pool. Her friend Katrina Beverly had a brother who had been in an incubator for a time as a baby, and that was the only reason he was still alive.

She trained up to eight hours a day in cold water at Camp Ak-O-Mak. Her trial swim on July 12, 2009 turned out to be like getting a face full of cold water. When she started the trial in Lake Ontario near Stony Creek, water temperatures registered in the mid-teens celsius. By the time she finished near the Burlington Skyway, the temperature had dropped five degrees to 11C. She was pulled out suffering from mild hypothermia. The goal of the trial swim is to show the swim master she can complete about one-third of the Lake Ontario crossing distance. She swam six and a half hours until she was pulled out, just shy of the 17 kilometre requirement.

She emerged from the trial with a new respect for Lake Ontario. "Lake Ontario was colder and wavier and a lot scarier than Erie." After the trial swim, training between her coach Nancy Black and Jade was quieter. Up to this point the process had been smooth; training had been tough but good. The trial swim was a reminder that this swim was serious. "It didn't make me think twice about my crossing. It just made me understand the extra training and conditioning I had to put in. The Lake knocked me down to ensure I was not too confident." She wasn't used to the rolling waves Ontario serves up. Though she was fit enough physically, she had to mature quickly mentally if she was going to complete the swim, because the Lake is so unpredictable.

She packed on 20 pounds, swallowing supplement drinks with each meal —a meal plus a meal in a box, six times a day. And still there was some panic she wasn't gaining fast enough. She ate entire cheesecakes on her own; the weight stayed on during the swim and she actually gained two pounds after eating about 1,000 calories an hour on the crossing. "I was so mad after that."

For nearly a week, weather delayed the crossing attempt. On July 31, 2009, she was in Niagara-on-the-Lake waiting in vain for the water to warm up, even just a touch. It never did and Jade was done with waiting. She didn't want to postpone the swim for another year. The swell of anticipation at the small beachfront park where swimmers launch their quest to swim Lake Ontario rolled in and swept the team out into the Lake. Everyone just wanted to get underway. They wanted to depart at 5:00 p.m. They waited out a storm. By the time the storm had rolled off, it was 9:30 p.m., and dark. Regardless, she left Niagara-on-the-Lake and began swimming into the morning of August 1st and the 15th year, 237th day of her life.

On her first night swim ever in training the normally level, focused swimmer had cried. She was trying to do 20 strokes at a time to get used to it. Then stop, then start again. Now she was entering Lake Ontario in the dark. She shot through the Niagara sandbar, throwing up the Tim Hortons donuts she had stuffed down just before leaving. "Me being stupid." Off in the distance, the CN Tower stood, a big protrusion just over the slight curve in the horizon. Her muscles were sore early. "This is going to be bad," she thought.

It did settle down, though. They struggled to keep glowsticks on her goggles and bathing cap to keep track of her. No one really likes cold water, she says. But after two years of colder showers, not to mention her trial swim, she was used to it. Still, swimming in the dark, alone, she was feeling depressed and trying to think about not complaining. Her swim was supposed to be about helping to buy an incubator.

From the lake the swimmer sees the arrival of the sun. It's quiet. Everyone is sitting, wrapped up in coats and blankets. Then the sun comes up. Everyone's mood lifts. As the water turned red in the light, Jade had the first hint that she would complete her swim. She had made it through the night.

Then the sun was up, and her best friend Katrina was in the water pacing beside her. Awakened at 5:30 a.m. from a good dream, she was told Jade was asking for her. She ate and jumped in, wearing a wetsuit for extra warmth and buoyancy in the water. "Jade has a lot stronger mentality than most people would. When I got in the water I was only there for a bit in the wetsuit. Otherwise I don't think I could have done it. You have to have a really strong mentality."

The tether training over the winter to mimic lake currents began to pay off in the final kilometres as Jade crossed the Humber River current. Her hip flexors, her muscles, her legs—everything felt like it would rip apart. Eventually, something did tear. Jade calculated she had done 60,000 rotations on the crossing; her left rotator cuff finally tore. She didn't know whether to stop, unsure of the extent of her injury. Could she fix it afterwards? Was this going to be more long-term? Would she ever swim again?

Her mother said she could fix it afterwards. She kept going. She had hit waves, boats were around. She doesn't recall feeling the current but did have to swim back for about an hour to get in. She could not understand why she just couldn't go straight in. She wanted to walk over the rocks she could see, just right there.

The swim was hard. But it was also memorable. She remembers the support she received, the people she met. The swimmer's perspective is different from that of her crew: she recalls the water, the side of boats, waves, and always the CN Tower. The tattoo on her hip of a sunrise and a swimmer reminds her of the moment when the dark Lake became bright again, the most beautiful moment of all, when she knew she would make it.

Having a charity to focus her swim helped focus her thinking. She raised $59,000: with $54,000 to Sick Kids Foundation, and the remaining $5,000 to Headwaters Hospital in Orangeville, the hospital closest to her home. She would remind herself in training that it was all for the incubator. On the swim, her nails were painted with the words Sick Kids on them. "Once I went to Sick Kids hospital, it really struck me emotionally." As she swam, she wondered why she was bothering to complain, this incubator could save people. But the drive to get in swims like Erie and Ontario is also about the end results. "It's also for self-satisfaction, the pushing, the challenge, knowing that all the training will pay off. You work so hard for something— then you get it. You've got to enjoy what you're doing."

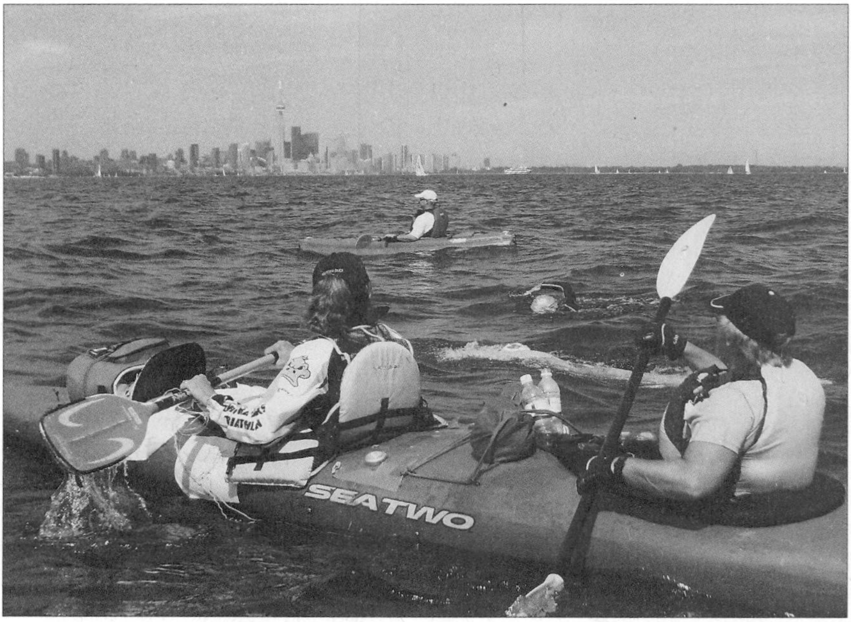

Jade Scognamillo almost naked, plus pacer Katrina Beverly in a wetsuit, on the approach to Toronto. Photo courtesy Jane Scognamillo.

Susanne Welbanks, Lake Erie, 2007; Lake Ontario, 2010

Water temperatures had been brutally cold in 2009, with Jade's crossing the only completed attempt. Colleen Shields pulled her own attempt that summer, fearing heart problems and tapping into memories of her mother's own sudden death in Lake Huron during a scuba dive. Susanne Welbanks of Kingston also watched a year's worth of preparation go into storage as frigid water temperatures prevented her swim from even leaving the beach.

The summer of 2010 saw five swimmers put their names forward but only two found the window of opportunity open. And even then, both swimmers encountered a different Lake. About 12 hours before Miguel Vadillo left Niagara-on-the-Lake on August 10, 2010, Susanne Welbanks was back in the water. She started her Lake Ontario crossing like it was just any other day. Indeed, she could have been like any regular commuter heading into Toronto: get up, have a cup of coffee, walk down to the beach, and begin swimming to Toronto. The IT professional from Bowmanville near Toronto, mother of two, and former lifeguard was about to luck out. And it's just that luck factor that freaked her out.

Susanne entered Lake Ontario's unpredictable waters at 7:32 a.m., having mulled over attempting this crossing for a year before committing to it back in 2008. She had raised over $5,000 for the Shriners but did so with minimal fanfare. She considered swimming across a Great Lake a private thing. "It's a goal I want to achieve. You can't do this type of thing for somebody else. It's something you personally have to want to do in order to accomplish it."

Susanne was a non-competitive swimmer growing up beside Lake Ontario. She loved being in the open water. As a teen she had wanted to swim the four kilometres from Nicholson Point to Amherst Island, right in her backyard. Just hop in for a little four k swim. But it never happened. When she was 30, her mother asked what she wanted for Christmas; she replied, she wanted to do that swim. Her mom contacted Vicki Keith, who was living in Kingston by then, and asked about the right way to do an open-water swim. Vicki told her to join a local swim club. Then they decided that the crossing wasn't good, that she should leave from another spot, at Bath, Ontario. "I took Vicki's advice," Susanne says. "She knows what she's doing, right?"

She swam 19.2 kilometres in 8 hours, 14 minutes across Lake Erie in July 2007 and planned for Lake Ontario in 2009. Susanne hoped to repeat her Erie experience on Ontario, and not be cold and miserable. She thought she could handle the cold but didn't want to cross badly enough to risk starting the swim only to get pulled due to conditions. "I wanted the challenge but I also wanted to make it a fun experience, for me, my family and my friends."

In 2010, like Miguel Vadillo, Susanne gambled on her swim date, and won. If you're interested in picking lottery ticket numbers, see these swimmers. Yet, this luck factor bothers Susanne. A self-admitted control freak, she thinks a lot of people who swim the lakes are A-type personalities who can (and probably have to) multitask. They enjoy being in control. The Great Lakes couldn't care less about that. You either luck out or you luck in.

The play of luck meant she would take her time before even deciding to attempt Lake Ontario. "Because I'm very analytical. Not many people complete it." It's not that swimmers just go into the Lake and swim for 24 hours, or 50-odd kilometres. If that was so, she would not have thought twice about attempting Lake Ontario. "If luck was not a factor and I didn't have small children and I had money coming out my butt I'd do it every year."

If luck is such a factor, then disappointment is luck's sibling. She never doubted her ability to swim 51 kilometres. Instead she feared the situation would let her down. In her circle of Lake swimmers that very thing was happening. In 2010, once again Natalie Lambert of Kingston put her name forward to attempt Marilyn Bell's route, only to have bad weather end her attempt.

Susanne had nightmares about being pulled and about the conditions that would derail her swim, the potential for thunderstorms, the cold water, the big waves. "For the team to make the decision that I'm pulled would break my heart. I didn't want that scenario. Not having control over that factor is definitely, for me, not an enticement. That is an absolute, huge negative."

For someone who likes to plan and control her situation as much as she can, she was extremely lucky. On both her Great Lake swims, water and weather cooperated. Erie was a fun adventure, a nice day out with her family. Ontario would give her the great weather, then the struggle she wanted.

Susanne swam under a hot August sun, over calm waters on August 10, 2010. She wasn't chasing a record, just trying to finish; her crew stopped in the middle of the Lake and swam with her. "It was just surreal. I didn't have any negative experiences at all for the first half, even the first three-quarters of the swim."

Overnight, the Aurora Borealis sparkled above in the moonless sky; the sunrise was glorious, she adds. With her course running pretty much parallel to that of Miguel Vadillo, she swam through the rush of cold water stirred up from the depths of the Lake by a midnight tanker.

But as she drew nearer to Toronto the cold water and current spilling from the Humber River began to take their toll. While she never felt like quitting, she had reached a critical point in the Lake and was stuck in the current swirling off Toronto. For Miguel, the currents didn't play a role. Susanne was unable to move though she was mere kilometres from shore. In Lake Ontario, the current on the Toronto side can be a corridor of frustration that rushes over the legs while the mind plays games: was that an eel? Is this the one spot in the lake with a significant lamprey eel population? What else is rushing over the legs? Surely this lake is deep enough to dump a body and no one would know?

Finally the decision came to land east of Marilyn Bell Park at Vicki Keith Point, also known as Leslie Street Spit. This enabled Susanne to move forward through the Humber current. As dawn approached, they discovered they were off course, floating about four kilometres east of Vicki Keith Point. At that spot there lies a large underwater shelf which causes another current to swirl, and which left Susanne swimming for two hours without moving forward, she explains. The switch of landing spots came late in the swim. Her coach Karen

Hillis worried that if the switch wasn't made, the swim would be called off, with mere kilometres left. "That's usually when they make the call. And I was fine with that. I didn't care. As long as I touched ground," Susanne laughs.

The change up also altered the distance. No longer would she do 51 kilometres; in the end it was about 45 kilometres. Along with the lack of progress so late in the swim, her sinus was dripping and she was gagging on the phlegm in the back of her throat.

Karen hopped into the Lake (McNair) and began to lecture in her no-nonsense, suck-it-up-buttercup way: "This is the point where you're able to make that call that you did it or you didn't. Stop whining, put your head down and pull as hard as you can."

Susanne had been swimming hard for 19 hours and now had to push even harder to break past the current. Pulling hard and long, she finally broke through, then refused to stop, swimming hard for another 200 to 300 more metres, not wanting to get sucked backwards into the current. Then they could see the landing at Vicki Keith Point. She touched shore, 24 hours, 28 minutes after leaving Niagara-on-the-Lake.

Lake Ontario was indeed different from Erie, dependent on so many factors from temperature to weather, food, hydration, currents. "There were so many ifs on that lake, that cause people not to finish. I was so lucky. Okay, you've got to have the physical ability to do it. You've got to have the mental determination to do it. I was born with determination. Some people call it stubbornness. I call it determination. But, you have to have luck."

Reflecting on just that rush of good luck, Susanne felt for the others who didn't complete their crossings in 2010. "I felt proud that I did it but there's part of me that feels bad they were cheated and I got across." She wondered if she would have made the crossing had she faced any waves.

Still, it was something she wouldn't challenge further. Being a double-crosser was enough. The time, the money, the effort—and "the luck scenario really starts to gain importance." She had found what she wanted: fun on Lake Erie, challenge in Lake Ontario. "Ontario was my Mount Everest… It was one of the most rewarding experience of my life."

Susanne Welbanks in a classic position. Photo courtesy Susanne Welbanks.

Miguel Vadillo, Lake Ontario, 2010

In the meantime, Miguel Vadillo's swim across Lake Ontario was splashed all over *The Toronto Star*, where he worked as a graphic designer, recalling the glory days of Lake Ontario crossings.

But there had been another story in the news, one that he hated, that helped inspire his crossing. A year earlier, in July 2009, 43-year-old Naila Yasmin, a mother of four, drowned on an early Sunday morning in a hotel pool in Gananoque, near Kingston. Her two daughters had been found floating in the pool with her. The Monday evening 14-year-old Kinza Kaianad died, and her 11-year-old sister Sunaila died Tuesday afternoon. They were survived by their father and two brothers. The family, originally from Pakistan but living in Toronto, had been on vacation to the Thousand Islands (Craig).

This accident appalled Miguel Vadillo. The graphic designer was reading the stories as he placed them on his pages at *The Star.* He read of Yasmin's death and was immediately troubled. The Guelph Marlins swim coach had been a swimmer in Mexico. He immigrated to Canada in 2004 to take over as Ontario's modern pentathlon coach. He wondered how it was possible that such an accident could occur in a small hotel pool, with the shallow end so close at hand.

Just about one month earlier, in June 2009, Miguel had been on a vacation of his own visiting Niagara-on-the-Lake with his partner Katie White. As they studied the plaque honouring all the crossings of the Lake, Miguel looked across the expanse of Lake Ontario and decided he would swim to Toronto.

One day.

Shortly after he made his decision, he learned of the devastation to Naila Yasmin's family. Convinced drowning is preventable—drowning remains the second-leading cause of preventable deaths in children under age five, says the Lifesaving Society—he decided to use his swim to raise money for Jumpstart. The Canadian Tire charity seeks to remove the barriers, usually financial, that prevent children from participating in and benefiting from organized sport and recreation. Jumpstart helps cover the cost of registration, equipment and transportation. His swim would raise funds for swimming lessons for disadvantaged children, for families who come from abroad and aren't in the culture of Saturday morning swim lessons. He would raise $13,000.

The compact 40-year-old athlete set August 10, 2010 for the attempt. He had gathered a crew of 21 to support him, including Katie, also a modern pentathlete, and Miguel's 12-year-old son, Santiago. Then with four days to the swim, he told his crew he would start his swim as dark settled on Lake Ontario. He feared swimming in the dark and what he might find as he swam with only the fuzzy light of glow sticks and support boats to guide him. He decided to deal with that head on, doing most of the swim at night. With the sun sinking imperceptibly into the western sky, he left Niagara-on-the-Lake, riding the Niagara River current. It was 9:00 p.m. The water was still warm from the heat and humidity of the day.

Near on midnight, a laker steamed by, miles ahead, and not causing direct danger to Miguel. But in this case, what you can see can bite. At the start of the swim, the water temperature had been about 18C. The laker churned up colder water from the depths of the Lake and now Miguel was swimming in water that ranged from 7-11C.

The cold set in instantly, aching and biting, and Miguel wanted out. He screamed it into the Lake, deep into the cold where no one could hear. He coached himself to continue on to the next feeding. He fed every 30 minutes. For about four hours he swam on like this, stroking through the cold, dark Lake until blessed relief rolled in around 5:00 a.m. Suddenly the Lake was warm again and growing brighter all around, the sunrise so incredible it left Miguel in tears.

As he neared the finish at Marilyn Bell Park, his pacers and boats pulled back and he swam to the breakwall alone. At 3:03 p.m., he touched Toronto, 18 hours, 3 minutes, 39 seconds after leaving Niagara-on-the-Lake. It was then the 11th fastest time. In 2010, five swimmers had listed their names to cross; Miguel and Susanne Welbanks (who had left from the same place 12 hours earlier than Miguel) were the only two who completed the swim. His swim master Alan Fairweather said conditions were as near to perfect as possible.

On October 1, 2011, at Niagara-on-the-Lake, Miguel and his partner Katie were among the throng for the unveiling of the new plaque Solo Swims helped create to update the list of all the lake crossings. Looking over to the Lake, as she

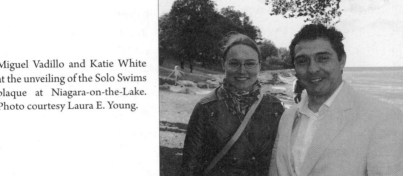

Miguel Vadillo and Katie White at the unveiling of the Solo Swims plaque at Niagara-on-the-Lake. Photo courtesy Laura E. Young.

clamoured for attention, rolling and thundering onto shore, Miguel remained amazed at the conditions he enjoyed for his crossing. "It was incredible," he says. Had this been his weather, the swim would never have left the beach. For his crossing, despite the hours of cold water from the laker, Lake Ontario was like thick, warm cream, lit by a lingering sunset and an invigorating sunrise, and laced with the smell of coffee and the sight of Toronto, oh so close.

For Miguel, success happens "when a little bit of luck meets with a lot of hard work in a specific time and space. That is what happened to us while we crossed the Lake." Still, a lot of things do fly out of one's control and you can't fight it, he says. "The fact that before we started many people already knew about the cause and the importance of knowing how to swim and be safe around water meant we already had success—even if Mother Nature wouldn't allow us to finish the crossing between Niagara and Toronto."

A swim on the Great Lakes raises money simply because it's a difficult thing to do, he adds. "Even when people may not realize how much work is needed, there is a notion that it 'must be really hard' (especially for non-swimmers) and there is a lot of respect for people that are brave enough to dare an attempt." People believe in the cause and find inspiration in such doings. He also thinks that, for some, there's this thought, deep in their mind: "I wonder if I would be able to do it."

His swim raised over $13,000 for Jumpstart. The word awesome applied to the entire swim, to the crossing, to the support of his family and friends, and, of course, to Jumpstart. "We achieved our financial goal to do something to avoid drownings in a country like this."

Rebekah Boscariol, Lake Ontario, 2011

Swimming across Lake Ontario seemed inevitable to Rebekah Boscariol. It was also a swim that touched all the right notes: her family shared in the story, all six children were involved in the swim, and she hit the right note with a fundraising swim for Sick Kids Hospital.

Then there was the fact of her athletic talent: she came within 24 minutes of a 37-year-old record for swimming Lake Ontario. Rebekah's time of 15 hours, 33 minutes, 15 seconds was closest in years to Cindy Nicholas' 1974 record of 15 hours, 10 minutes.

Rebekah was 17 when she swam Lake Ontario. Petite and strong, she had the body of a gymnast; she had even tried gymnastics and dance, but preferred swimming. When she was eight, she thought of swimming across the Pacific Ocean. In 2007 a teammate at Markham Aquatic Club suggested she swim across Lake Ontario and kept bringing it up. Rebekah did some research on the swim and the idea stuck. Eventually, she came to fresh waters with the appearance and shimmering horizon of the ocean. It made sense: she was a distance swimmer and liked swimming in lakes after all.

She mulled over the idea for about three years. Her parents had asked her to wait after they decided to do the swim. "It's a really big commitment for me and for my whole family," she says. She planned to swim in 2010 but wasn't ready as a swimmer, she reflects.

In 2011, the Lake was on. As her teammates prepared for national championships, she was putting in the distance intervals in the pool. She was swimming a combination of distance sets with power: 800-400-300-200-100 on a pace time of 1 minute 30 for the 100 metres or four lengths. That's 68 lengths, the swimmer's mile. Repeat. Repeat. Continue on with the workout. She laughs over how hard and nasty that kind of training can be, swimmers addicted to the pain. By now Lake Ontario was always on her mind. "I knew that I had to do it eventually."

There was another factor in this story: her youngest sister Sophia, four at the time of the swim. At 18 months Sophia had been diagnosed with a hole in her heart. On July 19, 2011 the hole was repaired at the Hospital for Sick Children in Toronto. "Her condition wasn't as bad as some of the kids at the hospital. I've read lots of stories online about kids with so many holes in their heart. My sister had one and it was pretty small too. We were really lucky."

By that time, Rebekah had already decided to swim Lake Ontario and thought Sick Kids was a charity worth supporting. She raised over $40,000 for the cardiac care unit at Sick Kids. "I knew that lots of people were giving up their money to support me and support the kids. It really helped that, like, that many people actually thought I could do it."

On Friday, August 5th, the swim was scheduled to leave Queen's Royal Beach Park in Niagara-on-the-Lake at 7:00 p.m. In the hours leading up to the departure, Lake Ontario wasn't looking conducive to a crossing. Boats were sent out to see what it looked like further out into the Lake and the decision was made to wait. Her swim master, Colleen Shields, said they needed to leave earlier because a storm was expected later the following afternoon. The time was advanced to 4:00 p.m. At the beach the waves rolling on the Lake from the east were big enough that the start was put back to 7:00 p.m. The waves kept rolling. Colleen had already spelled it out: the waves were coming at them from Kingston, broadside and about 1.5 metres high. Also, that Rebekah needed to know that there was a good chance that she would be pulled out. Rebekah went to consult with her parents. Colleen was close to calling the swim off. She says, however, that the Lake was "within the limits of going." It's difficult to swim with winds out of the east. "We go," she told Rebekah and her crew, "but we go knowing these things. You never know what the Lake will do."

Rebekah had completed her trial swim in two metre waves, but at the time Colleen had warned the Boscariols that the crossing wouldn't happen if Lake Ontario served up waves like that. For swimmers, bodies of water call out and tell them to come in. "I felt like we needed to at least try it," Rebekah says. She had another window, a just-in-case date set for August 21, 2011. Still, there were no guarantees. So, she started swimming in the waves. "I take waves pretty easily. I didn't mind it." She entered the Lake at 8:30 p.m.

First the waves ... then her support boats began to break down. She started out with five. One of the smaller Zodiacs died right off the start, so the swim started with four boats. During the night, another small Zodiac broke down. The Zodiacs do the running back and forth to ferry food and crew. With two boats down, the crew was unable to switch around regularly. A boat had to remain beside Rebekah to ensure someone was still watching the swimmer out there in the dark in the middle of Lake Ontario. "They could never leave me. It was really confusing but the crew did a good job," she recalls. She could see the blaze of lights from the boats. She knew her crew was trying to do everything as safely as possible. Her pacers hopped in after six hours, jumping off the sailboat and swimming back to meet her. "It was confusing, but it worked," she laughs. She tried not to let any confusion or breakdowns affect her. "I didn't know exactly what had happened but I knew that we were out a boat and the other boat was having to make all these detours and keep me safe, as well as everybody else."

Colleen was strict, Rebekah says. "I decided to try it because I knew that if she didn't think I could do it, she would have said, no, we're not leaving." Rebekah felt that if Colleen was giving her the choice, she must have some hope that Rebekah could still swim in the waves.

For Colleen, she thinks perhaps the swim should have been pulled. They were short on boats; the forecast wasn't great. And yet, there were other factors favouring an attempt: Rebekah was very aware, she says; Colleen trusted her own boat driver Tomas implicitly, and they had the two sailboats. The crew was solid.

Even a veteran lake crosser like Colleen can learn out on Lake Ontario. The weather settled down. Some swim masters would have pulled the swim when the boats broke down. Colleen made a judgement call based on the situation. Everybody was manoeuvring safely. Rebekah was safe. "I was safe so she didn't cancel. That was really nice of her," Rebekah laughs.

The worst part of the crossing came as the swim neared Toronto. It looks really close, Rebekah says. "But you're not really moving." The Humber current acts like a barrier to cross and it's still pretty far out from the city. All the pacers went in with Rebekah. The current was so strong the team went from swimming three to four kilometres per hour to 600 metres an hour—and then it seemed like they had actually stopped moving forward. "My dad was going crazy. Everyone was cheering us on so it was like we were almost there, but we weren't."

Rebekah had no idea how long it took to clear the current, only that she just kept swimming. One of her boat drivers said it was the strongest current he had seen. Training in the waves on Lake Simcoe with her father had also helped. Once their kayak had dumped and she had swum back, towing the kayak and her father.

When she touched shore at Marilyn Bell Park in Toronto, she was oh, so close to Cindy Nicholas' time, just 23 minutes, 15 seconds off over the 51 kilometres. "I was happy with it considering the waves and the current and everything." She hadn't set out to break Cindy's record. Still, in the heart of the night she was going so fast the record had entered her mind. In training the thought of the record, of perhaps even touching and breaking it, resetting a record nearly as ancient as Great Lakes swimming, lingered in her mind. She didn't pay attention to it because she just wanted to swim the Lake. "I just wanted to be able to finish it."

Besides, so many people try to swim Lake Ontario and it doesn't happen. Rebekah was happy she was able to complete the Lake on her first crack. "Things happened to me, too, and I was able to push through it and that was really great."

Colleen says Rebekah was swimming about four kilometres per hour. Then that torrid pace hit the walls of the Humber River current. Past Toronto Island, Rebekah's pace picked back up. And to think that it was almost all pulled amid the waves. "She was swimming really well. I just wanted to see how it would go," Colleen mused. "She was never once in danger."

Colleen didn't know Rebekah was that quick. Speed can be irrelevant if Lake Ontario isn't calm. The forecast hadn't been in their favour. Then Lake Ontario sighed its last wave. Colleen reads from her swim master's report: "two to three foot waves at 8:30 p.m., for the launch; then calm from 11:00 p.m. to about 1:40 a.m. Later, more one to two foot waves from the east, then waves settling to half a foot and finally to nothing." The Humber River current stopped the record-smashing aspect of the swim but Rebekah never varied from the line, Colleen says. "Her stroke rate was 60-64 per minute. Oh, to be 17 again," Colleen laughs.

Rebekah's swim raised over $40,000 and garnered a heap of deserving media attention. And why not: it was summer, it was a swim on a long holiday weekend over a truly Great Lake. Then for Rebekah it was on to shedding the ten pounds she had gained, just in case, following her nutritionist's suggestion. She increased her food intake in July, ate more chocolate, drank juice instead of water: "Everything the opposite of what a nutritionist should tell you," she laughs.

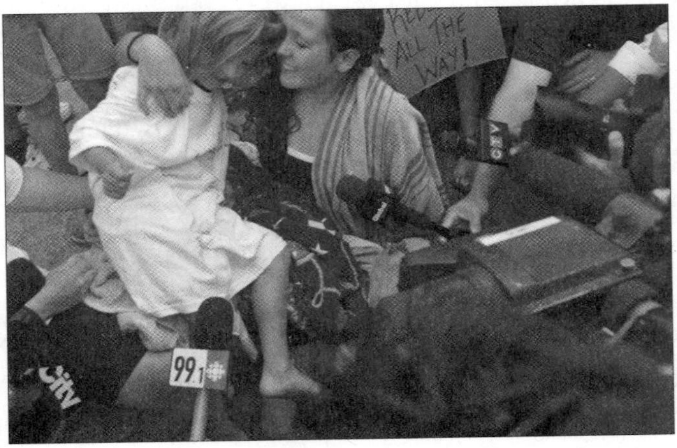

Rebekah Boscariol and her sister Sophia, at the finish. Photo © 2011 Tommie Sue Montgomery.

Christine Arsenault, Lake Ontario, 2011

Christine Arsenault's perspective on Lake Ontario was about the finish, the rocks, the weeds, the physical aspect of touching the other side. Two weeks before she crossed Lake Ontario in 2011, Christine wanted to get a handle on the wall at the finish on the Toronto waterfront. The social worker from St. Catharine's had come to practise the finish of her crossing. She slipped into the finish area at Marilyn Bell Park in Toronto with Miguel Vadillo, who had swum across in 2010. Christine needed to know what she would be swimming towards, right down to the wave of the algae on the rocks.

In 2011 Christine was one of only two swimmers to complete the traditional Lake Ontario crossing from Niagara-on-the-Lake to Toronto. She swam the 51 kilometres August 8th-9th in 22 hours, 22 minutes, with a titanium plate holding her collarbone together and a summer storm rolling in behind her.

Open-water swimming had been her passion for years as a swimmer, and then as waterfront staff at a swim camp in the Muskoka region of Ontario. A Lake Ontario crossing had lingered in her mind since she had watched Vicki Keith's marathon swims across all five Great Lakes in 1988.

In 1998 Christine cycled across Canada. Upon her return she met with Vicki who, at that time, was still living in Toronto. Vicki is open to anyone who wants help or direction in open-water swimming. Christine talked with her and decided to start training seriously about a year later. Three weeks into training she learned why she was so tired: she was actually pregnant with her daughter, Trinity; Michaela followed two years later. Christine went back to school and that was it for her Lake Ontario aspirations, not to mention her physique. She had gained weight; in 2009 she had to lose a startling 160 pounds from her six-foot frame.

What didn't help either were the curves life was tossing her family. There was the weight. She was feeling depressed after emerging from "probably one of the worst, horrible, yucky court experiences." The divorce and subsequent court battles "left us a bit of a mess." She went back to the water with no intentions and no grand design to swim Lake Ontario; she needed to reclaim her life.

With the training, however, came speed. Then she began to wonder if she could swim the Lake. She began to investigate the possibility. "Of course no one took me seriously; I'm not sure if I took myself seriously." Still, she was capable and putting in the training. She made an 18-month training plan and at Christmas 2009 decided to go for it. Her daughters were on board and joined their own swim programs. "We swam that big hurt in our lives away and we worked towards a place of healing. It was an interesting way to deal with such a big hurt but we did it," she adds, laughing. She focused her swim on raising funds and awareness for the Welland International Flatwater Centre and ultimately raised $8,000 for the centre on the old Welland Canal.

For Christine, when a swimmer reaches the start line for a Great Lake crossing, with his or her training intact, then that swim is already a success. In 2010, she wiped out on her bike, nearly taking her swimming with her. She broke her collarbone and had a pin inserted. She would see the Toronto Blue Jays trainer regularly to get herself to the start of the swim. He would thaw her shoulder capsule every week.

Her shoulder issues left her cautious about her speed; mentally that hesitation was difficult. One month before the swim she took a shot of cortisone to help get her through. And then she was there: standing on the beachfront in Niagara on August 8th, layered in grease and sunscreen. She had cleared that hurdle at least. At 12:10 p.m. she departed.

The weather window was tricky. While it had been nearly ideal over August 5th-6th for Rebekah Boscariol's crossing, once the waves calm down Lake Ontario only offers so much time before, inevitably, something blows up again.

For Christine, then 35, the first battle came after dark when a bout of nausea hit her hard and nearly ended the swim. She threw up for much of the night, well into the wee hours of the morning. With medication and ultimately food back in her stomach, she was able to get it under control; her energy returned just in time for the storm's advance party of wind and waves.

Her swim master Shaun Chisholm, who had crossed in 2008, told her she had to get a move on, that weather was approaching. She wondered if her crew even thought she would finish. "I didn't endure that night not to finish this. I don't care what we swim in. We're finishing this. That was an important moment for me." She swam into Toronto over waves up to 1.5 metres rolling in with her.

And then there it was: the end. Throughout the swim, the waves, the vomiting, she had kept a picture in her mind of what touching the wall would look like just beneath the waterline at Marilyn Bell Park. "I knew what I was swimming towards. You don't see anything beneath the surface the entire time." As she rounded the breakwall she could see the algae on the rocks—there it was: "and oh my goodness that picture had been in my head for 22 hours. I finally hit it." Overcome, she hugged Trinity and Michaela. Later that day heavy weather settled in on southern Ontario, dropping 47 mm of rain on nearby Hamilton; cars to the north in Vaughan were up to their door handles in rainwater.

Christine's was the 56th completed crossing since 1954 and Marilyn Bell. Her time of 22 hours, 22 minutes could have been quicker, she reflects. But every swimmer has a unique experience on Lake Ontario. Miguel Vadillo later told her that he could not have completed her swim had he faced the conditions she had. A seasoned athlete and pentathlon coach, he had swum Lake Ontario in 2010 on a glorious flat stretch of Lake that had chilled him to the bone. Christine's weather, coupled with the vomiting, would have been too much to his mind. Really, at the end of the day the time doesn't matter, she says.

Unlike swimmers who do one crossing and that's it, Christine is addicted. "I could do all of them." Shoulder surgery set those aspirations aside for a time. She had two surgeries in 2012. She was training to be a swim master to oversee the crossing attempts with Solo Swims and had joined the Solo Swims board of directors. It's natural for her to be around water. "Swimming the Lake and getting to continue some of the work I did as a teenager, I love it. Becoming a swim master is a small part of the doors Lake Ontario has opened for me."

Opening up Lake Ontario: Over the Vortex and Around the Horseshoe

So if a wider swath of Lake Ontario can deliver a rapid-fire punch of wind and waves, and send forks of lightning dancing, what happens when the Lake narrows?

At the eastern end of Lake Ontario near Kingston and heading out to the St. Lawrence River, ultimately to the Atlantic Ocean, the scuba diving is a descent into Ontario's marine history. Ships were built and wrecked at and near Kingston. In the Marysburgh Vortex some have thought there must be supernatural reasons for the ships sinking. Over the top of that vortex, Vicki Keith and her husband John Munro, as well as the swimmers at Penguins Can Fly in Kingston, have forged their own crossing routes for Lake Ontario.

Meanwhile, at the other end of the lake, in 2006 Rob Kent formed L.O.S.T. (Lake Ontario Swim Team) in Oakville, west of Toronto. Lake Ontario has a glorious marathon swimming history and Rob wanted to insure the Lake would have a bright future in the burgeoning world of open-water swimming. He launched a new route, a 41-kilometre crossing from Port Dalhousie to Oakville—the distance equivalent of a running marathon—spanning the proverbial "horseshoe" in the western end of Lake Ontario. (See the map on page 28, above.)

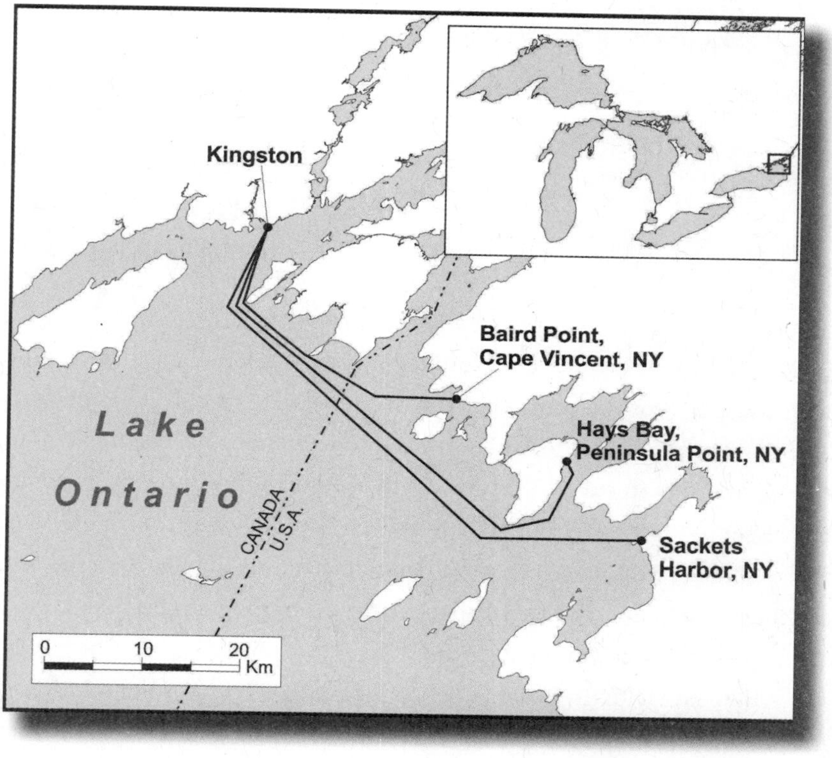

Lake Ontario east end crossing routes, developed by Vicki Keith and John Munro and Penguins Can Fly. Map Credit: L.L. Lariviere—Laurentian University.

John Munro, Lake Erie, 2003; Lake Ontario, 2003

Cutting the grass helps keep John Munro in shape. But the retired police officer isn't trimming any ordinary postage stamp plot of lawn. Along with his wife, world-record marathon swimmer Vicki Keith, John owns 1.6 acres of land on Amherst Island near Kingston, Ontario. The two don't mount ride-on mowers to cut all that grass, either. Instead they mow in tandem. It makes sense for athletes but it's also reflective of how they move off-island, with a shared passion for marathon swimming and their dedication to ensuring the continuation of YMCA Penguins, the swim program for athletes with disabilities that Vicki founded in Kingston.

A detective with the Toronto Police Service for 31 years, John came late to marathon swimming but he more than made his mark before he finally hung up his marathon suit and pitched the empty bucket of lanolin in the recycling. He swam the longest crossing of Lake Ontario—59 kilometres in 2003. He tried the traditional route along Lake Ontario in 1996 but pulled out due to shoulder injuries. After readjusting his stroke, he returned to marathons in 2001 when he and Vicki completed the first swim in tandem at the eastern end of Ontario. The 35-kilometre swim from Hays Bay, Point Peninsula, NY to MacDonald Park in Kingston took them 18 hours, 48 minutes.

In 2003 he named his own Great Lake challenges the Y Knot Marathon, raised over $80,000 for Y Knot Abilities programs in Kingston, and swam Lake Erie and Lake Ontario. He was 52. On July 13, 2003 he swam for 9 hours,

33 minutes to cross the 19.2 kilometres from Crystal Beach, ON to Sturgeon Point, NY. That August, less than one month later, he completed the 59-kilometre swim from Sackets Harbor, NY to Confederation Basin in Kingston in 35 hours, 15 minutes. He was the oldest man to swim the Lake and still holds a record for the longest single crossing of Ontario (Solo Swims).

It wasn't entirely obvious that the man who married Vicki Keith would become a marathon swimmer, but there is something called osmosis. Or, as Vicki says, it may well be contagious. In 1994 they married, but for the longest time John was a multisport athlete, into track, baseball, basketball, cycling. He was preparing for the National Capital marathon in Ottawa in May 1996 when his marathon running career was put on ice. He was working with Carlos Costas, a double-leg amputee.

Back in 1993, with Vicki's coaching, Carlos swam Lake Ontario in support of Variety Village. Carlos had made two attempts to swim the Lake, but lightning and cold water ended both. Finally, on his third attempt on July 23, 1993, he swam Ontario: he was 20 and then the youngest man and the first athlete with a disability to complete the Lake.

Carlos tries all kinds of things, John says. This time it was roller blades. As Carlos started to crash to the floor John made a grab for him, twisting and damaging his knee. John's specialist told him that if he continued running he would need knee surgery. He said to Vicki: "I can't do a marathon run, so why don't I try a swim?" Other than paddling around in the water, he wasn't a swimmer. He'd be with Vicki in the pool where "She'd do four laps to my one sort of thing because I hadn't done any swimming in years." He paced her on a couple of her swims. "But I hadn't thought much at that particular point about taking swimming seriously until the opportunity came."

In 1996 he attempted to swim from Niagara-on-the-Lake to Toronto and came within five kilometres of the Toronto shore before the pain in his left shoulder forced him out. Swimming in excruciating pain, he had torn his rotor cuff; the bloody bruising was visible under his skin. On top of all that he was seasick. He was trying to ignore everything until he feared he was at the point of "doing unbelievable damage." He told his crew he had to get out, that they would return another day. "It's one of those things you don't have that much control over. Health comes first. I was disappointed, but not overly disappointed. It's just one of those things that you have to deal with."

Over the two years it took to heal the injury, he and Vicki began to reconfigure his freestyle. Somewhere along the line of the stroke cycle from entry to exit, "it was a little bit wonky," he says. They figured he was pulling too hard and applying too much pressure on his shoulder. They adjusted his stroke, included more bent arm recovery with a more effective finish to reduce excessive pressure on his shoulder.

With the shoulder and stroke back in working order, he began designing another crossing attempt, this time in tandem with Vicki. Their tandem was not meant as a competition between them but first a fundraiser and as a means of putting John back into marathon swimming. They were raising money for their new program, Y Knot Abilities, and needed sport wheelchairs so their athletes could do their dryland training. Their first date of departure was postponed when they looked out across the water to see the waves on Lake Ontario rising higher than a sailboat. They eventually departed August 25th and completed the swim in 18 hours, 48 minutes. They raised about $5,000.

In 2003 John took on his own challenges to raise more money for Y Knot. He started with a trial swim in preparation for Lake Erie by swimming 6.6 kilometres on July 1st, becoming the first person to complete the crossing from Bath to Amherst Island. On July 13th he entered Lake Erie for a solid, fast swim. The Lake threw its standard choppy waves at him. "Getting a breath sometimes, I'd swallow a good part of Lake Erie. Other than that, it was a good swim." His time was reasonable considering his age and the weather. "Obviously there're people who've been across who are a lot faster swimming south to north. A lot of that has to do with weather conditions. I wasn't intending to set any records." He was out to ensure he passed his trial swim, thereby qualifying for the "big crossing" of Lake Ontario, from Sackets Harbor to Kingston which would ultimately go August 12th-13th.

With an eye to the sky that August the crossing team made the final preparations, with thunderstorms looming and black clouds forming in the south, just behind them. The team chatted on the dock; John wasn't sure about going. Thunder and lightning will stop a crossing attempt in its tracks, for obvious reasons. Would this storm come north with them? But Bob Boucher, his boat captain, is a veteran sailor on Lake Ontario who also teaches sailing. He predicted that the storm would stay on land. "I trusted him and off we went."

Luck is as much a factor in Great Lakes swimming as anything else and John was lucky. There were actually three thunderstorms around him but not one factored into the swim: behind him in New York, ahead in Kingston, and off in the east. He didn't see that storm forming as he swam up and down over metre-high waves. Vicki wasn't about to tell him either. "There was no safety issue there. It was amazing that I had the opportunity to get across without being pulled out for thunderstorms."

Still, Lake Ontario did its thing, growing rough towards the end of the swim. The support kayak struggled in the waves and smacked into him. His left shoulder began to protest. "I thought, 'Oh boy. We're not going through this again.'"

He told Vicki he was having trouble. She asked him to try a face-in dog-paddle. The drill stretched out his strokes and opened his shoulders as he stroked dog-paddle for 15, perhaps 20, minutes across Lake Ontario.

Perhaps the toughest challenge had been the doubters about John's crossing attempt. It was a huge swim for anyone, let alone an "ancient" 52-year old. There seemed to be a negative twist to the comments: Did he really think he could do that? Yes, in fact, he did. He had done the training; he was mentally prepared. "Knowing that I had great support and fantastic coaching I wasn't really concerned about it at all." It was funny to John that, amid the doubting, he also captured the imagination of people around Kingston. His was going to be a historic, record-breaking swim. People in Kingston followed the swim stroke by stroke into shore and came down to greet him. "When I got into shore I couldn't believe the amount of people." They were sitting on their boats, hanging off the balconies on condos nearby. He could hear them. He commented to someone that it was all totally overwhelming. "I couldn't believe that many people had come to see an old guy swim," he laughs.

Perhaps 52 isn't that old but coupled with that was the concrete fact of the distance of 59 kilometres and that until you're actually out there, with a crew, it's tough to get the mind around what goes into a marathon swim: "They just couldn't imagine that's possible," he says. It was the longest single crossing of Lake Ontario.

And then John was done with marathon swimming. He thought about another attempt at the traditional crossing to Toronto. He had come so close the first time. But, he wondered if he wanted to put the training into it. He would think about it "a number of times but I've never taken it seriously." People move onto other things, he reflects. He found other ways to stay active, running... and all that grass needs cutting.

Vicki and John also became swim masters with Solo Swims. John oversaw several swims, including Susanne Welbanks' 2010 crossing of Lake Ontario and Ashley Cowan in 2001 on Lake Erie, as well as Natalie Lambert's attempts on the traditional route of Lake Ontario. When he speaks to aspiring crossers he's curious: what captures their imagination, what's their motivation. "It's the 'why' that's crucial; having them understand what's involved in a swim, not only physically, but mentally and emotionally too," he says. He and Vicki like to spend a lot of time talking with the swimmers, getting a feeling for why they really want to do it, which usually boils down to simply the challenge of the attempt. Heading into a Lake crossing, swimmers need to know there's a serious amount of wear and tear on the body. "It's something that they can do if they are willing to put the time and effort and training into it. There are wonderful personal rewards for wanting to do something like that."

Lake Ontario is one of the most difficult marathon swims in the world, he adds. "For people to take on that challenge is really quite something to my mind. The other thing you have to take into consideration is the age of the person doing it and their maturity level." For John it's one thing to say you'd like to swim because somebody else did it. "But you have to be so careful with young people when they're focused on doing a swim like that."

Inevitably a crossing of Lake Ontario will see the swimmer passing through the night; when he started John was concerned about swimming "in the black in the dark" and getting lost. He practised at night to work through the fear but that didn't stop him from wondering about being lost on the Lake and never found. Lake Ontario is like being in the ocean, he says.

Still, there have been times out at night on Lake Ontario when it was never really dark. There was the spin and twist of the Northern Lights over Susanne Welbank's 2010 swim: "The sky was bright. With that light over the water I had no concerns at all and of course she had decent weather too."

For John, everyone trains really hard for these crossings; then the mental challenge begins as the swim starts. Handling waves, seasickness, and really cold water is as much psychological as physical. Susanne finished her crossing in 2010 in very cold water, he says. "Swimmers, in order to deal with it, they complain and complain. But they stay in; they don't want to quit. You just press on with whatever you have to deal with until you get to the other side."

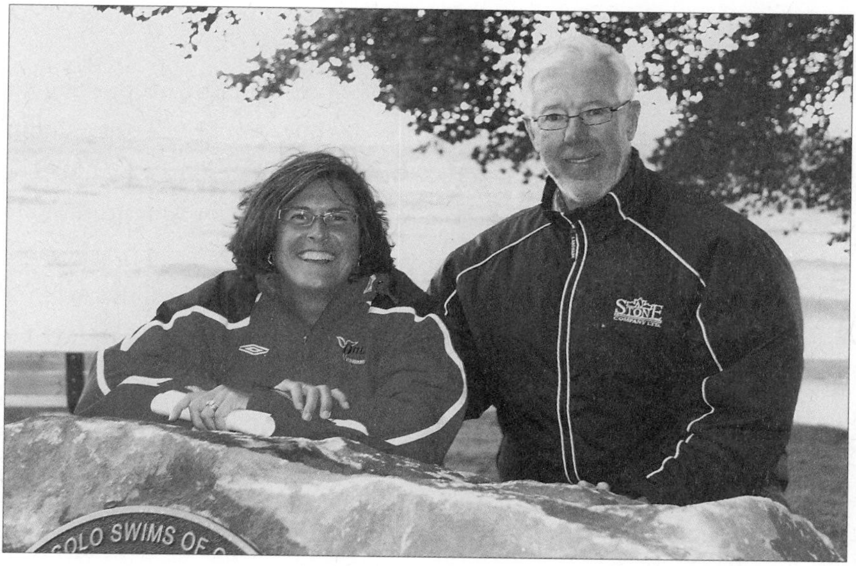

John Munro and Vicki Keith at the unveiling of the Solo Swims plaque at Niagrara-on-the-Lake, October 1, 2011. Photo courtesy Laura E. Young.

Jenna Lambert, Lake Ontario, 2006

Jenna Lambert's trip across Lake Ontario was just that, pressing on until she reached the other side. And yet, her crossing was only the beginning of her story. Over July 18-19, 2006, Jenna swam 33 kilometres from Baird Point, NY to Lake Ontario Park in Kingston, raising $210,000 for Kingston Family YMCA's Y Penguins and a new pool as part of the YMCA expansion. She became the first Canadian woman with a disability to swim across Lake Ontario.

A member of Team Canada since 2009, Jenna Lambert qualified for the 2011 Pan American Games in Mexico and is training for the Canadian Paralympic Swim team for the 2016 Paralympics in Rio de Janeiro, Brazil.

Jenna was an original member of the Kingston Y Penguins, part of the Y Knot Abilities program which Vicki Keith had founded. When she started swimming with Vicki and the Penguins as a ten year old, she had no intention of swimming across Lake Ontario. Then she met Vicki. "Vicki is an incredible woman and a fantastic coach. She has done amazing things for dozens of wonderful kids. Kids with stories just like mine. She helped me see the potential in myself, to reach for success in a way I didn't even know was possible."

The cerebral palsy Jenna was born with affects her swimming from the waist down: she doesn't use her legs to swim. Her muscles are tight and her coordination is off. CP makes for a complex Paralympic classification: there are 14 levels and each depends on that athlete's ability level. Jenna is a level six competing against other swimmers with CP and people with dwarfism, spinal bifida, and various other disabilities. Compared to Olympic swimmers with their spinning arms, her rotation speed is much slower. She developed the core strength to keep her body stable and balanced and streamlined in the water.

In 2001 the Lamberts connected with Vicki Keith at Merrywood Easter Seals Camp which is for families with kids with physical disabilities. Vicki gave a presentation at the camp; afterwards the Lamberts checked out the Kingston Y Penguins with Jenna and her younger sister Natalie. They loved the program and were members of this early pod, swimming in a 23 metre, 3-lane pool with five other athletes, and they loved it.

In the pool, Jenna could swim for hours and not get tired. It was all so different from life on land. About two years into her competitive swimming career, her passion for distance swimming was unearthed. It was also a case of thinking bigger. They swam in their tiny pool at the original Kingston YMCA. It was stroke, stroke turn, stroke turn, like swimming in a hotel pool. They needed more space; the team was also growing. Occasionally Vicki Keith comes out of retirement but it has to be for a truly great cause. Raising funds for a new pool in 2005 was such a cause. She swam 80 kilometres of butterfly to fundraise. The Lamberts went out to the Lake to cheer her on.

During that swim Jenna became convinced that she, similarly, could swim and support the kids who needed the pool space. "For me, God opened all the doors. He put the desire in my heart to do something that would benefit my friends and the people I watch get in the water every day and work their butts off. The swim was worth every minute of it."

After Vicki finished, she and Jenna discussed the possibility of completing a marathon swim, but Jenna was 14. Vicki told her they'd chat when she was 15. The following year when her 15th birthday rolled around, Jenna said: "So, coach what you think?"

And from there, she ramped up her distance; swimming 12 hours straight in a 24-hour relay for her first significant long swim. The trial was a 10-kilometre swim off Amherst Island. Jenna was blissfully unaware of what a marathon crossing entailed. She was 15, and she was going to swim and raise money for a new pool with the support of the city of Kingston. "They saw a need and they were so willing to support it. It was all over the radio and the TV; without people to say this is a worthwhile cause it wouldn't have happened."

She had hoped the swim would raise maybe a maximum of $100,000. That was her swim master John Munro's estimate. To a 15-year-old, it was all a lot of money and she would be happy to get half of that. The final tally came to $210,000. "I'm so thankful because every day that pool benefits people of the community. I feel so blessed."

On July 18th she stood on the shores of Lake Ontario at Baird Point, NY thinking, wow, this is going to be exciting. "I didn't honestly know what I had gotten myself into at that point, you know, looking at the water. You don't really understand how far it is until you get to the other side." Vicki had thought the swim might take 24 hours, but when the day passed she was still far from Kingston. At 11:56 a.m., she was nearing Simcoe Island, exhausted from battling the currents and wind, sleep deprived, and with every wave overwhelming her with the magnitude of the Lake. She was neither moving forward nor backward. She never thought of quitting; it was more like, "Holy, what I am still doing in the Lake?"

Vicki leaned in for a late-swim pep talk, eyeballing her swimmer, and laying out the options: touch land at nearby Simcoe Island. Swim and finish. Or she could pull out. "And Vicki is wonderful in that she understands where I am as a person and who I am. She knew her words would get in touch with my stubborn side, and encourage me to keep going."

Jenna interpreted this chat as "you want to give up?" She eyeballed Vicki back and told her she wasn't quitting. Vicki hopped in to swim a couple of kilometres beside her. "It was the fastest two k of my whole marathon. But I was in a mental struggle of "I'm so tired," and that was hard to shake. I needed the mental encouragement to get over that blockade." Vicki even encouraged Jenna by swimming without using her own legs.

Jenna cleared the rock wall into the beach in Kingston, leaving about 400 metres remaining. Vicki gave her the signal and with 25 metres to go Jenna finished in a blaze of butterfly. For Jenna, butterfly wasn't hot-dogging; it was a way of proving to herself that she had something left. "It says to my body and my brain, 'You know what? You gave it everything you had and you still could have gone on.' To me that's a really important message because that says nothing is impossible." She clambered back onto land at 6:44 p.m.

As a youngster Jenna was encouraged from the get-go to do everything. She joined neighbourhood hockey games, riding a sledge on the ice pond. Her parents, Christine and Ron, made modifications so she could play. She would also walk around the house. She used a walker on the pool deck. Two years after starting with the swim team, she had enough mobility, strength, and stubbornness to get rid of her walker. She switched to forearm crutches.

Although there is no timeframe, she hopes to be completely free of her crutches by her wedding day. Swimming is responsible for her upright state. "I would say swimming, in equal parts with determination, a really strong faith and a lot of prayer, and a heck of a whole lot of hard work has been responsible for the positive changes in my mobility."

The journey has been incredible, but it wasn't what she expected after a marathon swim. She thought she would swim Lake Ontario and go about her business. "For us it brought a community together. And we have a pool, which is probably the most exciting thing ever."

Jenna (left) and Natalie Lambert. Photo courtesy Laura E. Young.

Natalie Lambert, Lake Ontario, 2007; Lake Erie, 2008, 2009

As Vicki inspired Jenna, so Jenna inspired her younger sister Natalie to try open-water swimming. Natalie Lambert is credited with being the youngest and fastest swimmer to cross the longest Lake Ontario route, the 54 kilometres from Sackets Harbor, NY to Kingston, ON, first swum by John Munro. But when it comes to the traditional, 51-kilometre route from Niagara-on-the-Lake to Toronto's Marilyn Bell Park, Lake Ontario has not been inclined to let Natalie cross. Three times she has attempted to complete this long, tough, cold route. If you were to draw a line following those three swims, it would always stop just shy of Toronto, in a flash of lightning and rolling waves.

On Lake Erie, Natalie has had more luck. On July 6, 2008, at age 14, she set a women's record for butterfly and the women's north-south freestyle record swimming the 19.2 kilometres from Crystal Beach, ON, to Sturgeon Point, NY with a time of 7 hours, 47 minutes, 30 seconds. Six days later, Jade Scognamillo broke the freestyle record by nearly two hours, swimming south to north, instead. The following year, July 9, 2009, Natalie lowered her own time for the swim, completing 19.2 kilometres in 6 hours, 40 minutes, 59 seconds.

Her testing of Lake Ontario began in 2006 when Natalie had hopped in and paced her sister Jenna on the crossing from Baird Point to Kingston. "That was awesome. I was in there for about two and a half hours. It was just outstanding seeing her work so hard for 32 hours and give so much, number one for the Y Knot Abilities Program, and number two just to accomplish a goal she had." After Jenna finished, Natalie wanted to swim Lake Ontario, to make a difference by getting more children involved, but also to see just how far she could push herself.

So here's that magical fence that people cross from just wanting to swim some distance, perhaps across the local lake to a dock, to recognizing the need—and the necessary commitment—to swim across huge bodies of water. If Vicki's 80 kilometre butterfly was the spark, Jenna's swim was the gasoline. "And it just went whoosh!" Natalie laughs. Immediately, in the summer of 2006, she was getting into the water in preparation for a crossing. At 13 years old she was training to be the youngest person to swim Lake Ontario. But a month before she was scheduled to cross, Solo Swims changed their regulations. Swimmers now had to be 14.

Of course she was disappointed. But her commitment never wavered. Swimming for something made the difference. If she had just been planning to swim across Lake Ontario for a record she doesn't think she'd have done it. "Sure you want this. But you're also thinking about why you're doing this above yourself. Having the Y Knot Abilities there, with my main goal being to raise money and awareness for them, well, that made all the difference."

In 2007 her first attempt on Lake Ontario's traditional Niagara-on-the-Lake to Marilyn Bell Park route began on August 7th, less than a week after her 18 kilometre trial, and just a week after her 14th birthday. A nasty east wind blew in from Kingston down to Toronto but it was supposed to diminish. Instead, as the swimmer and her crew neared the halfway point the waves were at least 1.5 metres. She kept swimming but at about 17 hours the waves were hitting 3.5 metres, with a chop on the top. Natalie would swim three strokes, somersault backwards, swim three strokes, and somersault backwards.

One kayak was pulled out. Vicki Keith, who was Natalie's coach, pulled out her own kayak as she could no longer control the craft to stay with Natalie. Vicki hopped into the escort Zodiac with Natalie's father and worked to not only stay with Natalie but keep her eye on her. Natalie was throwing up, unable to hold food down. She swam in that mess for another three hours. She was still completing about 1.3 kilometres an hour. At that rate it would have taken her about eight more hours to complete the crossing. Without eating.

Around the 20-hour mark Vicki and Natalie had a chat. Vicki didn't want to stress Natalie's system with all the vomiting. Nor was the weather safe for the boats. "Vicki is amazing, especially with making decisions like that—to pull. She advises you but she doesn't force anything upon you. She states the facts and helps you make the decision but she does not make the decision for you, unless it's a safety call and then it's the swim master." Natalie got into the Zodiac, then into the larger escort, and that was that. She had swum 43 kilometres, and had only nine left. A similar—so near yet so far—scenario would play out for her on the traditional route twice in 2008.

Undeterred by the setback, Natalie turned her sites to the eastern end of the Lake, and on August 27-28, 2007, just three weeks after the aborted attempt at the west end, she swam 54 kilometres on the new route from Sackets Harbor, NY to Confederation Park in Kingston, a trip that one could drive in under 90 minutes.

Lake Ontario served up one-metre waves but that's relatively flat for the east end of the Lake. Instead the cold proved to be Natalie's biggest challenge as the air temperature dropped to 10C that night. And fatigue set in, forcing her to sleep: she lay on her back, pretending to stretch out her shoulders while she was actually napping. Vicki called from the boat for her to get swimming. Natalie's mother then grabbed a megaphone and began a game of trivia out there in the Lake. That proved more than impetus enough to get her moving and put her head back in the swim.

There was much more to see on this crossing compared to the west end where only the lonely beacon of the CN Tower is visible to swimmers. At the east end of Ontario, islands dotted her route, flickering lights from shore overnight, the sight of land reassuring for the whole crossing. Finishing in a solid 23 hours and 15 minutes of swimming, she couldn't help the adrenaline rush and started swimming butterfly into shore. As she emerged from Lake Ontario on August 28th she was tired but began to reflect that she could do more. "If I could do 54 kilometres, how much more could I swim? What's next?"

The swim raised $50,000 for charity, brought in new swimmers to the team—all benefits she was aiming for with her crossing. And she was listed as the youngest and fastest Lake Ontario swimmer at the time on a course 50 kilometres or longer. She was 27 days past her 14th birthday. "It was amazing. It was such a great experience that it made me want to do that again."

Not so surprising, then, that Natalie put her name forward to cross Lake Ontario on the traditional route in 2007, and twice in 2008, nor that she was back again in 2010, for yet another attempt at Marilyn Bell's crossing. For a Great Lakes swimmer, completing the traditional Ontario route is comparable to the Canadian media hoping for one of the founding six hockey teams in the National Hockey League to win the Stanley Cup. It's all well and good that the "expansion" teams get into the final but just once in awhile we want an original six match-up. It's the same with the traditional route; it's still the first successful crossing, still the one and only for many swimmers. For Natalie, it wasn't to be—yet. In 2010, weather again cancelled her swim, but this time even before she got underway. She was one of five aspirants and one of the three that summer who ran into weather issues. It's such a crap shoot: pick your date on the calendar, book everything and everyone, and take your chances. In July the Lake turned over two days before the swim, dropping an astounding 11 degrees in 12 hours, from a perfect, idyllic 23.3C to a frosty 12.2C. A whole week booked with boats, work, and schedules was sunk. The next time winds of at least 30 knots were predicted from the east. The boats couldn't get to Niagara-on-the-Lake because waves were so big. No Lake swims that summer; "which stank." She competed instead in Lac St. Jean, a world-famous, iconic site of marathon swimming. She also beat her own Lake Ontario trial swim time in an 18-kilometre jaunt along the shore of Amherst Island for a new personal best time of 5 hours, 20 minutes.

All her accomplishments are surely enough to make missing the traditional route on Lake Ontario seem like a hiccup, a minor one at that, in her life story. Still, there was some understandable frustration about the traditional crossing of that Lake. She has kept that in check by focusing on the positive aspects, including the fundraising for the Y Knot Abilities program. "That's a huge part, having a cause greater than yourself so you're not always relying on yourself and not focusing on the records. Having world records is nice but it's not the be all and end all."

Her Christian faith remains strong and a vital support. "I know everything happens for a reason. Even if we don't really understand that reason. Or, if we get frustrated that He can see the bigger picture and that He does have a bigger plan than we can ever imagine."

For Vicki Keith, Natalie's long-time coach, the word failure does not factor into the equation, even regarding the traditional crossing. "She has been so focused on that and has had such lousy luck." She *has* crossed Lake Ontario, Vicki says. She was the youngest to cross Erie, doing butterfly to set a speed record. On the traditional route she's simply had bad luck.

In 2010, despite her disappointment with the traditional crossing, Natalie still wanted to fit in a long swim, rewarding herself for all her training. She undertook to swim 59.5 kilometres from Belleville to Bath along the shore of Lake Ontario towards Kingston. It was one of the most challenging swims she had ever taken on but the challenge came from the mental effort to get through it. The water was warm this time around but this wasn't her goal. She hit a strong current and remained in place for about three hours she estimates. "It was the swim I've learned the most from," she says. At one point she was frustrated and it was obvious her mind was not in the water. She popped her head up to look around and Vicki was looking at her. "You need to get your head back in this," Vicki told her.

So Natalie prayed and reminded herself that she loved to swim. "I knew I was in this water for a reason, so I kept swimming." And then the sun rose, revealing the best part of any marathon swim.

And how does she feels about the traditional route on Lake Ontario? "One day..."

Melanie Price, Lake Ontario, 2011

On August 12, 2011, Melanie Price, then 38, completed the first-ever swim of the western end of Lake Ontario, from Port Dalhousie Lakeside Park to Wilder Park, Oakville, for 41.6 kilometres and 18 hours, 9 minutes, 24 seconds of swimming. She raised over $3,500 for Lake Ontario Waterkeepers (LOW). "People were very shocked when I said I was swimming in the Lake," she recalls. Growing up in the 1970s in Hamilton, the steel city along Lake Ontario's southwest corner with its own supposedly dirty harbour, she remembers how people went to the beach but there was no way anyone would go into the Lake.

But years later she was swimming in Lake Ontario and she wasn't sick. In fact it was in a smaller lake that she picked up swimmer's itch parasites. Still, people's concepts of Lake Ontario's environmental status intrigued her. She knew Ontario's water quality had improved significantly from its highly polluted days in the 1960s and 1970s, but also knew that popular belief to the contrary was hard to change. "I wanted to show that it was better." By getting in the Lake she was demonstrating her belief that the water quality was better and hoping her action would entice others to get in, thus making the water even better. Simply stated, her goal was to put the word Great back into the Lake—for Ontario to be a Great Lake in more than name only. "People don't necessarily think of Lake Ontario as a great place, as a Great Lake."

After several years on the busy triathlon circuit she was looking for some new challenges. In 2010, inspired by both the athletes she trained with and her love of open water swimming, she began toying with the idea of swimming Ontario. To see what it was really like out there she joined the crew supporting Miguel Vadillo on his crossing. Miguel's picture-perfect conditions helped finalize her decision.

As a member of the masters team in Oakville, the ironically named L.O.S.T.—Lake Ontario Swim Team—she opted for the new west end route that Solo Swims will also supervise and record. Although her crossing was not along the traditional route of Marilyn Bell and Vicki Keith, the further west side of Ontario—straight across the mouth of the horseshoe—meant something to Melanie. It was here that she trained, indulging her passion for open-water swimming. "It had a hometown advantage feel. Most of my crew lives around the area. That was helpful as well. It was convenient. All those things came into play."

The route itself is about 10 kilometres shorter than the traditional but, this being Ontario, shorter never means easier. The Great Lake's western end served up its usual banquet of challenges, unique to Melanie's swim. Since she was swimming closer to shore, the swirling currents played as much a role as her crew. Water temperature changes in big ways from day to day. "My swim wasn't easy. Every swim is different. I don't think the destination makes or breaks the swim. I think you can get a hard swim into Toronto one day and not the next, or vice versa. The neat thing about swimming in the Lake regularly, which is what we do with L.O.S.T., is you see all the differences. It's very temperamental."

She trained for one year, balancing her family, coaching, and work—pretty much every day was the Lake, the Lake, and the Lake. And then, at midnight on August 12th, greased in stinky layers of lanolin, sunscreen and Rub A535, Melanie left Port Dalhousie, swimming out into the flashlights from her support boats. A full moon lit the Lake, making for a beautiful night "for a little swim," she says. The waves were more than she was used to, however. After four hours she was calling for legal pain medication to help alleviate the strain in her back and neck from looking up to sight and breathe in the waves.

As the swim moved into daylight Melanie was unsure of how far she had come. There were no landmarks to gauge; she couldn't wear a watch as it's seen as a pacing tool in open water swimming and can give an unfair advantage, somehow. Eventually her crew told her when she had gone over halfway. But the waiting to be told she had passed the 20-kilometre mark drained any positive effect she had been seeking.

With her pacers looping through their first rotation, Melanie joked with her crew that they should turn their heads when her husband Bill Johnson, the last in the rotation, hopped in the Lake to swim beside her. They might indeed kiss out there, after all.

The rotation of pacers started again. Melanie switched to breaststroke, a more natural stroke for her but the slow pace isn't conducive to making headway in Lake Ontario. Her ankles hurt after the change from freestyle to breaststroke. Her shoulders were beginning to ache. For a time it seemed like she rode a tailwind but the winds shifted back around, once again becoming a headwind, as it would remain for most of the 41.6-kilometre swim.

As the waves picked up Melanie could see the shore but it never seemed to get closer. She realised she was going to struggle to finish, that she was neither strong nor fast enough. She was hungry; her bladder was full but she couldn't pee, a thought that began to wiggle around in her mind. Even with a mere two kilometres to go, she began to feel like quitting was the only option. "It's not like running where you can just walk. If you're being pushed back you're being pushed back," she says.

Time was hard to judge, and was likely different in her mind that what was really happening. It felt long. At one point she was judging the time based on the feeding breaks she was taking every half hour. "In the end I said 'the sun hasn't set; I know it's not 9:00 o'clock.' My team were all in there around me. They helped push me through and keep going." She had heard that Lake crossings can take 21, 22 hours to complete and she resolved to keep going until 21 hours had passed. Then she figured they could all re-evaluate her situation.

Since she seemed to be going nowhere, or worse, backwards, her swim master Colleen Shields made the call. Colleen figures that in terms of completed crossings, the swim master makes a lot of calls that will make a swim successful. The currents on that far western side of Lake Ontario had drifted

Melanie east, off her planned course. "She couldn't get back to where she was supposed to be coming in," Colleen says, "so I decided to take her in where she was. She would land wherever she would land." There's always a caveat though with Colleen. "If Mother Nature is against you it doesn't matter what the swim master does. You're not going to get in."

At least Melanie still had Mother Nature. Colleen directed the crew to land straight in at Wilder Park in Oakville. Fuelled on Reese's peanut butter cups and the support of her pacers, who all hopped into the Lake, she began swimming in to shore. The change in landing spot didn't disappoint her because she sees change as part of the experience of open-water swimming, a catch-all many swimmers use. Oh, that's part of swimming open water, they'll say. Instead, Melanie was thinking about how much Bill and their daughters Cadence and Dahlia meant to her, how all winter her training for the Lake had consumed their lives. She thought about how much her supporters on shore and in the boats meant to her. Then she could see the shore, the trees, her crew on shore, some in the crossing's official orange t-shirts. At 6:09 p.m., Melanie touched the rocky shore. Touching and clutching the rock on shore in Oakville was the moment.

For Melanie, it was great to catch up with her support team on land. She loved hearing the stories after her crossing, imagining the frantic run of her crew on shore when they caught word that the landing spot was changing. People drove and ran, some jumping through gardens to get to her in time for the finish. At the hospital Melanie met a friend who was getting his own medical treatment after her swim. He had been running along watching the Lake when he ran into a sign; he needed eight staples to close the gash in his head. "It was a fantastic experience being in the Lake, with my crew. They really were important. They don't get enough credit for sure."

Melanie took a beating in the Lake, too, for all that she was swimming for Lake Ontario Waterkeepers and to draw attention to the greatness of the Lake. She damaged her rotator cuffs, in particular on her left side, and would not swim for months after the crossing. She even wondered if she would ever be able to swim again. Out on the Lake she hadn't been able to ignore what might be happening in her shoulders, and questioned whether wrecking them would be worth it. No, she had decided, even if she did "get" the Lake. Yet as her shoulder healed in the months after the swim, she was able to use her injury as a lesson in how to learn to do other sports. "It's probably worth it, especially if you recover," she laughs.

The sense of "getting" the Lake seems even more powerful to Melanie when she takes into account all the other factors she had to negotiate in preparation for the crossing: family, work, coaching novice swimmers at the Hamilton Aquatic Club. "If I had had all the time in the world it wouldn't seem as big an accomplishment."

In fact, because "getting" the Lake depends on so many variables in open-water swimming, Melanie feels that just the serious attempt is the central achievement. "It's not just up to the person. It's so much Mother Nature. There's so much that can come into play. If you go for it, take the risk, if you put in the time and the work, then whether you get across or not you're successful in that you gave it your best shot."

Madhu Nagaraja, Lake Ontario, 2012

Having swum the English Channel, Madhu Nagaraja knew he could manage 13 hours of open-water swimming. Beyond that, all was unknown. Kicking off Solo Swims Great Lakes swimming in 2012, a short volatile season, Madhu Nagaraja, then 42, took advantage of some of the warmest temperatures Lake Ontario can offer. In relatively balmy 23.3C waters, the father of two swam from Lakeside Park Port Dalhousie to Coronation Park, in Oakville on July 28-29, 2012.

The 41.3 kilometre-crossing took 24 hours, 26 minutes, much longer than he had anticipated. Which meant that fewer than 12 hours after he completed the crossing, the computer programmer was back to work to meet a tight deadline. His boss told him he could take at least half a day off, but since he wasn't alone on this project Madhu had to complete his part of the assignment for a colleague who needed it by the end of the day. Then he headed out to party.

For Madhu, these marathons aren't about crossing things off a bucket list. Being with a team is the point; that's the fun part of any ultra-marathon. "I had the best crew. I'm lucky to hang with fantastic human beings who are great professionals in what they do. They are beautiful human beings. I looked for these personalities."

Madhu hadn't grown up dreaming about one day swimming a Great Lake or the English Channel. He was a swimmer, though, in Mysore and Bangalore. He had read about people of India who had completed the Channel, and was aware of the challenges swimmers go through on their open-water swims. As a young professional in California, though, he was not thinking about swimming, or his health—he was focused on work. Eventually, to get back into shape, he joined a master's swim club and entered his first open-water race, a mere one-mile jaunt across Spring Lake, California in May 2003. For Madhu this swim would take more mental preparation than any other that would follow.

About two weeks before the race he'd seen the film *Lake Placid,* which features a man-eating crocodile on the prowl in the Lake. In Spring Lake that day he was raw, with no clue how to navigate in open water. The water temperature was a numbing 18.3C. On top of all that the lake was full of weeds, tickling an over-active imagination. Every time a weed touched him, he'd freak out. "It was not a pretty swim," he says.

Since the monster never appeared to eat him in Spring Lake, he graduated to longer open-water races and then made a key connection. Later in 2003 he met Carol Sing, who in 1999 at age 57 became the oldest woman to cross the English Channel. "It was just matter of fact to her. I was awestruck when I spoke with her. It's that inner challenge to figure out what I can do. Is it something I can achieve, fighting against the odds and things I can't control?"

The English Channel became his secret goal. "It was difficult to explain that to my wife," he laughs (as wives and husbands around the world understand). He trained for a year with the support of his club: a special lane was set aside; he was given pool access at odd times. On one morning he needed to get in for 4:00 a.m. to complete a 20 kilometre trial swim. "The camaraderie, the team spirit are the little things that make these big events happen."

After one practice, Madhu took up the challenge of a teammate to race some butterfly. They did 10 x 50 metre fly sets and on the 10th and final set Madhu pinched his muscle in his shoulder and tore tissue. It was a hard lesson. He was training for mileage to complete a crossing of the English Channel, not butterfly sprints. "I was the stupid racer who took the challenge."

Despite a sore shoulder, he headed to England and on August 10, 2004, he stumbled ashore in France, having swum the English Channel in 12 hours, 31 minutes for the 37 kilometre crossing. Shortly after the swim, Madhu and his wife, Dr. Suman Joseph, moved to Toronto, Canada for work.

Through the Ontario masters swimming circuit, Madhu met Bryan Finlay. The conversation between two masters swimmers who love open water, and who had both challenged the English Channel, inevitably led to Great Lakes swimming. It was then a natural extension for Madhu to start thinking about swimming across Lake Ontario. He put his name forward to cross in 2006 but work interfered and forced him to back out. "It was haunting me for awhile."

He turned instead to the dry extreme, the elements of fire and earth, and prepared for the Marathon des Sables (MDS), a 6-day ultra-marathon across the Sahara Desert in Morocco, which he entered in 2010. Passing out, unable to eat any of the food he carried, he finished the 243 kilometre race by surviving on one package of sugar, chewing gum, and water. And then he couldn't drink any more water. "In the desert water is crucial." Too much water is also bad, sucking the sodium out of the system. Then he was throwing up water from all kinds of places on his body. "It wasn't pretty, yeah," he laughs.

Training for MDS had him up at 2:00 a.m., to run in a Canadian winter, but part of the training was figuring out how to fit it in with all the other small things that need to happen every day, he says. "That's one of the powerful lessons that I learned; respect everybody. Of course we all have our moments of stupidity but doing things like this has made me a better person."

Lake Ontario continued to beckon. In 2011, now a father of son Vivek and daughter Meghna, he worked with Christine Arsenault and Melanie Price as they prepared for their successful Lake crossings.

Madhu has said the hardest part of swimming Lake Ontario was the training. He was mindful, working to control what he could by holding several crew meetings, planning his nutrition, working at his weaknesses. Then there was the proverbial, even clichéd mind over matter, 90 percent mental, 10 percent physical. "I've rephrased it as 97 percent mental and 3 percent physical. You need to train hard to achieve that 97 percent mental. Many times we don't know if we have this kind of potential. That's the nice thing about training. The human body is so resilient it can do amazing things."

Finding enough boats to meet Solo Swims safety requirements was a struggle. In the end he opted to charter a boat, a $2,500 cost. Then his Burlington Masters Swim Club held a fundraiser and within a week they had enough money. After all that, as vulnerable as swimmers are at the edge of Lake Ontario, there was sheer relief to fling himself into the water. Once in, the job is easy; for the athlete—it's only about swimming. His crew would need to keep him on track, fed, and encouraged, to watch his mental state.

Madhu and his crew struck out from Port Dalhousie on July 28th at 9:00 p.m. and he struggled from the get-go. In theory Lake Ontario is likely to be calmer at night. The forecast called for winds of eight knots. When the winds began to blow, they registered higher, 10-15 knots. To Madhu, swimming steadily, it really felt like he wasn't going anywhere. Just before 5:00 a.m. he rolled over onto his back and asked his crew for a progress report. Between 10:00 p.m. and 4:30 a.m. he had hardly gone anywhere—13 kilometres.

He analyzed the speed and concluded this wasn't going to happen, or it would take him three days to get across. It was time to pull the plug on the swim. He wanted to have that conversation with his coach Alex McMillan, and tell him he didn't have it in him to keep going for the three days. He wanted to quit. "Alex," Madhu began. Alex interrupted right away and didn't let Madhu finish the sentence. Madhu settled his head back into the Lake and swam on. They would resume this conversation in another two minutes or so. "Alex," he said, and again Alex cut him off. After swimming another 100 strokes: "Alex." Again Alex cut him off.

In the meantime, Madhu was being bombarded, as if Lake Ontario had turned into the wash phase of a machine and was churning him back and forth. And what was up with the moon? He rolled over to look up. The moon, surging, grew nearly full in the sky...then up and set at 2:00 a.m. The winds were racing but the sky was clear. "That's Nature. That's what the Lake is all about. You can only study Mother Nature so much."

For Lake swimmers, sunrise is a moment they've been seeking and longing for over the long dark night. As daylight filled the sky and Madhu paused to experience the sunrise, he was going to convince his team once and for all that this swim wasn't going to happen and he should quit. He planned to tell his wife, parents, friends he'd never swim again, that he'd walk away from marathon swimming—this was it. Done.

Off near the horizon a cargo ship passed by and Madhu worried. They all knew that the lakers churn up cold water from down deep. Here it was; it was happening. How cold could it get? That would end the swim for sure, he thought. But as the sun rose and the freighter cut through his route, the scene blew his mind. "I just kept my head in the water and kept swimming." The daylight brought the pacers into the Lake with him, appearing like dolphins from nowhere.

And then there was joy, in hanging out with his crew. "It was a convergence of positive energy to get me across. I felt beautiful." Then he thinks he could return to the Lake and experience that joy all over again. "Then I stop thinking that way," he laughs.

He came ashore at Coronation Park at 9:26 p.m., 24 hours, 26 minutes, 3 seconds after starting. His crew had been critical to that swim. "My crew held me tightly from the minute I walked into the water until the moment I walked out. It was beautiful." The long hours over the previous months with his physical therapist Giulio Carlin, and the $700 per month it had cost was all worth it. "When I walked out of the swim I could have gone for another 24 hours. I had the energy. I didn't want to do that but I had the physical potential because of this guy. I was fine," Madhu recalls. The next day he was working, driving, carrying one his children.

Although Madhu dedicated his swim to his late aunt Valli Mudaliar who had died of breast cancer in 2010, and to his friend John Hathaway who had died of colon cancer in 2011, he doesn't swim to raise funds for charity. "Many times in life we talk about team work, camaraderie, all the good things that are supposed to be in life, in our workplaces." He wonders if that really happens at work. Could he create that opportunity where an entire team focuses and dedicates itself to one cause? It happened on Lake Ontario for Madhu. "We're against nature, there's only one way to do it—the right way. We all need to be humble. We all need to be good. We all need to be simple, and we all need to work together and create that special energy to get across." Real teamwork happens in barebones places like the Marathon des Sables and the English Channel. "I've read a lot but so far I have not found any one writer or any one athlete who has expressed it. It's beyond the potential of any language. I can't even describe that special feeling we all get. It's a special powerful feeling, believe me. It has taught me a lot about humanity, respecting people."

He would never compare the swims, but the worst of his open-water career was actually his first, thanks to the film *Lake Placid*. "In terms of difficulty, they're all monsters with their own characteristics. You can only get these bodies of water if they let you across. I've always known that." Still, the English Channel didn't punch his ticket across the Lake; it only put him on the shores of Lake Ontario. "These lakes and mountains are out there, standing, challenging you all the time, offering you all kinds of crazy things," he says. "The experience of working with people and with myself, that's the most important thing."

Rob Kent, Lake Ontario, 2012

Rob Kent, the founder of the L.O.S.T. (Lake Ontario Swim Team) route at the far western end of the Lake, also planned hard for his crossing, his crack at his own route coming over August 13-14, 2012. Based on what Rob Kent knew, what he had done, his respect for Lake Ontario, and the team he'd assembled to help with his swim, Rob estimated it would take about 15, maybe 17 hours to swim across Lake Ontario.

The father of three and currency trader from Oakville, Ontario, was a former member of Canada's national swim team and had raced Olympic trials. In 2006, he swam most of the English Channel before being plucked unconscious and bubbling with pulmonary edema. But hey, what an adventure.

In 2010 he redeemed himself in his own mind by finishing the 47-kilometre Manhattan Island Marathon Swim (in the Hudson River) where he learned that one year a swimmer had seen a dead giraffe in the water—and it wasn't the hallucination of the marathon swimmer—and where as he swam someone jumped off one of Manhattan's bridges; he could see the helicopter circling and looking for the body. He'd raced Ironman triathlons, qualified for the Boston Marathon, and run high and dry in Morocco for the Marathon des Sables in 2008. He set out to do his own crossing in 2012, coming in trained and primed after two shorter marathons, in April in Tampa Bay, Florida, and the Swim Around Key West in June 2012, where he was the fastest master.

And, so, well, not that Lake Ontario was going to be easy, but... On

August 13, 2012, Rob, then 47, spent nearly 21 hours swimming across the western end of Lake Ontario. His finish in the pitch dark interrupted a pair of trysting swans, kissing, making a heart shape with their necks. Swans can be aggressive but "at that point I didn't care," he reflects. "I would have taken on a swan to get to shore."

Rob Kent had the fortune and perhaps the frustration of swimming at the same time as the late Victor Davis, the 1984 Olympic champion who dominated breaststroke during his swimming career. In 1986 Rob finished second while Victor competed at the Commonwealth Games. In 1988 Rob raced Olympic trials, didn't qualify for Seoul, went home, and hung up his suit. He was burnt out and would not swim again for 17 years.

Still, he needed to channel his competitive energy. His days of taking a serious run "at being a good athlete" were done. Now sport was about the adventure, about finding cool and interesting things to train for, while not measuring his current self against the ghost of his former. He started running marathons where he had no benchmark and could set personal bests. He got into triathlon—not bothering to train for the swim.

In 2006 he decided to get back into swimming but didn't want to be in the pool. He decided to swim the English Channel. Like marathon running and triathlon, he had no real benchmark for open-water, marathon swimming. It was, he says carefully, big enough that he could potentially fail and not complete the Channel crossing, while having an awesome adventure. "So, I thought what would be cool is I don't know if I could swim the English Channel. That's a big enough challenge that it would be genuinely scary to go and try it." He wasn't out to improve his time: been there, done that. Now sport was supposed to be something fun, followed by a few beers and great stories to tell.

And sure enough he did come home with a great story, about how he was plucked unconscious from the English Channel after swimming 30 of the 34 kilometres towards France. For nearly two weeks Rob and some family and friends had waited out "brutal weather," and with only a day or so remaining their pilot suggested it was swim tomorrow or go home empty-handed. There was a small craft warning the entire time on September 5, 2006, but he managed to swim for 12 hours and get within a few kilometres of France.

As he swam, Rob began to hear gurgling in his chest. This can't be good, he thought. Yet thinking he was close enough to France that he could still make it, he neglected to tell his crew how bad things were. "It kind of went downhill fast from there." Later, he was pulled out suffering from hypothermia and pulmonary edema. "My thing is I like to say that I failed and I like to say that I didn't fail. It bugs me when people can't face up to the fact, that they sugarcoat everything. I'm still old school. I'm not afraid to say I didn't make it."

So on that day in 2006, the English Channel beat him. "Fair enough and move on. It was very disappointing. But I still live in the real world. I have a wife and kids and a real job. This is just something I do because I like the challenge of it. It's not the end of the world."

Ultimately it was about having a great adventure. He worried about getting on the plane in a few hours to fly home. Miraculously, by the time they reached the airport, he was starting to feel better. As he left, the Channel was flat as glass and all crossings that day were successful, he adds. "Yeah, but coulda, shoulda, woulda. It makes me crazy if I ever catch myself doing it. I didn't do it. Fair enough, it sucks, but it is what it is. That's why it's great if you do make it across."

In 2010, he qualified for the Manhattan Island Marathon Swim where he also enjoyed the moment, as they say in sport, and rolled over to swim backstroke as he crossed under the Brooklyn Bridge. He saw and heard helicopters buzz overhead, later learning someone had jumped off the George Washington Bridge. "It's a unique race," he says. The Manhattan swim was redemption for the English Channel.

Living a block from Lake Ontario in Oakville, he would train for cold water in the Lake. People told him he was crazy, that among other things the Lake was too polluted. But that's not what he found. After the English Channel, he returned to the Lake for training, with his triathlon buddies joining him. He incorporated the L.O.S.T. route for people wanting to swim Lake Ontario and watched Melanie Price finish it in 2011, in a time that would be three hours faster than his. He recalls Lake Ontario's open-water history, the crowds watching CNE swim races, Cliff Lumsdon taking home thousands upon thousands of dollars with his victories. Rob wanted that sense of grandeur back for swimming Lake Ontario; he wanted to grow the sport on the Lake.

"I love the adventure of it. I think it's cool if as many people as possible get to experience it." He looked into ways to get boats, to make the crossing less of the "logistical nightmare" it can be for swimmers in Ontario—let alone someone coming from abroad.

"I want to make it more feasible to bring back the nostalgia and glory of open-water swimming in Lake Ontario. There's the triple crown of Marathon swimming: English Channel, Catalina Channel, and MIMS (Manhattan Island Marathon Swim)," he says. Time to make it the Four Classics, with Lake Ontario up there with the other three great swims, and back on the world map of open-water swimming. "But for me, and same with Melanie, open-water swimming in this new era is all about L.O.S.T. swimming. I wanted to swim to Oakville. Toronto doesn't mean as much to me."

Past experience taught him to get some sleep before a big event, so he settled down over three pints of beer with his crew, then a fourth to be sure. He slept over four hours then got up at 1:45 a.m. on August 12th. He headed to the Dalhousie Yacht Club in St. Catharine's and the swim launched into the wind at 3:45 a.m.

At first his team had navigated him to the west, thinking the winds would blow him back on course into a straight line. But he was swimming strongly enough despite conditions and ended up heading off into the west through the waves. The water temperature was relatively good, 21C. "It wasn't a big surprise but it's still interesting that you go through all kinds of weather patterns as you're going across," he says. Lake Ontario changes a lot over a day.

Though the first eight hours of his crossing had been rough, from about 10:00 in the morning until 2:00 p.m., the Lake went flat, like a beautiful watery mirror, "and everybody wanted to be my pacer." His daughters Jillian and Maisey were on the boat; his wife Joanne had been on shore, apparently too nervous to be in the boat, so he was stunned when she popped up beside him to pace for a time. Their son Dylan was working but had also been coordinated with the support crew to come and pace with his dad.

After 11 hours, however, the fun of the crossing evaporated. The weather changed again and pouring rainstorms appeared ahead and behind the crossing. "It was literally the calm before the storm." The weather hit and the Lake roughed up again, with chop on top. Rollers broke over him. As if he was hearing the voice on a GPS, Rob recalculated his crossing time every half hour as he took his feedings, frustrated that he wasn't going to make the 15 hours, that this swim was taking much longer than he had anticipated.

As tempting as it was to quit, he was having no issues that would justify ending the swim: the water temperature was still the relatively good 21C. He wasn't hypothermic or injured. His nutrition was good. The rough waters carried on until near 10:00 p.m. It was now the hardest thing he'd ever done. As he swam he thought about what made it so hard, and concluded that it's the combination of distance and the time. "I'm usually pretty good about keeping my wits about me and staying in the same personality mode as I'm going along. I was getting really frustrated near the end because I was going so slowly and I'm not used to that." The last six hours were simply pain.

Then Lake Ontario settled down, turning perfect, a black, flat glass at angles to the pitch dark sky. A lighthouse twinkled ahead of the running lights of the lead sailboat. Headlights of the cars sparkled onto the water from shore in Oakville. He had hoped the ending would work out in this way, so that the boats can jet ahead to the pier, tie up, and then the crew can come down to the beach to watch the final few metres of the swim. As he swam across, recalculating his math equations for his finishing time, he worried that no one would be waiting. "I was thinking at least the crew will be there and see me finish."

About one kilometre off shore his coach Alex McMillan asked him from the Zodiac if he could hear the noise. He listened and picked up the sound of several hundred people on the pier, his L.O.S.T. teammates, friends, family. "Having the crew there to be able to see me finish was wonderful; it was also really nice to have people who were staying up that late," he laughs.

He emerged from Lake Ontario all "unnatural colours." His legs had turned a ghostly white since his blood had left his legs in the effort to warm his internal organs. That explained why it felt like he'd been swimming like the letter L, with his legs dragging through the Lake. His back was purple in an effort to keep blood flowing in his core. Still, his core temperature read 31.9C after the swim, with normal being 37C.

Fortunately, he had been rigid about his feeding and nutrition on the crossing. Here his experience in Ironman and around Manhattan Island would stand up to the test of Lake Ontario. He fueled on his apple-cinnamon gel packs every half hour. With about ten kilometres left, the team ran out of his gels and had to dispatch to shore for more power gel-take-out. "Having 41 gels is gross," he says. But it all stayed down and he never felt sick or lacking in energy. "That's what I call a success. I was pleasantly surprised because I've done Ironman events and not been able to keep that many gels down. You end up bonking [losing energy] if your nutrition goes sideways." In a triathlon or marathon, an athlete can sit on the curb, take a break; out on a Great Lake, bonking can lead to serious trouble and signal the end of the swim.

Usually Rob Kent would be encouraging everyone to try a swim, a run, a bike, a triathlon. He can talk swimming forever—but Lake Ontario? Wait, now. He had a deep respect for Lake Ontario going into it; the degree of difficulty of swimming Lake Ontario is refined, etched in his mind. Given his own swim, and with the media attention that focused on Annaleise Carr's crossing the same summer, the popularity of marathon and open-water swimming might well increase, he says. "Having said that, the Lake didn't get any easier and it isn't any easier than it was 60 years ago. It's still a bloody hard swim." Patience is a key for endurance athletes, and he says it's best to avoid wallowing in the misery of Oh, God-how-far-is-it-I'm-going-to-be-out-here-forever-I'll-never-make-it. For Rob, the swimmer must not travel down that road of misery. Just plug away to the next half hour, to the next feeding. "Certainly if I knew it was going to take me nearly 21 hours to swim I'd probably never have started it."

Rob likes challenges that are big enough to allow for the real possibility of a failure, even a spectacular failure, where completion is not a guarantee. Lake Ontario exceeded all that, and he laughs about that fact afterwards. After all, he had attempted the English Channel with no real idea of what the Channel was about. On Lake Ontario, he was experienced and carried the appropriate measure of respect for a body of water that he well knew can measure 23.3C one day, then flip over and drop to 14.4C the next day. So sure, 15-17 hours seemed like a reasonable expectation for himself, considering everything. "I was way off. It was way harder than I thought. In my mind it adds credibility to the degree of difficulty of that swim."

And yet, people are wont to compare. Having swum his marathon on Lake Ontario, Rob figures that the swim is equivalent to racing three Ironman triathlons back to back to back. At least. "It's still not going to have a high success rate, which is good. It makes it that much more, I don't know, honorable or prestigious or just select. It's arguably one of the hardest swims in the world." If he was to recall accurately how hard every race he'd ever done really was, he would likely have avoided more ultra-distance events after his first running marathon. "Swimming Lake Ontario was the hardest thing I've ever done and when I completed it I swore I would never do anything that hard again."

In the weeks after his crossing, the pain and struggle began to fade. He knew it had happened but figured the human brain is smart enough to selectively forget. "That allows us to always try to achieve more and do better. I'm getting the itch again," he says. "I guess it's just how people like me are wired. Enjoy the training, the moment, the challenge and the adventure... because win or lose, it is always worth it."

Reflections on Success when the Great Lakes are in Charge

Perhaps it seems odd to include chapters focusing on swims that remain incomplete, and even on some swimmers who have not (yet) completed a crossing. Doing so conflicts with our usual way of seeing things: black or white, failure or success. But Great Lakes swimming is grey. As Michèle Benoit says, no one comes to the shore without the intention of making it to the other side. And it's no simple feat to swim Lake Ontario, let alone any of the other four Great Lakes, as swimmers and swim support crews have known since 1954 when 16 year old Marilyn Bell proved it could be done.

From another perspective, though, the Great Lakes don't seem so Great—in fact they appear extremely fragile. They seem to shrink as our human footprint on this planet inexorably grows. Over the last 100 years the Great Lakes have been "done to" in a big way: everything from climate change and human pollution, to eels, and zebra mussels, or the real possibility of annihilation of fish stocks by Asian carp if they get a gill-hold. Not to mention dredging, shipping, or the sheer fact of 40 million North Americans depending on their water.

And yet...

Swimmer versus Lake remains the one human-lake interaction where the Lakes are in charge. For all the technology, navigational advances, safety policy, knowledge in nutrition, training, fitness—a crossing finally comes down to one swimmer, wearing nothing more than a bathing suit, goggles, cap and a greasy mix of sunscreen and lanolin for protection against some of the elements. Swimmers have been pulled unconscious from the Lakes, their bodies beginning to self-cannibalize; the best and fastest swimmers have needed reassurance and efforts at sports psychology to finish. In all crossing attempts, the equation is basic, simple, and stark: a Great Lake plus a swimmer, a human being who is virtually naked, and alone. Yes, there is a crew for support—a crew who is not allowed to touch the swimmer without ending the crossing.

All the aspects of swimming a Great Lake—the memorable highs, as well as the heart-breaking lows—also come into play in the incomplete attempts: the luck of the weather—for good or ill; the unpredictability of support boat mechanics, or support boat crew, as well as the ingenuity of the team in adapting to fickle weather; physical surprises, despite the training; psychological experiences one couldn't have foreseen—all the circumstances we sum up as earth, wind, fire, and (of course) water, whether metaphorical or real. They all play into the definition of success, and of failure. Those who did not complete crossings looked ahead to another season, another Lake, other ways of being in the water. Never say never, they would add, say what if…

Bryan Finlay, Lake Ontario, 1992 attempt; Lake Erie, 2001

Before Greg Willoughby's 2011 attempt at Lake Ontario, Christine Arsenault would have thought of success and failure on a Great Lake in terms of completing or not completing, in black and white terms. Talking that night on the crossing with swim master Bryan Finlay, though, Christine learned that his uncompleted swims were as much successes for him as his completed ones. "Every single one was a success because of what he gained from each."

Bryan Finlay carries an international résumé packed with stories of early exits from freakishly cold water, salt and fresh, around the globe: the Irish Sea, Loch Ness, the English Channel, Lake Ontario. It's true to say that there's nothing like getting plucked out unconscious, hypoglycemic, and hypothermic—not to mention tired—to keep Bryan hooked on open-water swimming.

But that résumé shows completed and record-setting open-water swims too, a lot of them for the long-time swim master at Solo Swims. These have come not from the traditional freestyle stroke, but from, of all things—the breaststroke. Swimming at the western end of Lake Erie, he crossed from Leamington Beach to Pelee Island lighthouse in 2001. Then 58, Bryan swam the 22.1 kilometres in 10 hours, 44 minutes, eclipsing Canada's Ian James' own remarkable record of backstroke, again 22.1 kilometres, though he swam from Pelee Island to Leamington. In 1993 James swam backwards across Erie for 14 hours, 46 minutes. For Bryan Finlay, swimming Lake Erie using only the breaststroke was about setting records.

His affinity for breaststroke persisted from when he was young, despite attempts to dissuade him from it. His first swim coach, his uncle Roy Sutton, used to send the 10-year-old Bryan up the ladder of the three-metre diving board. Then Bryan would dive, reluctantly, into the pool in Coventry, England. This was his "punishment" for being caught out yet again swimming breaststroke when his uncle wanted him to work on his freestyle.

The many records Bryan holds tend to the oddity side of things, including the breaststroke record for the 8.4-kilometre course in Lake Coniston, England in 1960. He completed the distance in exactly three hours. The following week he led from the three to five kilometre mark of the Lake Windermere championships, a 16-kilometre race that he didn't complete. The heady start ended poorly with Bryan being pulled from the water unconscious and hypoglycemic near the 11 kilometre mark. He credits this particular incident with hooking him for good on open-water swimming. He swam for Great Britain in Holland. In 1963, he lowered his time on the Lake Coniston course to 2:31:54, which stood until 1988 when Bryan, now a Canadian, returned to improve the time by 20 seconds. The Lake Coniston record has been his for over 52 years, from 1960 into 2014.

Bryan always stresses that times in the pool cannot be compared to swimming the same distance in open water; these are great bodies of water, after all. On Lake Erie, for example, there's Point Pelee to contend with. "When you've got something like that sticking out into the lake and the St. Clair River is running down into that area, currents are quite common." And their impact depends on numerous unpredictable variables, not easily controlled for.

In Lake Ontario, the changing temperatures are notorious. Bryan lasted only six hours in Lake Ontario in 1992. "It was pretty pathetic," he says. The cold water was unlike any he'd ever felt. He swam from a hot afternoon into a night where the air temperature dropped below the dew point, raising bubbles of condensation on the boats. Each time he came up for a stroke, cold water ran from his neck into the small of his back. He figures it's easier to start in cold water and then swim into warmer temperatures. But then, the team's inability to predict the changing temperatures with any degree of certainty is simply part of swimming Lake Ontario. If your otherwise well-planned and well-prepared-for swim gets pulled due to cold water, well, you can still count yourself part of the Lake's history.

Failure on the Great Lakes becomes a point of discussion for Bryan Finlay. He recalls a conversation with Gerry Forsberg, a Canadian-born marathon swimmer who set the English Channel crossing record in 1957. Forsberg's time of 13 hours, 33 minutes was 22 minutes faster than the previous record. In his trademark "Otter" bathing suit, Forsberg won every major championship, and completed some 219 swims. He was the president of the Channel Swimming Association from 1962 until 1988. Bryan says Forsberg, a naval officer, took a military approach to failure. The swimmer, having reviewed the situation, strategically "retires" from the swim (offering reasons like waves, cold, currents, jelly fish, lampreys, etc.). "You didn't necessarily wave a white flag," Bryan says.

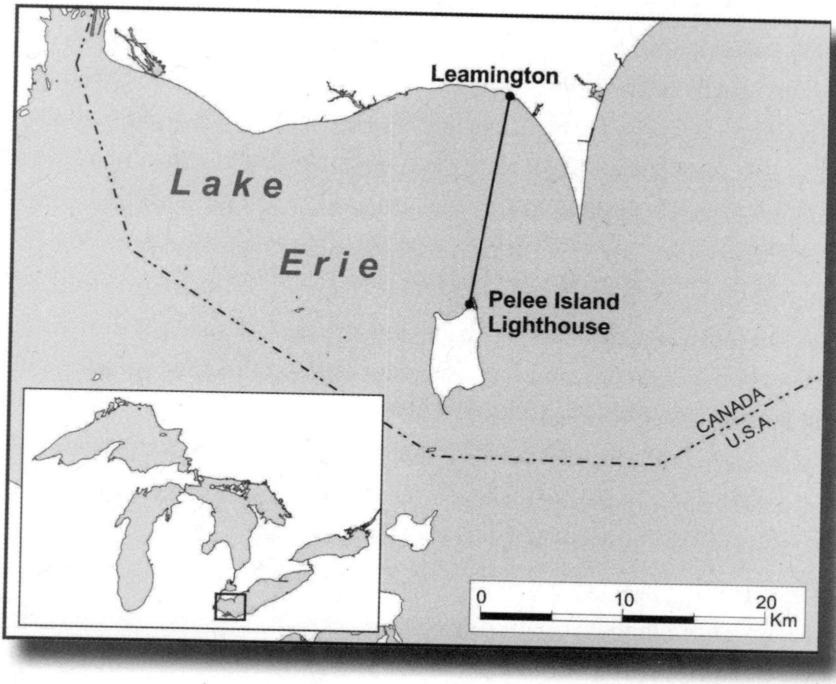

Lake Erie west end crossing route, swum south from Leamington to Pelee Island lighthouse by Bryan Finlay in 2001, and north from Pelee Island lighthouse to Leamington by Ian James in 1993. Map Credit: L.L. Lariviere—Laurentian University.

Thie Convery, Lake Erie, 2010; Lake Ontario, 2010 attempt

If a swim is planned and trained for with intelligence, foresight as far as possible, and the heart in the right place, is it a failure if the swimmer doesn't touch the other side, but touches a hand, a boat, a paddle in the middle of the Lake, and is pulled out? It's a question for Thie Convery, who completed Lake Erie in 2010, but had weather end her Lake Ontario crossing later that summer. Regardless, she achieved something else en route to the lakeshore.

It cuts to the marrow of Rotarians, indeed into their DNA, that they exist to eradicate polio from the face of the earth. And they fundraise relentlessly, because the next penny may well be that lucky one that finally pushes the disease over the edge. One more vaccine, one child less likely to contract polio. Let's rally! Let's go team!

It was in precisely that spot that Thie Convery found herself in 2009, tossing fundraising ideas around with fellow Rotarians in Dundas, Ontario, near Hamilton, as well as tossing back some Irish whiskey. And so what came out of her mouth was supposed to be just another idea. Raise money, grab attention and continue the steady march towards eradicating polio. A tumbler of whiskey in hand, Thie said, "I'll swim across Lake Ontario." Then, startled, the wealth advisor asked, "Who said that?"

No one let her off the hook. Her friends and her life-partner Frances Manias leapt on the idea: let's do it, let's raise money for polio. "And I was, 'Whoa, whoa, whoa. Wait a minute here.' So the words were out of my mouth.

I didn't know where they came from," Thie recalls. What was the problem? Well… Thie Convery was not a swimmer. She was a retired body-builder. She and Frances had competed in drug-free body-building events; Frances was competing on the international stage. But Thie was done with the extreme dieting that came with her sport. She liked to train and lift weights, and eat.

Growing up in Sudbury, Thie knew all about lakes and indeed had paddled in the waters of Sudbury's gem, Lake Ramsey. She took her Red Cross swim lessons deep in the east end of Sudbury at the Nickel District Pool. So, hers was not a particularly special swim background considering she was living in Sudbury during the 80s, the glory years of Olympic champion Alex Baumann's swimming career. When Thie moved away to McMaster University in Hamilton for her studies and then to set up her life there, she played at various activities, including soccer. Her soccer days came to an abrupt end when, as goalie, she leapt for a bad shot during ladies' league action. When she landed, her knee could now bend both ways. After that accident she needed an activity or sport that was no-impact, safe and controlled. She didn't want to gain weight and wondered what she could do. Body-building fit the bill. For five years she competed in various shows. Then she was done. For Thie there's weight training and there's bodybuilding; the two are separated by the dieting, she says. To compete she needed to be 30-35 pounds lighter. "And you have to diet to get there."

After 2007 she was onto other things, something always catching her fancy. And so along came 2009. It now seemed that she was going to swim across Lake Ontario to raise funds for polio vaccines. But how? Of course she knew about Marilyn Bell, the first crosser, and knew that she had fought off eels. "We all know that. I say it's Canadian folklore. Those are stories that have been passed down, even subconsciously." The rest of the details were uncertain. After opening her mouth about a lake crossing, she rose the next morning and proceeded to search for information. She found Solo Swims of Ontario, a course, a distance of 51 kilometres, and a whole process for crossing. "And I thought, 'What have I done?'" she laughs.

Next up on the research: eels in Lake Ontario. Thie doesn't do sucking things, like eels or blood suckers. She learned the eel population has declined about 95 percent since the 1950s to the point where the Ministry of Natural

Resources may restock some eels. The MNR knows some immigrant populations like to fish and eat them, she says. "I said as long as they do this after I do a swim, I don't care what they put into Lake Ontario."

It never crossed her mind to drop the idea at that point. She'd said she'd do it, so she would. She figured her non-swimmer status actually helped. "If you're going to do something crazy, knowing nothing about it is actually a good thing." But being a non-swimmer didn't look good from a lot of angles. She looked more like she was drowning, Thie laughs. She didn't know why anyone wore a bathing cap except to keep hair out of the eyes, not that it might keep the head warm and let people see the swimmer. Goggles? Initially when swimming in Lake Ontario she'd raise her head to sight, and then close her eyes. She had to get goggles.

Thie learned to swim as efficiently as possible, knowing the crossing wasn't a race. She thought about how she could train to swim the 51-kilometre distance. First it was swimming 51 kilometres over a week, or roughly seven km in a day, nonstop for 2.5 hours. "Now all you've got to do is swim it tomorrow." Eventually she could do the distance in a week, then four days, down to two, and then 51 kilometres in one day. She is self-employed so has some flexibility with her schedule. "This is my whole thing: anybody can do what I did. Anybody. Maybe not in the timeframe I did, but all you've got to do is swim one kilometre. If you know how to swim, which I did, swimming one kilometre takes the average person 30 minutes. All you've got to do is do that again and again and again."

When Thie applied to cross, Solo Swims of Ontario thought her application was a joke. Surely she had been put up to it. In a way, that was true. Solo Swims was going to reject her application. "I did send a cheque but they don't care about the money." Without a shred of swimming background to be found, no masters club affiliation, nor a long-expired bronze medallion certification, Solo Swims wasn't impressed with Thie—at first. Born out of a drowning tragedy on Lake Ontario in 1975, Solo Swims is primarily concerned with safety. If they don't think it's safe, there's no swim. Then they reviewed Thie's training logs: the fine details included the number of hours she slept, her weight, heart rate, etc. She came from a competitive body-building base. She was, indeed, serious.

Sso requires all aspirants to complete a 17 kilometre trial swim prior to the Lake crossing attempt, one-third of the Lake Ontario journey. Since her escort boat, a 16.7-metre-long diesel-powered fishing tug, was already on Lake Erie, her swim master Marilyn Korzekwa suggested her trial be on Erie so she could become a Great Lake crosser at the same time. On July 4, 2010, and now with an actual background in swimming—albeit only a year long—Thie completed a slightly different version of the traditional Lake Erie eastern crossing, 1 kilometre east of Sturgeon Point, NY to Crystal Beach, ON—18.5 kilometres.

The distance was fine but the steady chop of the shallow waters of Lake Erie banged Thie constantly during the 7 hour, 20 minute crossing. The problem for Thie on Erie was the water temperature. She had trained for Lake Ontario's chilly depths; on Erie the air temperature was a sunny 28C and the water was at 23C—in short, too warm. Then as she approached shore in the shallow Great Lake, she could see and touch the bottom of Erie. She stood up only to be told the swim wasn't over. Keep swimming. When she finally touched the rocky shore on the Ontario side, she became an official Great Lake crosser and gave in to her nausea. She was sick from the heat, so nauseous in fact, she couldn't even remember if she vomited during the swim. In retrospect, she feels the waves were a good thing. A calm day on Lake Erie might have made her over-confident for Lake Ontario, and she might not have made adjustments in preparation for her Rotary-sponsored Swim to End Polio crossing, scheduled for August 6, 2010.

As the time to depart drew closer, the weather stepped up to play a role. Later Marilyn Korzekwa, charged with overseeing the Lake Ontario swim, would write that it was the most difficult weather-related start decision in her 25 years as a swim master. It seemed like every station was forecasting a different weather picture. Yet they all seemed to promise a bumpy crossing. High north-westerly winds and a small craft warning on Friday postponed the swim to Saturday morning. Strong winds were predicted for Sunday. The only 24-hour window of opportunity creaked open on Saturday morning but it was tough, like trying to push open an olden wooden sashed window frame. Wave predictions were confusing. Over the phone prior to the swim, Marilyn told

Thie her chances of success were declining by the minute. Frances asked Marilyn what Thie's chances of success were. "About 30 percent." Meaning a three in ten chance of getting across. Frances said, "A year ago Thie had a zero in 10 chance of getting across. She didn't know how to swim." The team was light years from 2009, Thie added. "I said, 'Let's give it a go.' And thank goodness Marilyn agreed to do it."

Marilyn would later note how well organized the crew was, with large, seaworthy boats, and how well Thie had done in the waves in Lake Erie. Thie thought she had nothing to lose, that what the heck, they were all on the beach at Niagara-on-the-Lake anyway. The sense of anticipation and pressure at the start of a swim is incredible, all focused and positive to get the swimmer across. At 9:38:46 a.m., precisely, the swim began.

Shot off the start with the aid of the current from the Niagara River, Thie began crossing the murky waters of Lake Ontario just over the Niagara sandbar. Grey and choppy, it looked like some things were down there on a feeding frenzy. The waters were worse than usual and gave Thie a ride. She was turned left, and took in a mouthful of water, then turned right, and took in another mouthful. For two hours it went on like that. "I thought, 'Oh man I'll never get across the lake like this.'"

The chop eventually settled down, leaving the Lake rolling, sending in waves about a foot high out of the west and southwest, but to Thie they didn't seem like much, really. She could breathe on both sides and not take in any water. It was wavy but she was breathing and all seemed fine. She was on her way to Toronto.

Around 4:00 p.m. the southwest wind picked up, kicking up whitecaps. Thie remained solid through the two-metre high waves. Had the waves come at her more to the front, they might have challenged her breathing more. Though she was handling the weather change, the high winds and waves were making it harder on her crew. They would lose Thie in the waves, only to see her head pop up 3.5 metres ahead, she recalls. The Zodiac would scoot up, and then think Thie was under the boat. Feedings were increasingly difficult because the crew couldn't get close enough without the fear of actually hitting her. The forecast predicted winds up to 20 knots with a small craft advisory. The Bayliner escort struggled in the waves and requested permission to leave the crossing. At 6:45 p.m. Marilyn Korzekwa made the decision to end the attempt.

Thie looked up to see the Zodiac with her partner Frances, a non-swimmer herself, hanging off the side, wanting to talk to Thie before a scheduled feeding. It seemed odd to Thie. Frances delivered the bad news. "We're going up and down. Marilyn's called off the swim."

Thie was beside herself, wondering if her support crew thought she was having a hard time. She didn't know why until Frances told her Marilyn was calling the swim for safety reasons. There were three boats escorting Thie. The yacht captain had never seen waves like this. They were losing sight of her in the waves and not only was the weather forecast getting worse, night was coming.

The boats formed a semicircle around Thie. Crying along with her crew, Thie tread water. Frances put a ghetto blaster on the side of the boat. Every hour on the hour she had been playing a song for Thie. She couldn't quite hear it but she would catch the tune and keep it in her head for awhile. This time Michael Jackson's "Man in the Mirror" played across the waves of Lake Ontario. Thie asked for a few minutes to take a swim, have a cry.

Then she swam over to Marilyn's boat. She didn't think there was any room for discussion with the swim master once the swim has been called due to safety. Thie told Marilyn she wasn't calling off the swim and that her swim master would have to touch her to end it. Marilyn said, "Fine," and touched Thie. "I didn't want to get in her Zodiac. I wasn't pissed off. I was sad. I went back to Frances' Zodiac. They pulled me in." She had been swimming for 9.5 hours and was 1.6 kilometres from the halfway point in Lake Ontario; she'd swum over 25 kilometres, just a year after "learning" how to swim.

Up in the Zodiac Thie's perspective shifted with every bounce. Oh, it was rough. Transferring crew members between boats had become more dangerous; a team member had been slightly injured on a transfer. Even the evacuation of the team when the swim was called off posed difficulties. Down in the water, Thie hadn't realized. She was prepared to keep going. "I had lots in me. In fact I said I could have gone to Newfoundland. I was fine. I swam the next day." Lake Ontario had ended the Swim to End Polio. Not to mention anything else that was on the lake at the time. Less than two hours later there was a may-day call outside Port Credit. The Coast Guard successfully rescued a 24-foot boat that had not been part of the swim attempt.

It remains unclear whether Thie will try again to swim across Lake Ontario, striving to complete the full 51 kilometres. People tell her that she went halfway, nearly 26 kilometres. But it doesn't feel like that for Thie. There's no tattoo she can get, she says, to mark a half-swim of Lake Ontario. "You don't get a badge. I wasn't exhausted the next day. There's nothing ingrained in my mind. What I can tell you is how sad I felt. That's ingrained in my heart. But there was no way I reached my physical limits."

She believes she still would have completed the crossing despite the conditions, but the safety of her crew was called into question. Two of her boat captains were scared in weather they'd never encountered before. But as a non-swimmer, there were other things to consider. She hadn't spent a full weekend with Frances in a year because of the training. She wasn't sure if she was prepared to adjust her life again for another year to take another crack at Lake Ontario. She also wanted to see what else the world could offer.

Without a complaint: Lake Erie's chop and heat made for an unsettling crossing for Thie Convery in 2010. Photo courtesy Frances Manias.

Thie Convery has not yet put up her name as an aspirant for Lake Ontario again. She did, however, stick with the Solo Swims community she linked with in 2010. In 2011, Thie and Frances supported Marilyn Korzekwa as she became the oldest Canadian woman to swim the English Channel. They were also there to support Marilyn when she swam the Catalina Channel in 2013.

Whether Thie attempts Lake Ontario again also isn't the issue, really. Her primary concern was doing what she could to rid the world of polio. She learned to swim. The Swim to End Polio achieved what the Irish whiskey had set in motion. The Dundas Rotarians raised $52,000 and inspired other Rotarians to raise another $143,000 for a total of $195,000. The Bill and Melinda Gates Foundation matched all monies raised through her swim to bring the final tally to $390,000. That is enough to vaccinate 650,000 children against polio, Thie says. The oral vaccine would go to children in the endemic countries of Pakistan, Afghanistan, India, and Nigeria.

Regardless of the outcome, Thie would change nothing about her swim. She felt great, despite the bad luck with the weather.

Greg Willoughby, Lake Erie, 2011; Lake Ontario, 2011 attempt

The end of Greg Willoughby's 2011 Lake Ontario crossing attempt is vivid in everyone's mind, except his. For hours he had been unable to eat enough to fuel his body. By the end his pacers were anxiously trying to squeeze gel packs of nutrition into his mouth and painting his face with the goop in their effort. He was communicating less. An hour before they would evacuate the swim he refused to answer a hypothermia test and wanted to swim. Christine Arsenault, who had crossed Lake Ontario two weeks previously, was pacing beside him. They talked, tried to get him to swim 100 strokes. This worked once; the next tries never reached 100 strokes. He would stop, struggling to keep his mouth above the water in the developing swell. His final attempt at 100 strokes reached five. He told Christine he was sinking. The warning signs of hypothermia can be confused with sheer exhaustion, too; either way, recalling her lifeguard training, she grabbed him and ended the swim. She told him to lie on his back, then swam him over to the Zodiac support. There were three kilometres remaining to shore. He doesn't recall the heave-ho up the side of the Zodiac nor being put into an ambulance and taken to St. Michael's Hospital. He awoke the next morning, saw bright lights staring down at him and thought, "This is probably a hospital. I'm probably in the hospital." He was in a heavy warming cocoon, unsure of where he was, unable to move and sweating profusely, suddenly hot when all he could remember was being cold. "Everything felt like cement."

"So, you know, in those ways I can say I gave it my all. I think if I had swum faster through the night I would have had more energy and finished the lake before it got too cold."

In 2011, Greg, an immigration and refugee lawyer from London, Ontario, was attempting to be the first man that summer to cross Lake Ontario from Niagara-on-the-Lake to Toronto, the 51-kilometre traditional route of Marilyn Bell in 1954, and where John Jaremy became the first man in 1956. Greg had already become a Great Lakes crosser in 2011, setting the men's freestyle record for Lake Erie in July, a swim that had seemed almost easy. Lake Ontario, however, was a different swim altogether. "I got so close. I could taste it. I could almost touch the shore," Greg says.

On Lake Ontario that August morning the police escort was arriving towards the end of his struggle. Greg's supporters on shore could see them out on the Lake. Then the boats dispersed; everything stopped. At St. Michael's Hospital in downtown Toronto medical staff had rarely seen people come in with a body core temperature of 29C who were still alive. His CK (creatine kinase) blood levels were through the roof, at 11,000 units per litre. The normal range is from 60-400. For his kidneys, it was like throwing mud at a screen and hoping it would go through. His kidneys were on the verge of shutting down because they had been working so hard to keep his blood clean, he says.

He was in the hospital for four days on an intravenous to flush his kidneys. He grew bored, and since he was feeling better he wanted to go home. Hospital staff would come in and do a blood test. No, Mr. Willoughby, you're not fine. If you go home right now your kidneys will shut down. He would come to laugh at the dark situation. He would talk to his crew, asking them to help him remember. "I take it with kind of a sense of humour. Worst case scenario? Next time the same thing will happen, but it's not dangerous in any way; it's just an inconvenience."

The seed to try the Lake was planted in 1992 when he joined the support crew on Bryan Finlay's attempt at Lake Ontario. Bryan's swim was pulled due to weather and cold but even though Bryan had not touched the shores of Toronto, Greg thought the whole thing a great adventure. He wondered if he could do something extreme. He wasn't a mountain climber, but as a former lifeguard, instructor, competitive swimmer, and waterpolo player, swimming was up his alley. "What's the toughest swim that I could do?" Lake Ontario? Now that was an accomplishable challenge, he says. "And a challenge that I highly respect that other people have done, and almost more now that I see how tough and unpredictable it is."

Eighteen years later Greg made something of a snap decision to cross Lake Ontario. Suddenly in late 2010 it seemed like a now or never situation. He was looking at the average age of people who had done it and, at 40, he was moving past that average. It had to be now, sooner rather than later. His attitude was "I'm just going to do it and we'll see how it goes." In March 2011 he announced to his wife Dawn that he planned to swim the Lake. Most people were skeptical at best or, conversely, rightly, thought he was insane. His wife and coach supported him. He made the commitment, announced it publicly. He wanted to raise funds for St. Joseph's Health Care Foundation, to gain that accountability that would keep him swimming. "I knew quitting would be so easy, either quitting in June, or July, or 2:00 o'clock in the morning when I was halfway across the Lake. I knew if other people knew that I was doing it, I had a bit of pride on the line; then I wouldn't quit."

And in retrospect that was a good thing. He wasn't a mountain climber but he and coach Ken Fitzpatrick, captain of the 1984 Canadian Olympic swim team, ramped his training up like a vertical climb. By May and June 2011 the training was a drag, Greg rising every day at five to swim "my ass off" (literally, as he dropped 20 pounds in training) for two to three hours, then working all day as an immigration/refugee lawyer, then home to the family life: four kids under age 11 at the time. He figures he didn't miss out on too much with his children. "It was mainly just exhausting. And more taxing on my wife as well." Some days he would tell Dawn he was going to the Lake: "see you in eight hours." Then just the daily grind of rising, swimming, working, running things at home, and doing the next day, the next, and the next.

Solo Swims requires a trial swim of one third of the distance of the main swim to be challenged, in this case Lake Ontario. Like Thie Convery Greg chose Lake Erie, which meant that, upon completion, he had swum a Great Lake and had become an official crosser. During the planning, he began to have the delusion that with Erie complete, that meant only four more Great Lakes. “Then once I do Lake Ontario, that’s a big one.” That left three more, and no man had ever done all five lakes. “I had those delusions of grandeur, but I’ll have to revisit those ideas.”

As it turned out, Lake Erie was, he says carefully, kind of a piece of cake. The shallowest of the five Lakes can be rough with a constant smack upside the swimmer’s head. His conditions on Erie started out with about one-foot waves, then out in the main body of the Lake the surface flattened out like glass, a summer millpond. Everyone was having a great time on the crossing, he recalls. Within a few kilometres of the American side, the water was even shallower and the water temperature shot into the upper 20sC. “It was weirdly kind of hot—like swimming in a bathtub.”

He set a men’s freestyle record of 6 hours, 17 minutes, 40 seconds for the 19.2 kilometre crossing from Crystal Beach, ON to Sturgeon Point, NY, at the popular east end of Erie. Unsure of how much he had to give, he clipped along; his crew asked him to slow it down, that this was still a long swim. He adjusted his pace, not wanting to expend all his energy at the start. At the end, he ran up the beach and did a handstand on the rocks. He felt great. “I was doing jumping jacks; the going was that easy. I should have gone harder; I should have gone a whole lot faster.”

He drove home, put away the boat, and told Dawn it had been like a regular day, the swim was fine. In reflection, as so many athletes do, he figured maybe he had held back on Erie, whereas on Ontario he thought this is the real swim and he had to be patient because he didn’t want to blow it in the beginning. “Then I think I was too patient and I should have pushed it more at the beginning just to get as many kilometres under my belt while it was still nice.”

Greg’s swim across Ontario launched at 7:41 p.m. on August 26, 2011. His was the third crossing attempt of the summer; Christine Arsenault and Rebekah Boscariol had crossed earlier. Now Christine was a pacer. The rest of the team was seasoned as well: the lead paramedic, Stephen Turner, had been in the Coast Guard and carried an AED in his kit for the crossing. Bryan Finlay, the swim master, noted a great spirit among the crew and Greg. Under clear skies, Greg darted across the spongy beach into the pinky blue waters of Lake

Ontario. His main goal was to finish, with a secondary goal of not quitting. He figured it would be so easy to pull out. He had told his crew and Bryan Finlay not to pull him out until he was unconscious.

Weather on Lake Ontario is tricky at the best of times. It looks great, like a promise, then something moves in. Greg had been anticipating waves. Instead, fog dropped like pea soup by early morning, becoming denser and never leaving the horizon. Navigation became tricky in part because a stationary GPS doesn't always recognize issues of orientation, says Bryan Finlay. Equally frustrating was the zigzagging, with occasional 90 degree turns in the fog.

That would become a minor irritant. Over the swim Greg was becoming nauseous, a state he couldn't shake and had not accounted for in his preparation. He couldn't take in and keep in enough food. Combined with nausea, he was hypothermic. As he neared Toronto with shallower water closer to shore, the currents rose from the bottom, rounded up over the beach and then bounced back out from the beach. "It was like this big wave coming up from the bottom. It would kind of be like a punch in the face of cold, cold water, and then it would subside."

Christine Arsenault hopped into the water, trying to feed him in the final stages of the swim. At one point the crew asked Greg to do something that would indicate his level of coherency. He refused, saying he had to swim, don't make me count, and she took that as a good sign. The team could see traffic on the parkway leading into Marilyn Bell Park; they could see the shoreline, the people waiting. Greg was transferred to the police launch and then onshore to St. Michael's Hospital where he would shock doctors with his body core temperature, blood levels, and the fact that he was still alive. He figures doctors were impressed that he wasn't the usual gunshot or crime victim they would see at that hospital. "I think it was more interesting that they had someone who was athletic and who had tried to do something that just went wrong."

The final swim report shows Greg swam 46.9 kilometres in 23 hours, 32 minutes, and change. Officially he was 3.74 kilometres from Marilyn Bell Park. He took a beating, sure, more than he'd expected, but at the same time, he had "complete faith" in his crew. Going into it, people had said to him, isn't this kind of dangerous. He said in the worst case scenario he'd be pulled out and rushed to the hospital. "Which is not what I expected to happen, but that is exactly what happened."

His emotions are mixed about his Lake Ontario swim. He couldn't control the currents off Toronto, nor the nausea that hits some swimmers and leaves others alone. He remains thrilled that so many supported the St. Joseph's Health Care Foundation, the charity, raising $11,000. "Yeah, at least I can look back on it and say I didn't quit. Mentally I didn't quit. I gave it my all. So, in one way I'm pleased that I didn't quit and I swam nearly to the point of unconsciousness. And I can say, there are few things in life where you give 100 percent. I swam until I couldn't swim anymore."

He was left with a sense of work incomplete. He sees himself going again in the future, "but to get it requires an awful lot of selflessness from my family and my kids because I have to be training so long." The decision to swim Lake Erie as a trial swim paid off. He will take his record. "I'm proud I got that Lake and I'm torn about doing Lake Ontario again."

The commitment to him from his crew was huge. He remains surprised that people said yeah, Greg, I'll support you. Greg's swim has two sides to success and failure. On the one hand, for so many swimmers just making it to the start line, to the dubious sandy beach at Niagara-on-the-Lake, is one of the biggest accomplishments. On the other hand, there is the swimmer against the Lake, regardless of completion: "You have to give it your all and not bail out, not wimp out and just quit because it's too cold, or it's too wavy or whatever." But, of course, no one can downplay the fact of touching in Toronto at the far, far end. "Those who do touch must be so exuberant, and for the rest of their lives... because it really is a phenomenal accomplishment."

The 2012 Attempts: Finding the Success in the Failure

In 2012, seven swimmers aspired to swim "Marilyn's Lake." They lined up in a steady parade at Lake Ontario's south west side. In order of start dates: François Hamel, Madhu Nagaraja, Rob Kent, Annaleise Carr, Michèle Benoit, Amanda Lee Kelessi, and Colleen Shields. François, Annaleise, Amanda Lee, and Colleen were tackling the traditional route of Marilyn Bell's 1954 crossing, a 51-kilometre swim that, on average, on a good day, with all the stars aligned, can take 18-22 hours, sometimes more and sometimes—though rarely—less. Madhu and Rob were swimming the L.O.S.T. (Lake Ontario Swim Team) 41 kilometre route from Port Dalhousie to Oakville. And Michèle Benoit, from Burlington, was hoping to establish another crossing on Lake Ontario, a 45-kilometre swim on the extreme western side of the Lake into the park near her home in Burlington.

That was the plan, those were the swimmers registered with Solo Swims. And then the summer swimming season began. Annaleise Carr, Rob Kent, and Madhu Nagaraja completed the journey. Here's what happened to the other four.

2012 Lake Ontario Aspirants: (from left) Rob Kent, Annaleise Carr, Madhu Nagaraja, Colleen Shields, Michèle Benoit, and François Hamel. Absent: Amanda Lee Kelessi. Photo courtesy Maisey Kent.

Michèle Benoit

If Michèle Benoit had been a surfer she might have rejoiced. But as she looked across Lake Ontario she could not believe it. This was crazy, and this is where months of training, mild hypothermia, a 12-pound weight gain on her five-foot-five body, and all the charity work had been leading to, a 45-kilometre crossing of Lake Ontario. Here she was, late in the afternoon of Friday August 17th, ready to swim, and it was more than clear that the crossing was not going to start that night. Two-metre high waves rolled and a headwind ranging 15 to 25 knots blasted the lakeshore. Perhaps, she reflected, she would be fine in the water. Swimmers think like this sometimes; but her crew—the boats brought along for her safety—were likely going to be unhappy at best and in danger at worst.

And so they postponed the attempt. Several kilometres down the way Annaleise Carr and her crew at Niagara-on-the-Lake waited out the weather as well. Michèle and her crew returned to the weather forecast to look for another opening. Saturday the 18th near midnight showed promise, but now there was another problem. In order to be safe according to Solo Swims of Ontario, she required four safety boats as escort. With the postponement, her sailboat captain couldn't chance the crossing starting on Saturday night and rolling into Sunday morning since he had to be in Europe for business on the Monday.

What had first been a weather issue was now a resource issue. As it was, the weather was so bad that the sailboat spent the night tied up in Port Dalhousie.

It took the captain seven hours to sail back to Oakville, a crossing that normally takes four hours. On the other side, over 40 kilometres away near Burlington and her home near Lake Ontario, the Lake lay flat. She did consider a change in the route but Burlington was home. Nor was she going for time and speed. Besides, anything can happen in Lake Ontario. "It's about doing it safely, and doing it successfully, and just raising awareness about why I'm doing it."

Still, it was tough to call it off. She tried to explain to people that no one gets to the edge of the Lake without intending, physically, mentally, emotionally, to reach the other side. She looked for another date and remained optimistic until the Thursday of the Labour Day weekend. Again, a shortage of boats was her biggest issue. She found a solution on the Wednesday; then Hurricane Isaac touched down in the U.S., shifting weather patterns. What had looked good for Labour Day Saturday was now the weather on Sunday, but then another boat, her paramedic, and her swim master couldn't make that date.

It had been like this all summer as she solved one issue only to have another arise. She was sleeping three hours a night. A crossing attempt didn't make sense, since by now she wasn't in a great mental space to go. She decided it wasn't meant to be in 2012 and looked to completing her unfinished business with Lake Ontario. One day.

The effort of shifting another year took its toll mentally and emotionally, with the impact of 25 knot winds whipping across her face. She hadn't thought of things finishing this way, without even leaving the beach. She had been so focused on training to swim the Lake and raising funds for Waves for Water, a charity she created in partnership with Compassion International. Michèle hoped to generate funds to help provide a project in Togo, Africa with wells, water tanks, hand-washing stations, and training so the facility could be maintained, as well as hygiene education in Compassion's partner churches. Just prior to her swim, in yet another "you've got to be kidding me" moment, she learned the project cost had doubled to $40,000.

In the end, though, the health care practitioner found blessings. She raised $14,000 through her efforts and would continue to work towards creating an annual swim-a-thon that would also raise money for Waves for Water. She was disappointed but not discouraged. "The swim isn't about me. It's for the cause."

François Hamel

In 2009, François Hamel and his wife Julie Maltais found out the hard way that their son Pierre-Luc has juvenile diabetes. Pierre-Luc, then 10, was thirsty after playing hockey, but this went beyond an athlete's usual thirst. He wanted to drink all the time, rising several times at night for relief, and to drink again. Yet he was still thirsty. Alarmed, his parents looked up the symptoms, had him tested; when his blood sugar registered 37 (the normal range is 70-100 mg per decilitre), and he was close to lapsing into a diabetic coma, they flew south from Yellowknife to Edmonton, Alberta where they spent many emotional days riding a big learning curve.

Pierre-Luc is in good health and happy, growing taller than his father, François says, but what better way to marry his desire to support research into juvenile diabetes with his passion for marathon swimming than by swimming a Great Lake. François was a recent convert to swimming. The former runner turned to swimming after nagging running injuries put him in the water. He grew up in Roberval, Quebec, site of the legendary Traversée internationale swim across Lac St. Jean. The race had inspired him since he first started watching. He would swim Lac St. Jean in 2006. After he was stationed at Canadian Forces Base Borden near Barrie, he heard stories of marathon swims on Lake Ontario. For three years he had wanted to do the Lake. He decided to swim in 2012 and set himself a goal to raise $10,000 for juvenile diabetes.

He trained, took cold showers to acclimatize just in case he faced Lake

Ontario's mercurial rolls in temperature, secured boats and crew for the crossing attempt on Lake Ontario. He worked barbeques, car washes, and sport-a-thons to fundraise, finally, $12,000. "When you want to do something you have to work hard. It's a big puzzle that you have to put together."

He was scheduled to leave August 3rd but Toronto Port Authority, which can turn a crossing away if it doesn't have the correct paperwork, did not want any swimmers coming into the waterfront that weekend. It also happened to be Caribana, Toronto's massive Caribbean festival. François' crossing attempt was slated to occur as Caribana headed into the Grand Parade, the pinnacle of the festival on August 4th. The swim was moved forward one week to July 27th.

He was ready, regardless. His training had gone well, he had raised more money than he had hoped, his trial swim has been perfect, everyone was happy. Lake Ontario beckoned, welcoming, as the team prepared to launch. As he slipped in at Niagara-on-the-Lake at 7:00 p.m., the Lake was warm at 22.7C. He swam the first five kilometres in an hour thanks to a helpful push north courtesy of the mighty Niagara River current. Though things looked so hopeful, François knew the stories of sudden shifts in events on the Lake. And he was determined to not complain about anything, to be kind and polite to his crew, thanking them at every feeding and refreshment break.

After three hours Lake Ontario did what it does best and changed, with waves rolling to two metres, the wind picking up to 16 knots. François felt ready for this. With military precision he had planned for as much as he could in this crossing, right down to his stroke rate. Usually he swims 70-72 arm strokes per minute. He instead determined to keep his stroke rate at 60 per minute, designed to be steady and sure across the Lake. His coach Melanie Price kept track; indeed he held to a 60 stroke rate, about one arm stroke per second for the duration of his attempt.

The wind turned out to be the least of François' concerns. A few hours into the crossing a fuel line broke on his lead sailboat. No one told François so as not to distract him. In the dark night, he could taste fuel and smell it. He thought that perhaps a tanker had gone by ahead. A headache was blossoming. He couldn't eat, couldn't figure out why. He just knew if he ate something he'd be sick. Normally he ate well on marathon swims. Instead he asked only for liquids. Still, he never complained and swam on. Besides, by now there was this weird sound in his shoulder, signalling something else, something serious.

About 20 kilometres into the 51-kilometre crossing, the fuel line in the coach boat broke. The swim was paused for about 20 minutes as the team took time to make the repair. François rested his shoulder and hoped for the best. Maybe the shoulder just needed to rest.

When the swim resumed, François' shoulder muscles were cold. As he began stroking, the pain was still there and it was bad. He thought about it as he swam on. If he stopped now, would treatment take care of things? Or would this mean surgery and possibly the end of his swimming? He had already left running because of injury. At 3:40 a.m., deep in the heart of the night, he decided to stop, 22.5 kilometres and 8.5 hours after starting.

He was disappointed; he hadn't even been tired. It was his seventh open-water swim and the first one he'd been forced to end before completion. It was also his most important one. In the beginning, in the days after the crossing attempt ended, he said he'd failed. Then the positive comments flooded in. "A lot of people said you didn't fail because you showed up at the start. You try. Yes, it's kind of a fail but it's also a decision we took together to stop the swim. Now, with time, I'm not happy but I think it's a good experience and I will learn."

Amanda Lee Kelessi

On Friday, August 24th, after many starts and stops and a steep learning curve, Amanda Lee Kelessi at last felt like she was soaring. As she swam from Niagara-on-the-Lake, she crossed hundreds of feet over the Niagara sandbar. This pile of sand deep at the bottom of Lake Ontario has accumulated over the centuries and can lead to choppy, mucky conditions at surface almost right off the start of the swim across Lake Ontario. Some swimmers have panicked in the midst of the waves. Amanda swam on. Three hours later the 22-year-old lifeguard was pulled incoherent and in big trouble out of Lake Ontario.

Amanda Lee Kelessi of Toronto had been a competitive swimmer, then left the sport after loving it but not feeling that she had the drive for it. Her mother encouraged her to complete her lifesaving and swim instructing certifications. Here she found her calling. After graduating with a diploma in theatre she returned to instructing swimming. By chance she was working with swimmers with disabilities. One child in particular with spina bifida forced her to rethink everything, including her career path. "Everything about this kid brightened up my life." Connor was nine and had never been in the water before he started lessons with Amanda. He was petrified. "It was incredible watching a kid go from not handling being in the water to swimming on his own nine weeks later."

After that, she took on more swimmers with disabilities. She loved theatre but wasn't into the competitive life of an actor, living show-to-show and paycheque-to-paycheque. She needed something steady. She turned to studying emergency telecommunications, while still teaching swimming. In the end she loved working with children with disabilities and planned to study to be an educational assistant.

She was always interested in swimming Lake Ontario. Her paternal grandmother Mildred had talked "all the time" about Marilyn Bell's achievements. "I didn't know what was involved at the time." She turned it all into action in September 2011 after her friend Brett Clemance was killed in a car accident on the 17th. At the funeral a speaker talked about how Brett wouldn't want people to sit in their sadness and grief; he would want his friends to go out and benefit others.

Two days later, Amanda decided to swim across Lake Ontario. She would raise money for Sick Kids Foundation in Toronto in Brett's name. Sick Kids had given her young swimmers a second chance so it only made sense to Amanda to fundraise for them. She set up her website, set a modest goal of $5,000, and began to prepare. She thought she could just get in and swim. She recruited her friend Kathleen Dennis, who was also coach of the lifeguard team, and paid the Solo Swims $1,000 registration fee. It was two 22 year olds: let's do it, let's sign up and figure it out.

They learned as they went along but felt like everything was a shot in the dark. But she couldn't pull out either or wait another year. She had started raising money, she had dedicated the swim to Brett, and everyone knew. Over the next seven months she often wanted to give up. Then she would think of Brett and pull herself together again. "I didn't want any of my kids to be disappointed. I really wanted to show them that, no matter what life throws at you, if you're determined to do something, and you really want it, it's going to happen."

She relied on Colleen Shields, her swim master, who actually didn't pass Amanda's first trial swim. The Great Lakes are interconnected and the story of the swims is also a story of connection. Her fellow Lake crossers came to help. Her sailboat and powerboat cancelled out but then the charter boat captain for Madhu Nagaraja`s crossing stepped up and connected Amanda to people who eventually sailed her lead sailboat.

On her second trial swim, Shaun Chisholm, the Toronto firefighter who had swum the Lake in 2008 and raised money for the Sick Kids Burn Unit, stepped in, and along with his wife Allison, gave advice on food and training in general. He offered his cottage near Bala, north of Toronto in the Muskoka region, for the site of her second trial swim. "They were awesome people to have around," Amanda recalls. There was likely a sign of things to come in that trial. In the final kilometre, Amanda felt cold. Still, she passed this time.

So, on August 24th when she was finally out on Lake Ontario it was a relief to just get swimming. The crossing had been delayed by nearly three hours with winds and half- to one-metre waves from the northeast. Solo Swims had banned swim Mp3 players midway through the crossing season after most athletes had used them in training and in their crossings. Amanda depended on hers and had never been in open water without it. It helped her slip into the head space for the swim. Still, she was off and swimming in 24.4C water, moving as if the sandbar was mere grains. Kathleen told her she flew through it.

Around about her second feeding, about an hour later, she asked for her Swimp3. Kathleen told her no, that she didn't want to get to the other side and not have her swim recognized. Amanda didn't seem to care about the official recognition. She was doing this for Brett, for Connor, her swimmers, for the fundraising. She asked Colleen Shields to take her out. Christine Arsenault, who had swum Lake Ontario in 2011, was training to be a swim master and had come along on the crossing. She stayed in the boat while Colleen hopped in to swim with Amanda. Colleen told Amanda the feeling would pass. After swimming a few kilometres with her, she returned to the boat.

Amanda felt fearful; she was cold. A pain crept up her left side but she thought it was just a cramp and kept swimming to work it out. At her next feeding she told her crew she was really cold. Colleen told her no, she was fine, the water was 24.4C. On her final feeding Amanda threw up. She couldn't keep anything down. She threw the bottle back and kept going. She didn't want her crew to see her being sick.

Her crew on the Zodiac noticed her slowing down. Then her coach Kathleen began to ask the pre-arranged questions whose answers Amanda should know without really thinking. Amanda answered them, in fact she remembers answering. Kathleen told her to keep swimming but Amanda remembers, despite her haziness at the time, hearing the note of concern in her friend's voice. Her condition mirrored severe hypothermia, Colleen recalls. Which was weird. The Lake was warm. Kathleen turned to Colleen and told her, "None of those answers were right. Something is wrong." Amanda couldn't even recall Connor's name. Colleen leapt into the water and told Amanda the swim was over. She fell into Colleen's arms, wrapping herself around Colleen, her eyes rolling back in her head.

The swim evacuated south to Niagara, the crew working to keep Amanda awake. Amanda doesn't remember much, just images of the ambulance, the hospital, the tests staff ran on her. Nurses told her mother there was no way Amanda was going home, something was really wrong. Her boyfriend Justin Curlew slept on the floor in the emergency department as nurses came in regularly to rouse her. Later that morning a cardiologist told her that she had likely had a heart attack. Eventually it was determined that she had demand ischemia, a type of angina, where the heart is so over-exerted it can't pump hard or fast enough, leading to a switch up in the supply and demand of oxygen.

Still, she felt better enough that Saturday night to attempt a walk in the hospital, towing her IV bag on a pole. She looked down to notice blood in her IV. The next thing she knew she was on the floor. Her heart, she would later learn, had stopped for four to six seconds. She had been wearing a heart monitor; when she fainted her heart had stopped. "You've got to be kidding me," Amanda says.

She was in the hospital for five days but left with everything looking better; she was told she should go back to regular life. She asked her doctor if she should swim again. He asked whether she meant for exercise. She said no, she meant going across the Lake. The doctor told her it would not be a good idea to try and swim the Lake again. Though she can still teach swimming, lifeguard, run, and do what she was used to doing, she's still "really, really disappointed with everything that happened," she says. "I don't want to see myself as so fragile now. It wasn't a full out cardiac arrest."

She wondered if she put some stress on herself and somehow made the whole incident happen. Perhaps she swam too fast in the beginning. She then looked at her fundraising, which secured over $10,000 when the goal had been $5,000. "I didn't think I would make that kind of money." Her swimmers were thrilled for her, she says. One youngster told her he wants to swim the Lake and be in the Olympics. When she asked why, he replied, "Because you did it." At first she thought she had failed. "But after hearing from all my kids, who are so young and just so mature, I suppose I didn't fail. I was successful in raising the money for Sick Kids and inspiring my kids to go out and conquer their fears and live their dreams."

Colleen Shields, Yet Again

After her dramatic leap into Lake Ontario to help the floundering Amanda Lee Kelessi, Colleen Shields returned to her ongoing quest to complete her business with the Lake.

Unlike the other swimmers of 2012, Colleen has seen Lake Ontario from just about every angle. She loves it, respects it, can't seem to stay out of it. She has overseen swims as a master for 20 years, and swam the Lake herself in 1990 and 2006. She holds the record as the oldest woman to cross, but she was quietly hoping at age 60 definitely to become the most senior person to swim Lake Ontario.

In 2012 she was training for what she said was her final attempt to cross Lake Ontario. While checking out her friends' recently redesigned backyard in July, she tripped and fell heavily. She tore muscles and popped ribs out of place, for the second time in less than a year, though this time it wasn't from the whip of a roller coaster at Wonderland. She didn't swim for three weeks. She was lucky, however, when the weather for her first departure date in August postponed the swim and gave her a chance to recover fully. She looked ahead, planning to go sometime between September 7th and 9th. But again it wasn't to be.

Colleen found a pocket of weather open to her on Wednesday, September 5th. But on September 4th she still had so much to do. The change in dates meant she had to reapply to the Toronto Port Authority. All the paperwork was in her computer at the travel agency where she works. She thought that maybe she could let the paperwork slide. But she didn't want to chance getting into Toronto and have the authority turn her away on an administrative oversight. She remained at work waiting four hours for authorization, four hours she could have been resting.

She drove to her chiropractor's home for an adjustment, spending several hours on the commute and appointment. Word reached her of boat problems. A sailboat had broken down in the Lake. The team discussed applying the three-boat escort rule with a powerboat leading the swim. That was confirmed, but then word reached her again that the boat was fixed and they would rendezvous at 1:00 a.m. in Niagara-on-the-Lake.

Her coach had gone to London for the Paralympics so Lisa Anderson, coach of Annaleise Carr, by now the youngest swimmer to have completed the traditional route, stepped in at the last minute to coach Colleen across. Marilyn Korzekwa, one of the few swimmers to have swum Lake Ontario both ways, was swim master. They watched the weather and the whitecaps on the Niagara River as it spilled into Lake Ontario. Colleen opted to stay on shore for a few more hours and finally slept.

In what felt like minutes, she was awakened to check conditions again. She said she'd go at 5:00 a.m. It was back to bed, but she barely dozed. Then Marilyn came down to announce it was time to go. Already? She was exhausted, and not even in the water yet.

The crossing started at 6:17 a.m. Nicole Mallette, Colleen's long-time friend and fellow crosser, had been ill with food poisoning and was vomiting into the bushes nearby. Colleen fought the waves at the beginning of her crossing, feeling like she didn't even want to be there. The chop was confusing, as waves came every which way.

She had told Lisa not to expect anything out of her until at least five kilometres of swimming because it can take her that long to warm up. She swam for five hours and then told Lisa she needed something to give her a second wind. Immediately Lisa changed her diet to apricots and Swedish berries which gave her incredible energy.

Then Lake Ontario flattened out and turned glorious, even hot. "It was gorgeous," Colleen says. After sleeping off the food poisoning, Nicole hopped in to swim with her as a pacer. The Zodiac lingered behind as crew members got in to swim themselves and enjoy the Lake. Colleen laughs that they were probably going for a pee.

Then the winds came up, raising 1.2 metre waves; instead of forecast south-easterly winds which would have pushed her right into Toronto, the winds came easterly and the waves pushed her broadside. Her crew wanted her to swim to the right of the CN Tower; then she could body surf into Toronto. "I just didn't have the energy. I was exhausted. I hit the wall and I never got around it."

In an effort to motivate her, Lisa called upon Colleen's days at Camp Ak-O-Mak, a girls' open-water swim and triathlon sports camp in Ontario's Muskoka region. Colleen had spent seven weeks every summer for a decade at the camp. The directors, Buck and Rosemary Dawson, were like a second set of parents and "a very important part of my life," Colleen says. Rosemary had been particularly disappointed in Colleen after one incident which Colleen hesitates to specify. It was bad enough that Rosemary wouldn't even look at Colleen. Decades later, Lisa played that disappointment card on Lake Ontario in a desperate attempt to get Colleen into shore. "It made me go for a little bit."

Then she lay back and listened to her father's opera music on her SwimP3 headset. Her father had been a professional singer. His voice kept her going. On her right hand, she wore her mother's rings. Always her family is with her on these crossings. Colleen was perhaps 14 kilometres off Toronto, her back arched like a bow, and sore. She figures she's so buoyant when she swims that her body is arched, the front and back ends are up with the middle down. "There's nothing I can do about that because that's the way I swim."

At 9:43 p.m., the swim ended.

She picked through and found joy in details from the swim. There was her speed, how her efficient stroke, which rarely strayed away from 52 strokes per minute, had placed her ahead of the speed record. Conditions had been okay, and would have allowed her to get close enough to body-surf into Toronto. She had picked the right window. "I'm glad the weather was bad in August because I wasn't healed to do it." She attributes everything to being exhausted before she ever even went in the water. She was disappointed, but happy with the way she swam. "I've never swum that fast. Ever. In any of my crossings. I worked really hard and it showed."

Marilyn Bell Di Lascio: the Changing Winds of Success and Failure

Back in Toronto after her famous crossing in 1954, the craziness of her post-Lake Ontario swim days had Marilyn Bell living in a fishbowl. She had been adamant on a few points: she would personally sign all the letters coming to her, return to school at Loretto College, and return to the swimmers with disabilities she was teaching at Lakeshore Swim Club. As offers came in and stories were churned out about Marilyn and her family, the executives at the Dominion Stores where her father worked were concerned for the family. "They wanted to ensure that we were protected."

There was good reason. In 1926, George Young, then 17, hopped in the sidecar of his buddy's motorcycle for the ride to California for the inaugural Catalina Channel crossing. William Wrigley, Jr. had put up prize money of $24,000 for the first swimmer. Despite the presence of a black fin swimming beside him, George bested the impressive field and broke through powerful tides to touch the California mainland first. Headlines across the continent in this different era feted his accomplishments and he became a target for every promoter standing (McAllister, 83). His next swim was to be the CNE's first marathon swim in Toronto in 1927. Everyone assumed it would be a coronation for George, a repeat of his California victory for the unbeatable Canadian. This CNE marathon swim would be his showcase. Lake Ontario was having none of that celebrity nonsense and set its temperatures to bone-numbing cold (McAllister, 84). George was ultimately pulled out, half frozen, without finishing the swim. Then he was slammed and shamed in the media for quitting, for even being a fake. In 1928, the water was so cold no one finished. In 1931 George won the CNE race but it was too late to turn the tide back in his favour (McAllister, 85).

George Young's rapid rise and inglorious fall was still fresh in the minds of the marathon swimming community and no one wanted to repeat it. A group of attorneys and two men from an advertising agency became the advisors to the Bell family. "There were all kinds of offers and presentations and contracts that were being submitted. Marilyn was going to Hollywood—that was all true. It was absolute bedlam," Marilyn says.

In England for the Channel crossing in 1955, another priceless moment presented itself to Marilyn. Florence Chadwick was also in England training for the third crossing of her remarkable swimming career. After the Lake Ontario crossing in 1954, Florence had sent a telegram of congratulations to Marilyn but the two never did meet. Much of the training for the channel crossings was in Dover; one day Marilyn was swimming back and forth with her escort boat. She stopped for a moment to adjust her goggles, eat something. Gus pointed back towards shore and told her Florence was in the harbour training. "I would have loved to have met her but I'm sure that would have been pretty difficult for her. And I certainly understand that." Over the years after the swim, Marilyn would reflect on how hard the summer of 1954 had been for Florence, not completing a swim of the Strait of Juan de Fuca and then "the big brouhaha" of the Lake Ontario crossing "which certainly wasn't a taste of Canadian hospitality, that's for sure." As she grew older she felt that the way the press had written about Florence "was really a shame. I really did feel sad about that. And there's still a part of me that thinks there was something that wasn't quite right about that." After all, on Lake Ontario Marilyn seemed to appear without an invitation. It might have seemed pushy of "the little kid from nowhere. Of course, there were forces-that-be that were certainly instrumental in that. But it had to be an unpleasant experience for her and I'm sorry still about that. She was a wonderful swimmer. My goodness, she was world-renowned."

On July 31, 1955 Marilyn swam from France to England in 14 hours, 36 minutes becoming the second Canadian (after Winnie Roach Leuszler), the 14th woman, the youngest swimmer, and the 32nd person to complete the crossing. Florence completed her third Channel crossing and finished in a record-breaking 13 hours, 55 minutes.

Over the winter *The Toronto Telegram*, in partnership with the *Victoria Daily Times* (Hawthorn) made another offer, this time to sponsor Marilyn's crossing attempt on the Strait of Juan de Fuca, the bitterly cold waters between Canada and Washington State on the Pacific Coast. Water temperatures hover around 11.6C. The Race Rocks near Victoria add some excitement when the ebb and flood tides race, with the potential for carrying the swimmer with lousy timing into the barnacle covered rocks. The fame of this swim, touted as tougher than the English Channel, drew Marilyn's attention. It would be her last. She didn't want to get sucked into a swimming career. She and her "lifeguard," from the Atlantic City swim, Joe "Chipper" Di Lascio, had developed a friendship which had evolved into something more. They were planning to marry as soon as he finished college.

On August 10, 1956 she set out from Victoria. The tides pushed her east and the cold water took its toll (Wennerberg 285). Her finish point was moved to Green Point, east of Port Angeles, to compensate for the effect of the tide. With just over eight km to go she was pulled unconscious from the water.

In his otherwise clear account of open-water and marathon swimming, *Wind, Waves and Sunburn*, Conrad Wennerberg adopts a tone to Marilyn's failed attempt that bears out the concerns the advisors to the Bell Family had in the wake of George Young's experience. Wennerberg grants no quarter, almost relishing in the defeat. Large men are fine specimens of both man- and swimmer-kind in his book while women, represented by Marilyn, suffer from the social clichés prevalent at the time: "She was now 18 and running to fat. She was no longer the demure 120-pound girl she was when she made that swim [across Ontario]. She was now 150 pounds and it didn't look good on her five-foot two-inch frame. Marilyn made that swim her final effort and within the year she was married" (286-87).

As she recovered from the initial attempt, Marilyn watched the shocked faces around her. No one knew what to say. "Even my own parents! They couldn't string any words together." The media, her coach, her friends were at a loss. To this point, it had only been success: Atlantic City, Lake Ontario, the English Channel. Perhaps she was due for a failure. No one knew how to deal with this because it hadn't happened before. "By then, everybody that knew me had discounted all the times I had failed as a short distance swimmer," she laughs. There's a distinct photo, a grainy black and white image of Marilyn being hauled into her support boat on this crossing attempt. As she would later say, it's one thing to fail when no one knows you; it's another when the whole country is paying attention.

Years later, Marilyn would reflect that her 18-year-old self gave up in Juan de Fuca. That first attempt was a failure. Everything had been in her favour that day, except her head. She accepted her aborted crossing as a failure because she hadn't done what she'd been trained to do—to focus and not let negative thoughts or feelings get in the way of her goal.

Had she not failed, and then forced herself to go back, she might have missed an important experience in growing and living, in facing failure and using it in a positive way to spur herself forward. "For me it was important to go back in the water when people were telling me no, no you don't need to do that. You've already proved you're worthwhile, and you've got the prize money."

But she did go back. On August 23, 1956, at 11:30 a.m., Marilyn dove into the rough waters of the Strait at Port Angeles, and headed north to Victoria. The water was barely 10C. It was windy. She had to time the landing so she wouldn't get dashed into the rocks. Ten hours, 39 minutes later she came ashore with a new speed record. Bonfires lit both the shore and the faces of the people of Victoria who had cheered her every stroke over the weeks she had spent training for the crossing (Hawthorn). "I was very lucky it worked out that way. But, I do think, in retrospect, that if it had it not worked out, I wouldn't have come back the following year. I was ready to leave swimming. I have such admiration for people who see this as an ongoing enticement. They want to do it, they want to do it faster, they want to do more of it. And I'm amazed by that."

For Marilyn, a now retired teacher living in New York State, mother of four and a grandmother of five, newness brought challenge; she liked trying new things, even if there was always the possibility that it wouldn't happen, a lesson she took home from the Strait of Juan de Fuca. "Life doesn't work out the way you expect it to on any given day but the secret for me is learning from that experience and then reworking it in my head, approaching it from a different direction." It was a message she tried to impart to her children and her students, to not be afraid to try, that when there is failure—and everyone has to fail at some point—then you appreciate success. "I learned early on to appreciate lack of success in my swimming career," she laughs. From there, it's about learning and reinventing either the situation or the swimmer. "But some change has to take place."

Of course, all the swimmer's best intentions and planning then have to face the forces of nature in open-water swimming. If someone has good conditions on Lake Ontario, or any of the Great Lakes, does that lessen the accomplishment of that swimmer, she wonders? She reflects on two crossings in 2010, where Miguel Vadillo completed the swim in ideal conditions while Colleen Shields' attempt ended with a shoulder injury in rolling waves kilometres off Toronto. "The fact is, they were both there, ready to go. They started with the greatest intentions of doing their best." There can never be a guide to swimming across a Great Lake. Everyone who steps into the Great Lake waters—relieved at last to be just *doing* it—shares the true intention of swimming over the curve of the earth to the other side of the inland seas. What happens next?

We humans have been doing what we want to the Lakes, turning parts of Georgian Bay off Lake Huron into grassland that needs to be mowed, not swum. As for the swimming, we think we have more knowledge. Training has never been more available: there are dozens of books and articles on training. YouTube has swimming videos on proper technique up the lane and back down. It's clear what to eat, what to wear, how to train, rest, raise money… and on it goes. There's business potential here for forming a charter company, similar to the Channel Swimming Association crews that escort swimmers on the English Channel, or the team that organizes the Catalina Channel crossing. All that would be true.

But as to the final outcome, it comes down to a swimmer, barely clothed, and the Lake. And always the Lakes decide.

Appendix: List of Crossings to 2013

Below are listed the Solo Swims of Ontario, Inc. ratified crossings by amateur swimmers—Canadian and foreign—not included in *Solo, Yet Never Alone*. Information was drawn from the Solo Swims of Ontario website, www.soloswims.com. Used by permission.

Lake Ontario swims (Toronto)

John Jaremey, Canada, 23 Jul 1956
Brenda Fisher, England, 12-13 Aug 1956
Bill Sadlo, USA, 23 Aug 1957
Jim Woods, USA, 26 Aug 1957
Jim Woods, USA, 02 Sep 1961
Diana Nyad, USA, 30-31 Aug 1974
Debbie Roach, Canada, 16 Aug 1975
Angela Kondrak, Canada, 22-23 Aug 1976,
Kim Lumsdon, Canada, 27 Aug 1976
Cam Kamula, Canada, 03-04 Aug 1984
Rick Wood, Canada, 19 Aug 1989
Paolo Pinto, Italy, 28-29 Jul 1990
Rick Goodwin, Canada, 27-28 Aug 1994
Ingrid Martin, Australia, 11-12 Aug 1996
Dan Foster, Canada, 15 Aug 1998
Peter Gibbs, Barbados, 7-8 Aug 2004
Kim Lumsdon, Canada, 5-6 Aug 2006
Ashleigh Beacham, Canada-USA, 18 Aug 2013

Lake Erie swims

Rick Wood, Canada, 25 Aug 1990
Chris Stockdale, England, 21 Sep 2006
Daniel Nichols, Canada, 4-5 Aug 2007

Works Cited

Unless otherwise noted, the direct and indirect quotations are drawn from the author's personal interviews and correspondence with the swimmers and members of their support teams.

Alamenciak, Tim. "Annaleise Carr: Lake Ontario swimmer's team key to her successful crossing." *The Toronto Star*. 26 Aug. 2012. www.thestar.com.

---. "Exhausted, but jubilant Annaleise Carr completes Lake Ontario crossing." *The Toronto Star*. 19 Aug. 2012. www.thestar.com.

Blatchford, Christie. "Race commitment takes second place: New York Teenagers double escort flotilla." *The Globe and Mail*. 17 Aug. 1974: 35.

---. "Tears, then cheers—Cindy conquers the lake." *The Globe and Mail*. 17 Aug. 1974: 1.

Canadian Press, *The Globe and Mail*. 29 July 1988: A8.

Channel Swimming. www.channelswimmingassociation.com.

Craig, Anne. "Three Dead After Drowning Incident." www.gananoquereporter.com. 18 July 2009.

"Florence Chadwick." http://www.answers.com.

Great Lakes Information Network. http://www.great-lakes.net.

"Guy Lafleur, Hockey, 1977." http://loumarsh.ca.

Hawthorn, Tom. "'Canada's sweetheart': Marilyn Bell, the great strait swimmer." *The Globe and Mail*. 22 Aug. 2012. www.theglobeandmail.com

Jenkins, Mark. "Maxed Out on Everest." http://ngm.nationalgeographic.com. June 2013.

Kennedy, Patrick. "Queen of the Lakes Celebrates Silver Anniversary." 14 June 2013. http://www.thewhig.com.

Keith, Vicki. "Marathon Swimming." TEDxWaterloo. April 2007. www.youtube.com.

Ketcheson, Graham. "A Brief History of Georgian Bay." www.whitesquall.com.

"Loreen conquers the lake, but weather denies record." *The Globe and Mail*. 3 Sept. 1979: S7.

Mallick, Heather. "Eels main worry for swimming star in lake crossing." *The Globe and Mail.* 19 August 1985: 13.

Martin, Lawrence. "Sets speed record in calm, warm lake then heads for bed." *The Globe and Mail.* 17 Aug. 1974: 1.

McAllister, Ron. *Swim to Glory. The Story of Marilyn Bell.* Toronto: McClelland & Stewart, 1954.

McGammon, Andrew. "Connecting the Great Lakes to their Headwaters." *Great Lakes News.* 31 Aug. 2009. www.ohwi.ca.

McNair, Brian. "Bowmanville Mom Tames Lake Ontario." www.durhamregion.com. 19 Aug, 2010.

Nolan, Mary K. "Swimmer, 41 braves crossing to Manitoulin." *The Toronto Star.* 23 Aug 1993: A2.

Nyad, Diana. *Other Shores.* New York: Random House, 1978.

"One may be in water now: Teen-agers complete training for Lake Ontario test." *The Globe and Mail.* 16 Aug. 1974: 27

Ontario MNR. "Great Lakes." http://www.mnr.gov.on.ca.

Openwaterpedia. www.openwaterpedia.com.

Penguins Can Fly. www.penguinscanfly.ca.

Rowe, Michael. "After the Swim: Kim Middleton looks for new challenges." *Highlights Kitchener-Waterloo.* (July-August 1990): 15-18.

Science North. "Mysteries of the Great Lakes." http://sciencenorth.ca.

Solo Swims. www.soloswims.com.

"Toronto in Time." http://citiesintime.ca.

Waites, Al. "Determination Brightened Journey into Darkness." *The Globe and Mail.* 17 Aug 1974: 35.

Wennerberg, Conrad. *Wind Waves, and Sunburn. A Brief History of Marathon Swimming.* New York: Breakaway Books, 1974.

Bibliography

Cox, Lynne. *Swimming to Antarctica. Tales of a Long-Distance Swimmer.* New York: Knopf, 2004.

McAllister, Ron. *Swim to Glory: The Story of Marilyn Bell and the Lakeshore Swimming Club.* Toronto: McClelland & Stewart, 1954.

Nyad, Diana. *Other Shores.* New York: Random House, 1978.

Serdula, Jay. *The Ambition of an Aspie.* Kingston: Jay Serdula Publications Co., 2009.

Wennerberg, Conrad. *Wind, Waves, and Sunburn—A Brief History of Marathon Swimming.* New York: Breakaway Books, 1997.

Laura E. Young is a writer and journalist based in Northeastern Ontario. She is also a lifeguard and an experienced open-water swimmer. She lives in Sudbury, Canada with her family.